# LANGUAGE
# & NATIONHOOD

# LANGUAGE & NATIONHOOD

## The CANADIAN EXPERIENCE

# RONALD WARDHAUGH

☆
**NEW
STAR
BOOKS**

Vancouver

First printing October 1983
1 2 3 4 5   87 86 85 84 83


**Canadian Cataloguing in Publication Data**
Wardhaugh, Ronald.
Language and nationhood

Includes index.
Bibliography: p.
ISBN 0-91957-316-9. (bound). -- ISBN 0-91957-317-7 (pbk.)

1. Canada - Languages.  2. Canada - Population -
Ethnic groups.* 3. Minorities - Canada.  I. Title.
FC104.W37 1983     305.7'0971     C83-091357-2
F1035.A1W37 1983

44, 743

The publisher is grateful to the Canada Council for assistance
provided through the Writing and Publication Section.

Printed and bound in Canada by Gagne Printers.

New Star Books Ltd.
2504 York Avenue
Vancouver, B.C.
Canada V6K 1E3

*For Chau,*
*my bicultural, multilingual companion*

# Contents

# Preface

This book is about various aspects of language and ethnicity in Canada and certain attendant issues. It is also about government policies concerning bilingualism and multiculturalism and some of the inadequacies of such policies. It is not an optimistic book, but no one who looks seriously at such matters in Canada can be heartened by the view.

The contents draw on readily accessible resources such as information available through Statistics Canada in order to show the kinds of issues which continue to interest Canadians when they consider the mixture of languages and races in their country. Canadians do not lack good scholarly works describing their society and indicating both its strengths and weaknesses. Unfortunately, most such works find a very limited audience: colleagues in the academic world and a rather small number of students in institutions of higher learning. They also do not enjoy wide "foreign" circulation. On the other hand, the mass media in Canada continue to feed a variety of myths to the public. Non-Canadians, too, are very likely to be unaware of certain realities of Canadian life. It is part of a scholar's responsibility to attempt to bridge the gap between the world in which he or she lives and makes discoveries and the world that others inhabit. This book is such an attempt. It strongly questions many Canadian myths and some of the messages which political and economic leaders would have Canadians believe. Many of their contentions are demonstrably unsupported by facts; indeed, often the facts indicate a situation which is almost the opposite of that which is declared to exist.

This book offers no ready-made solutions, no panaceas. It asks Canadians to look at what is happening in their country, for only if they can do so objectively and dispassionately can they hope to find solutions. To find the right answers, you must ask the right questions. This book is directed toward deciding what those questions are.

Finally, a word about the use of *English* throughout the book to refer at times to those who are not French and at other times to those who are either English, Scots, Welsh, or Irish. Ethnic labels are difficult to use accurately in the absence of any clear definition of ethnicity. There is a sense in which there is a *French* Canada and an *English* Canada (the non-French part) and there is also a sense in which the similarities among the English, Scots, Welsh, and Irish are far more important than their differences. These are the senses in which *English* is used in the following pages, being less clumsy than either *non-French* or *Anglo-Celtic*. In a real sense too, Canada's most conspicuous problem is that of *English-French* relationships, though its shame is its treatment of its native peoples, and its tragedy its people's willing acceptance of a seemingly perpetual colonial status.*

> *R.W.*
> *Toronto*
> *August, 1983*

---

*In this text, standard French diacritical markings have not been reproduced due to technical constraints.

# LANGUAGE
# &
# NATIONHOOD

# 1

# NORTHERN SOLITUDES

Although Canada is a modern nation state, it is one made up of at least two "nations," that is, it consists of at least two distinct groups of people whose members are bound together by ties of loyalty reinforced through identification with particular territories. It is also likely that one of these nations, the French, has an even stronger sense of group identification than the other, the English, because of its geographic isolation in North America and its religious, linguistic, and social cohesiveness. In contrast, the English nation is really little more than a collection of different peoples, with those of English ancestry dominant over a variety of ethnic groups, many of which have their own national consciousness, particularly, of course, the increasingly recognized nations of the native peoples, that is, the Indians, Metis, and Inuit. An enduring problem, one faced by Canadians throughout their history, has been the need to grapple with just what it means to be a citizen of a state such as Canada, and then to reconcile that citizenship with views of nationalism derived from considerations of ethnic origin.

Internal conflict has been an abiding hallmark of Canadian history. While Canadians have managed to avoid bloody civil war, English-French conflict has nevertheless been a dominant theme in Canada's political and social life. One interesting aspect of English-French conflict has been the ability of each party to the conflict to write and rewrite the history of the relationship to suit its current needs. Of course, all history is interpretation of the past and interpretations do change. However, in this case the English and French have two quite different histories of the same events in the same country. Each of the two "charter" groups in Canada, that is, the original immigrant-groups, has its own interpretation of certain historical events, one that is at complete variance with the other. If both interpretations are to be allowed to exist in a truly pluralistic approach to both past and present, there is hope of a future for Canada. But each party appears to be as intransigent as the other in its rectitude about its particular views of the past. And, at present, talk itself has all but ceased.

The Engish and French in Canada have written their settlement histories quite differently, as though two separate countries and series of events were being described. In the English version, what can be called the "Loyalist" tradition is very apparent. In it, the story of Canada really begins after the conquest of the French in 1759, and it is one of a people growing from colonial status to nationhood while retaining a strong connection to the motherland across the ocean and maintaining an ever-present wariness of all things American to the south. The French were conquered in 1759 but they were treated well. Immigrants have also been welcome to the new land, and the opportunities afforded by the Canadian way of life have been theirs to enjoy if they so wished. In the French version the focus is on the survival of a nation with a long and proud existence in North America prior to 1759, but a defeated nation nonetheless and one which has had to look to its own resources to preserve its identity in the face of discrimination, British imperialism, and isolation. In the English version political and economic development loom large as themes; in the French version the cultural, religious, and linguistic survival of a nation are the equivalent themes. Doubtless, neither version accurately reflects the facts (if any history does), but each serves the purpose of those who use it and each continues to influence the course of events in contemporary Canada.

It is also part of the folklore of the two groups that the other group is antagonistic and unco-operative. Consequently, contacts between the groups reinforce rather than mitigate those beliefs. Small shifts in government policy tend to become magnified into major disruptive changes, as do any adjustments in rights and privileges. The Official Languages Act of 1969, which established bilingualism as official Canadian government policy, and Quebec's various proposals to preserve the French language in the province, particularly Bill 101 of 1977, which compelled a reduction in the use of English in Quebec, changed the relationship between the two communities and tended to arouse and even anger many of the English. That most French Canadians saw these measures as almost life-and-death moves to protect their language in Canada, but particularly within the province of Quebec, went unappreciated. Not surprisingly, the English reaction confirmed any feelings the French had about their inferior position in Canada and encouraged them to try even harder to preserve what they felt was rightfully theirs within Confederation, that is, the overall federal system of government.

There are widely conflicting views between the charter groups and even within the English group itself about what Confederation is, that is, about the basic political framework of the country. One view is that Confederation is a kind of compact among a number of autonomous provinces to form a country in which the central government is to do only those things which the provincial governments cannot do. In this view the central government should really do as little as possible while the provincial governments retain all powers not expressly granted constitutionally to the central government. A second view is that the central government exists as a partner of the provincial governments, having been created by the same original statute, the British North America Act of 1867. Therefore, it is at least an equal of the others. Moreover, since it alone has a "Canadian" perspective through countrywide representation, it is obviously the first among equals. Still a third view, one particularly espoused by most French Canadians, is that Confederation is basically an agreement between two equal founding peoples to live together in the territory north of the United States. In this view, Canada is "founded on the duality of races and on the popular traditions that duality involves."[1] This last position finds little support in English Canada, where most of the disagreements concerning Confederation turn on the correctness of the first two views; a "two nations" concept of Canada or a "special status" for

Quebec within Confederation is not seriously entertained.

It is unfortunate that the English in Canada pay so little regard to this French view of Confederation because it is one that cannot be ignored if viable solutions to problems of nationhood are to be found. As Ramsay Cook, a leading Canadian historian, has written:

> Either Canada will be a federation of provinces in which, wherever practicable, the French and English cultures are recognized as equal, or it will be two separate nations, one Francophone, the other Anglophone. To return again to the fantasy that there is some supposedly typical Canadian compromise between these options would be a monumental waste of time and creative energy.[2]

However, it is also Cook's contention, reiterated on numerous occasions, that what Canada does not suffer from is a lack of feelings concerning nationalism; rather there is a surfeit of such feelings. Nationalism actually increases English-French antagonism and confuses all other issues. Canada is a modern nation state but one in which two nationally conscious peoples must learn to co-exist within a federal system which affords that opportunity. Neither can dominate the other, so co-existence is the only feasible alternative to the dissolution of the system and of the state itself. Since any heightened "national" consciousness tends to break the federal system apart, a fundamental Canadian concern must be to resolve disputes before irreparable damage occurs.

To date it has proved impossible to devise a system within which the English and French have been able to live harmoniously in North America. Several attempts have been made. Indeed, "Canada" has had more than one constitution. For example, the Act of Union of 1840 tried in its way to produce a form of government which would protect the rights of each group, but that attempt proved unsuccessful. The British North America Act of 1867 was a further attempt to devise an alternative solution, known this time as Confederation. That Confederation has lasted over a century is testimony to the wisdom of those who wrote the British North America Act; that the basic issue of national unity continues to surface is an indication of how difficult finding a permanent solution really is, particularly since that solution must now address itself not only to the demands of the English and French but also to the claims of millions who are of neither English nor French origin and to those of the native peoples. The Constitution Act of 1982 is Canada's latest attempt to address some of these issues.

It is also possible to argue, however, that in some almost perverse way Canada's greatest weakness, her ethnic composition, is also her greatest strength. Perhaps the only real distinction between Canada and the United States is that Canada is a bilingual and either bicultural or multicultural country whereas the United States is neither. In this view, that difference alone accounts for Canada's claim to a separate identity and protects the country from becoming, even more than it is at present, just another satellite or appendage of the United States. But to the extent that this view is correct, it is also proper to observe that the very same situation is internally divisive for Canada. Ironically, the internal division which protects Canada from the United States also prevents the development of any kind of cohesive Canadian identity and even, at times, coherent policy making. If the French fact in Quebec, English intransigence outside, and a strong ethnic consciousness everywhere make Canada undigestable for the United States, they also cause chronic pains and upsets within the country.

To someone who had more influence than anyone else on political issues in Canada in the 1970s and early 1980s, Pierre Elliott Trudeau, Prime Minister of Canada for most of that period, all disagreements based on feelings of language and ethnicity are to be deplored. Following Lord Acton's example, Trudeau has long been critical of nationalism:

> . . . in the advanced societies, where the interplay of social forces can be regulated by law, where the centres of political power can be made responsible to the people, where the economic victories are a function of education and automation, where cultural differentiation is submitted to ruthless competition, and where the road to progress lies in the

direction of international integration, nationalism will have to be discarded as a rustic and clumsy tool.[3]

According to Trudeau, an acceptance of a federal state based on reason is to be preferred to claims for the recognition of national entities based on appeals to emotion. Consequently, he has long berated both the English and French in Canada for their obtuseness and unwillingness to see reason, that is, his point of view. One can only surmise how far Trudeau's persistence in trying to impose his vision of Canada onto others has contributed to keeping the embers of discord hot in the country. Certainly, as Prime Minister of Canada at a critical period in the country's history, he chose much of the agenda for political debate within the country and must accept much of the responsibility for the consequences of his choices. Canadians may regret how far they are today from the vision of Canada held by the pre-Prime Ministerial Trudeau:

> The die is cast in Canada: there are two main ethnic and linguistic groups; each is too strong and too deeply rooted in the past, too firmly bound to a mother-culture, to be able to engulf the other. But if the two will collaborate at the hub of a truly pluralistic state, Canada could become the envied seat of a form of federalism that belongs to tomorrow's world. . . . Canada could offer an example to all those new Asian and African states . . . who must discover how to govern their polyethnic populations with proper regard for justice and liberty. . . . Canadian federalism is an experiment of major proportions; it could become a brilliant prototype for the moulding of tomorrow's civilization.[4]

It is possible to appreciate some of the characteristics of the two charter groups in Canada if one looks closely at some of the beliefs that have guided each group during its history in the New World. For example, English histories of Canada tell how the English came to this country as conquerors of the French. Once established, they tried to impose their culture on all other Canadians. This can be seen as early as the Royal Proclamation of

1763 which abrogated French rights, in the francophobia of the early Loyalist settlers, and in the Durham Report, which preceded the Act of Union. It can also be seen in the history of the settlement of the West, where English and American settlers were to be preferred to any others: they were to replace settlers of French descent, the Metis; and they were to found there a kind of new Upper Canada (Upper Canada being the old name for what is now, with small changes, Ontario).[5] British imperial policies were also to be followed, as in the Boer War and in World War I. Immigrants were to be chosen on the basis of their assimilability into English ways of life. French minority rights throughout Canada were to be removed, particularly at the turn of the century, because the survival of the French and their language was an obstacle to the English. Later still, the Official Languages Act of 1969 was to be resisted in English Canada, often on such grounds as: "Canada is an English-speaking country" or "the English won in 1759" or "the French are plotting to take over a Canada that does not belong to them."

The English in Canada have also been conservative in their views. The influx of Loyalists during and after the American Revolution served to strengthen existing conservative tendencies and to further cement ties across the ocean. Suddenly Canada's English population more than doubled with the arrival of people fleeing the liberal, democratic ideology of the revolutionary United States, preferring instead British authoritarianism and colonialism. Consequently, progress toward independent nationhood was much slower in Canada than in the United States and developments occurred within a framework designed and approved by the British, for example between 1867 and 1982 through the umbilical cord which the British North America Act provided. Ultimately, "responsible government" was gained only when the country became "mature," a situation one can contrast with the way the people of the United States threw off the colonial yoke in favor of radical "constitutional government."

That many English Canadians still identify very strongly with the "old country" was seen in the fierce debates that raged as recently as two decades ago over the adoption of a Canadian flag and national anthem and is still seen in the reluctance of the federal government to tamper with Canada's ties to the United Kingdom through the British monarchy. Even if a majority of Canadians appear to favor ending the monarchical connection with the United Kingdom, as some recent polls have indicated, the old Loyalist tradition is still so fiercely entrenched among those who exercise political control that such a move appears to be virtually impossible. Part of the opposition to patriate the British North America Act and give Canada a completely Canadian constitution also arose from a belief that somehow leaving Canada's constitution in the hands of the parliament of the United Kingdom offered greater protection to traditional ways than bringing it to Canada, where it might be changed in ways that no British government would ever possibly consider. In other words, an unpatriated constitution would afford guarantees a patriated one might not.

These then are some of the characteristics the English in Canada exhibit in their behavior toward Canadian people of other origins. They have serious consequences for the political and social climate of the country. However, the statistical dominance of the English has fallen gradually but consistently during the twentieth century. While the English comprised 57 per cent of the total population of Canada in the 1901 census, they fell to under 45 per cent in the 1971 census. When the figures for the 1981 census are released, they are expected to show a further decline. The English are no longer in a majority in Canada, so they must tread more carefully than before, and, since the English population is an "older" one than, for example, the French and also draws on non-English sources for replacement, it is not as powerful as it once was. Of necessity the English have had to become more accommodating to the wishes of others. As one observer has remarked, "old-stock Canadians, particularly those of British origin, increasingly accept the attainment by individuals from other backgrounds of positions of stature and power in various aspects of Canadian life."[6]

English life in Canada was not born in an ideology; there was nothing corresponding to the American Revolution. Instead, it evolved almost by accident and in a series of pragmatic, even defensive, moves. English life in Canada therefore lacks a unifying theme and a controlling set of values and symbols. The internal history of the English in Canada is a history of compromise and accommodation; moreover, it is one shared by a mosiac of peoples and lacks any really central theme. On the other hand, French life in Canada is rooted in an ideology, that of the survival of a nation after its conquest by another. This theme provides a purpose to French existence in Canada which English existence lacks.

The French in Canada are descended from the 60,000 or so people who were abandoned to English rule by the Treaty of Paris in 1763. They were French people from the pre-revolutionary era, mainly habitants, somewhat feudal in their social organization, and strongly under the influence of the Church. The French found themselves a minority in North America and faced the prospects of dispersal (as with the Acadians) or absorption (as with various small, scattered French outposts). The twin pillars of their survival were their religion and their language. These they could maintain only if they stayed where they were, living as it were on their own vast reservation, and only if they were prepared to struggle in order to preserve as many of their traditional ways as their new colonial masters would allow them to keep. Essentially then a conservative society with a kind of garrison mentality evolved in Quebec, a society soon isolated from France by the French Revolution of 1789, which curbed the Church, and from the English by a different language and culture.

For more than two hundred years then the English and French have lived physically side by side but psychologically really quite far apart in Canada. Their relationship has been anything but amiable. Beginning in defeat for the French on the Plains of Abraham, it continued through the Constitutional Act of 1791, which while confirming the Quebec Act of 1774 and therefore the rights of the French to much of their distinctive way of life, nevertheless subordinated the French legislature of Lower Canada (Quebec) to an English executive and established a separate Upper Canada (Ontario) for the English, who thereby became Canada's first "separatists." The Rebellion of 1837 was a French protest against the ways of the mercantilist minority who controlled them and threatened to subvert their culture, religion, and language. In his report to the British Parliament on the troubles in Canada, Lord Durham said that he had found "two nations warring in the bosom of a single state"; however, he damned the one and praised the other. To give the one which he damned the benefits of the one he praised, the British Parliament joined Lower Canada to Upper Canada in the Act of Union of 1840. Although the Act of Union brought a brief period of peace and prosperity, the need for still further changes became necessary in the 1860s when the French saw that the arrangement threatened them with assimilation and the English saw that a broader based Canada was necessary both for economic development and to protect the north from a post-Civil War United States. Consequently, a series of compromises and agreements led to Confederation in 1867.

The Canada that was formed in 1867 was essentially a compromise, designed to protect a number of British colonies in North America and to open up lands into which the new country could grow. Quebec became one of its four founding provinces, at once the homeland of the French and to some extent a partner in the government of the whole country. But as the number of provinces expanded, or various conflicts arose (e.g., the Riel Rebellion of 1885 in western Canada, the Conscription Crisis of 1917 caused by French resistance to fight in an "English" war, and the various moves over the years against the use of the French language in the schools of Ontario and Manitoba), and as the powers of the central government grew, French discontent with Confederation also grew.

The basic disagreement today is about the place of the French in a country which the English seem bent on dominating. Many French regard Confederation as a compact made between two equal nations, certainly one between two founding races, the English and French; the English want to break that compact and usurp powers. Others see Quebec reduced in status to a province just like all the others in the eyes of Ottawa, but claim that it has a special place in Canada, being the homeland of the French. Moreover, as the population of French origin in Canada has shown a marked decline—from 30.4 per cent in the census of 1961 to 28.7 per cent in the census of 1971—that homeland required strengthening. Still others resent the post-World War II growth in power of the federal government in Ottawa. For Premier Rene Levesque of Quebec the solution is separation: only a separate Quebec can guarantee the survival of the French in North America, and Canada would gain too, for without Quebec the country would be rid of its most divisive issue.

Opposed to this view is the federalist position, most strongly associated with the long-serving Prime Minister, Pierre Elliott Trudeau. To federalists all the French in Canada, wherever they reside, are Canadians. They happen to be spread from coast to coast, with the largest concentration in Quebec, and it is the responsibility of the federal government to protect this French minority within a country dominated by the English majority. Hence, the official policy is one of bilingualism throughout Canada. Such a policy provides no special status to Quebec. The province of Quebec is unique only in that within it the English must be protected just as the French must be protected elsewhere. However, Quebec itself is just one of ten provinces in a federal system and any claims for special status must be dismissed as spurious. To recognize any such claims would be to risk the balkanization of Canada.

The consequent language disagreement seems to resist solution. Disputes are the order of the day and confrontations of one kind or another occur with predictable regularity: a dispute over the language of air traffic control in 1976; Quebec's Bill 101 to restrict the use of English in the province; Toronto baseball fans' booing a bilingual "O Canada" in May, 1978; and letters to the English press almost everywhere deploring "having French rammed down our throats." Even when the English make a move to accommodate the French, it always seems to be too little, too late, and too grudgingly given: by the time the federal government adopted a distinctive maple leaf design for the Canadian flag, Quebec had adopted the fleur-de-lys; by the time the country as a whole adopted "O Canada" for its national anthem, the people of Quebec had adopted "Mon pays" as the song which best gave expression to their feelings; and by the time Ottawa decided Canada should be a bilingual nation, Quebec had begun to opt for a policy of unilingualism in the province.

Of course, the North American pattern of national development has tended to favor societies which foster majority concerns to the point that minority interests must give way to those of the majority. One language, one culture (or no culture), and one social system is to be supported, and minorities must conform in all important respects. Any differences they have must be somehow supported outside the officially approved system and largely on a voluntary basis. Tolerance rather than support is the best that can be expected. Until recently this has been the predominant pattern in the United States, certainly until the recent era with its legislation to attempt to ensure the "collective rights" of certain minorities (e.g., Blacks, Hispanics, and women). In Canada the French presence has long tended to frustrate the intent of the larger English society to accomplish the same goals. Any "two nations" concept of Canada would allow for the existence side by side of two somewhat equal systems, one for Quebec and the other for Canada outside of Quebec. Such a concept is firmly resisted by a majority of Canadians outside of Quebec.

In the long run though, minorities are unlikely to ascribe legitimacy to a system in which majority will must always prevail, "the tyranny of the majority," particularly when one of the minorities is as large as the French minority in Canada and has a solid geographical base in Quebec within which it can act unilaterally largely in defiance of majority will. Even in a democracy the majority must from time to time give way to a minority to avoid democratic dictatorship. Accommodations must be made, and patterns of compromise must be available.

Canadians, however, have not been particularly successful in developing the kinds of structures and institutions which make accommodation and compromise easy. The English and French necessarily have contacts with one another and one might expect such contacts to reduce differences and encourage the development of a common "Canadian" viewpoint. In fact, almost the opposite happens. Many contacts tend to occur in such a way that differences become accentuated, positions harden, and the two charter groups are encouraged to grow still further apart. Even when the groups have joint institutions in which they meet regularly, such institutions as for example the Royal Society of

Canada, almost independent sections develop, an English one and a French one. The norm for a meeting of the English and French in Canada is almost always a situation which necessarily promotes rather than diminishes conflict, as in meetings of first ministers (the Prime Minister of Canada and his provincial counterparts, the ten premiers), or in one or other public forum. It is almost as though the parties had long ago given up the idea that they could possibly work together or they no longer see any point in trying. It is a remarkably different system from that of Switzerland for example, where consensual arrangements are not merely a norm but almost the very life blood of the federation.

Perhaps there are only two viable choices in the situation in which Canadians find themselves, in which an inability to compromise has resulted in policies which have obfuscated issues and heightened rather than reduced tensions. Given that there are two Canadian groups which differ strongly in matters of language and culture, one view holds that "good fences make good neighbors," i.e., that contact between the groups should be minimized so as not to exacerbate ill feelings. Contacts should be left to selected negotiators from each group who will iron out difficulties and reach accommodations, thus allowing the masses to go their separate ways. This kind of pattern is seen in Japan's deliberate isolation from the rest of the world until the mid-nineteenth century, in Burma's current isolation, in the establishment of ghettoes by immigrants in some societies, and to some extent in French-Canadian withdrawal inside the boundaries of the province of Quebec. The forms of segregation vary from case to case and differ in the degree to which the segregated group has freely chosen its isolation.

The opposite view is to remove barriers and encourage contact at all levels with the goal of enhancing mutual understanding. Such a policy requires affirmative action programs, declarations of human rights, encouragements to mobility, and so on. Individuals would be protected by law in the moves they make. However, such accommodative strategies may be very expensive for society, very threatening to entrenched interest groups, and very upsetting to individuals who see their traditional supports eroding at a time when others flourish in the new climate.

A key issue between the charter groups, of course, is the issue of language and ethnicity, the basic English-French dispute. Neither charter group can dominate the other; each has the power to break the country; and neither seems willing to relinquish what it conceives to be its rights. The language-ethnicity issue is a powerfully divisive one, but not one unique to Canada. Language and ethnicity have both proved to be very real problems in modern nation building.[7] The examples are many. For example, Jawaharlal Nehru had the following to say about the subject of language divisions in India as he wrestled with the problem of establishing a new nation: "Some of the ablest men in the country came before us and confidently and emphatically stated that language in the country stood for and represented culture, race, history, individuality, and finally a sub-nation."[8] Nehru clearly saw the threat posed by linguistic conflict to decades of work and sacrifice.

Language is a powerful tool of both social control and political identity. It is to be expected that different groups in society will attempt to control use of that tool. The majority group will see it as a means of bringing minorities to heal or into the fold. Minorities will see it as a means of preserving what collective rights and powers they have. Conflict is to be expected and so are appeals to "natural rights," "fairness," and "justice" by both sides. Since such appeals are also likely to be answered differently from time to time, as interpretations of the basic concepts involved change over the years, it may be unwise to think that fundamental issues could ever be settled once and for all. Resurrection in a different form may be expected.

Currently, the official Canadian position is that the country is bilingual in English and French. But this vision of Canada is plainly defective. It goes against the everyday experience of the vast majority of Canadians, who hear only one of the official languages, not both, as they go about their lives. Indeed, the forced intrusion of the other official language by decree has a profound irritant effect on many, whether they are English or French. The majority of Canadians do not live in bilingual, bicultural settings, and of those who do, the second language and culture is unlikely to be either English or French, but rather

Chinese, Portuguese, Italian, Greek, and so on. The official policy therefore is possibly divisive rather than cohesive. While it does little or nothing to help the French in Canada, it also is somewhat unattractive to those who are of neither English nor French origin. Any discussion of the language and cultural rights or aspirations of non-charter groups in Canada, that is, groups who are not of English or French origin, must inevitably find itself in the larger framework of the English-French dispute. Any move to preserve their language capability must take place in the context of an official federal policy of bilingualism in English and French, one which is now enshrined in the constitution. Any attempt to preserve a cultural distinctiveness through an official policy of multiculturalism immediately confronts the reality of the predominant English and French cultures. And, inevitably, any discussion of what will happen ultimately to the non-charter groups in Canada must take place in either the English or French language within a dominant institutional framework controlled by the English outside of Quebec and the French within.

The English-French dispute is therefore likely to remain close to the centre of any debate on Canada's future, its continued nationhood. In some ways it is the very similarity between the groups which separates them. As John Porter, one of Canada's most important sociologists, once observed:

> English and French Canadians are more alike in their conservatism, traditionalism, religiosity, authoritarianism and elitist values than the spokesmen of either group are prepared to admit.[9]

The result is a kind of shared conservatism which produces in the charter groups a stiff-necked unbendingness which makes any easy accommodation unlikely. It also makes dubious the successful implementation of a multicultural society, which is the official policy of the central government and the hope of many ethnic groups. It certainly makes impossible the realization of the policies of Anglo-conformity leading to the creation of yet another "English" nation in North America, a desire still espoused by many. Perhaps Canada is just a collection of various peoples suffering a permanent identity crisis and so lacking in confidence about the future that traditional ties to Britain, France, and other parts of the world must remain unbroken. Unfortunately, such ties may tend to choke rather than free the development of a distinctive Canadian voice unless, as did the Pepin-Roberts Report of the Task Force on Canadian Unity of 1979, one wants to consider the resulting "diversity as a source of strength" for Canada.[10]

Perhaps the only solution to Canada's dilemma depends on developing a feeling of nationhood which does not rely on language and ethnicity. To achieve this end, of course, governments at each level would have to curtail drastically their involvement in promoting any kind of "official" language and culture. Diversity would become the best guarantee of a national consciousness not based on the concept of the "rightness" or "superiority" of a specific language or culture. The result would be a truly pluralistic society. As Ramsay Cook has observed:

> A pluralistic society, if it values and understands its plural-ism, cannot be a nationalist society. Without the homogeneity which nationalism assumes, it cannot develop that sense of mission which characterizes all modern nationalisms.... Canada can exist only as a pluralist society for geographical and economic as well as historical and cultural reasons.... What Canadians must come to understand is that our nation-state is more seriously threatened by appeals to nationalism than by the lack of nationalism. The value of the Canadian experience is, or at least could be, its explicitly non-national-ist, pluralistic character.[11]

Crawford Young, a distinguished student of the problems of language and ethnicity in modern states, has pointed out the importance of learning to agree to disagree. He concludes his influential book *The Politics of Cultural Pluralism* with the following statement:

> The tensions built into this process are obvious. But nation-building can only move forward through an ongoing con-

sociational bargaining and compromise. There is simply no escape from the existing state system, as the political frame within which mankind must seek a better life. Conflict, some argue, is creative; that may well be, yet endemic civil strife along lines of cultural cleavage is surely not a pathway to either peace or prosperity. There is no single prescription; each plural polity has its own unique configuration of diversity. The sensitive application of wisdom accumulated in the observation of the politics of cultural pluralism is not beyond the reach of statesmanship. There is, of course, no other choice.[12]

Canada is beset with problems other than the English-French dispute but most observers agree that it is that dispute which looms largest in Canadian consciousness. Certainly the central government's concern with bilingualism has kept it embroiled with English-French relationships for well over a decade. Attention which might well have been given to other parts of Canada has instead been focused almost exclusively on relationships between Ottawa and Quebec City and between Ontario and Quebec. The needs of both the Atlantic provinces and the West have been overlooked. The West has never been particularly interesting in Ottawa's definition of what constituted the crisis in Canada's existence (the English-French relationship) and in a real sense has been excluded from full participation in Canadian political life by the agenda set by the governments of eastern Canada. High on the agenda have been language rights, a subject that grows less and less relevant the further one moves westward from the Quebec-Ontario border.

It is of considerable interest to observe that the aforementioned Pepin-Robarts Task Force on Canadian Unity arrived at conclusions somewhat different from the earlier Royal Commission on Bilingualism and Biculturalism, which did its work in the 1960s. The emphasis of that Royal Commission's report had been on the need to achieve equality between the two founding peoples of Canada. While the Pepin-Robarts Task Force acknowledged the basic duality of Canadian society, it also recognized that this duality is less apparent today in many areas of Canada because of the development of strong regional feelings. Indeed, to a considerable extent the Pepin-Robarts Report of 1979 played down the English-French problem in Canada and treated it as but one of half a dozen problems that confront Canadians when they consider the future of their nation, the others being the future of the native peoples, the state of the economy, the alienation of the Canadian West, the growing ethnic consciousness, and the increasing role of the central government in Canadian life. Nothing came of the Report; it was quite predictably shelved. Apparently, the Task Force had been established to buy time and its Report did not say what the Prime Minister was saying: it dared to acknowledge the duality of Canada. Consequently, what it said went unheard, and Prime Minister Trudeau continued to treat English-French intransigence as Canada's key problem and to lecture all parties on the rectitude of his solution to it and the inadequacies of all other proposals.

Keeping the language issue almost continuously on the national agenda has at least one other drastic consequence for Canada. It tends to conceal the basic issue of who really owns and controls Canada and the purposes of that ownership and control. Observers of Canadian society such as John Porter, Wallace Clement, Peter Newman, and Dennis Olsen have amply documented how certain elites control Canada, how they are "English" in origin, and how they perpetuate themselves.[13] They have also shown how false the belief is that social mobility in Canada allows those with talent to become members of the elites regardless of ethnic origin. In reality, the elites are closed to all but a select few, and their continued hold on power is a basic fact of Canadian life. However, few Canadians seem to know or care, and, even when public attention is drawn to members of the elites, it is usually in a not unfavorable light (as in a 1980 Canadian television series based on Newman's very successful book *The Canadian Establishment*).

Porter, Clement, and others have shown quite convincingly that the Canadian economy is controlled by a very small group of people, whom they refer to as the economic elite. This group numbers about a thousand but it manages to control (or jointly control with Americans and sometimes British) most of the economic institutions in the country. It is also heavily involved in activities which now spread far beyond Canada as various kinds of multinational arrangements have developed in recent years. Almost needless to say, anyone who seeks to find in it wide representation of French Canadians, indeed of members of any other group than the English, is doomed to disappointment.

Studies which have analyzed the ethnic composition of the boards of directors and senior executives of the hundred or so dominant Canadian corporations repeatedly show that Canadians of English origin dominate in numbers far beyond their proportion in the total Canadian population. The French are considerably under-represented and ethnic groups other than the Jewish are hardly represented at all. Even the Jewish group depends for its representation mainly on the success of half a dozen families who have managed to succeed in business by successfully swimming against the mainstream.[14] This situation has not improved with time, for as John Porter observed in his Foreword to Wallace Clement's *The Canadian Corporate Elite*:

> The economic elite of 1972 is more exclusive in social origins, more upper class and more closely knit by family ties than in 1952. Nor has there been any sizable entry into the board rooms of our major corporations of Canadians who are not British in their ethnic origin. So social structures are slow to change.[15]

According to Clement, a major reality of Canadian life is that corporate business controls government, not the opposite.[16] Moreover, corporate business shows a strong interlocking between the economic and mass media, one which grows more powerful and self-serving each year, and one which successive governments have encouraged rather than discouraged. The highest and most influential positions in Canada are well protected and almost hidden from view behind popular myths of opportunity, mobility, prosperity, and a mosaic in which all benefit according to what they bring. The reality is that Canada has a rigid social system, the top levels of which are virtually inaccessible except through inheritance and the members of which use Canada as a means for perpetuating private, acquisitive ends rather than promoting public, national goals. Clement writes:

> By developing a powerful national base in the circulation sectors, the indigenous Canadian elite has been able to operate internationally among the most powerful world capitalists. By servicing U.S. control of most of the resource sector and much of the manufacturing, the indigenous elite has reinforced its position within Canada and in the international capitalist system. They have accepted an international "division of labour" and their role in it as mediators.[17]

Clement concludes his book as follows:

> Top decision making positions in the economy and mass media in Canada are dominated by a small upper class. Through dominant corporations they maintain a hierarchically ordered corporate system by which they are able to extract surplus allowing them to continue and expand their control. This same surplus provides them with a life style much different than that experienced by the vast majority of Canadians and the privileges that accrue to them are passed on to their children. Despite severe erosion of the Canadian economy by U.S. based corporate capitalists since the early 1950's, the Canadian upper class remains intact. In fact, it has further consolidated its traditional commercial forte. . . . With all the changes which have been experienced over the last two decades, Canada has not fulfilled its promise as a society with equal opportunity. As long as corporate power is allowed to remain in its present concentrated state, there is no hope for equality of opportunity or equality of condition in Canada.[18]

Olsen's survey of the background of what he called the political elite in Canada between 1961 and 1973, comprising federal cabinet ministers, senior judges, and provincial premiers, led him to conclude that while the English were over-represented, all other groups were under-represented, particularly those who were neither English nor French:

These other groups increased their representation in the elite by 4 per cent over the previous study [1940-1960], but their share of the population increased by more than 5 per cent between 1951 and 1971, so that their position *relative to the population base* was actually worse than before. These are the blunt realities behind the image of equality among ethnic groups conjured up by "multiculturalism."[19]

Olsen argues that the elite comes from a middle class "that is generally content to leave the small upper class dominant in society while elite members themselves *individually* aspire to move up the ladder."[20] This ladder is the corporate ladder. In addition, since there is a considerable turnover of personnel in both federal and provincial governments, certain individuals gain considerable power, particularly premiers and the prime minister because of their ability to act as "chiefs":

> It is clear, then, that the Canadian political elite changes very slowly and not at all in some respects. The elite is still dominated by male lawyers and businessmen of French- and British-Canadian origins who came from middle- or upper-middle-class families. Most spend a relatively short time in politics, and, apart from a few individual "chiefs," few turn it into a regular lifetime career. The continuity of class and ethnic backgrounds suggests that the Canadian state creates, internally, a structured alliance between the two charter ethnic groups and between the middle and upper classes. This being the case, very little effective state power accrues to other ethnic groups or to the working classes.[21]

Olsen maintains that the political or state elite acts on behalf of the powerful corporate upper class, which does not directly involve itself in politics; in this sense it acts as a kind of broker or mediator between the upper and lower classes. But it never seeks to ally itself with the lower classes against those who control the economy since that would disrupt the somewhat delicate balance that has evolved, socially and politically, within Canada and, financially, without.

The various elites in Canada seem well able to perpetuate themselves. A series of studies shows that their characteristics have remained remarkably consistent over periods of many years. It is still very difficult for outsiders to penetrate them; what penetration has occurred might also be called nominal. The elites are above all the bastions of English power in Canada. What this means for members of other groups is that they must seek alternative means of creating power. The French have attempted this in Quebec by taking political control over their destiny. Individuals in other groups elsewhere have gone the route of entrepreneurship with the hope of gaining some kind of ultimate legitimacy for their descendants as members of the elite.[22] But such opportunities diminish each year as "big" business becomes more and more the only kind of business that has the resources to develop new ideas and technologies and therefore new wealth. What this apparently means for those groups now virtually excluded from the elites is that the doors to entry are just as firmly closed as before to almost all who seek to enter. The only hope is to create new opportunities outside the system but these too are limited. Leadership of minority groups is one kind of power and prestige, but ultimately it must prove frustrating if the prizes society awards are never finally available to such groups.

The worlds of big business and politics live comfortably with each other in Canada, as they do in many other places in the world. Big business even looks to government for help in fulfilling what it regards as its raison d'etre: the maximization of profit. Canadian big business has long had government support in its endeavors and has dipped even more bountifully into the public purse than has any other interest group in Canada: the building of the railroads is a prime early example, but every major economic sector has been the beneficiary of government funding programs. If a business is sufficiently big, it cannot be allowed to fail, as was revealed in the "bail out" of Dome Petroleum in 1982. Periodic ritualistic outbursts between business and government do occur, largely one suspects for appearance's sake. In reality, Canadian governments do little to interfere with monopolistic corporate capitalism, their regulatory agencies being notoriously weak, and big business does little to interfere with governments so long as profits are not endangered.

Canadians go along with this system, although the majority do not even seem to be aware of it, and many of those who are do not seem to care. Most Canadians regard themselves as consumers who require jobs to be able to buy and pay for what they buy in various kinds of financial arrangements. They therefore have a vested interest in stability and a suspicion of any change which might jeopardize their ability to consume. This attitude leads them to prefer the *status quo* and to adopt a conservative attitude toward the social system: any redistribution of shares must proceed slowly for fear that the result will be a loss rather than a gain. This approach is apparent even in Quebec, for the Parti Quebecois government has constantly reassured investors that they do not wish to change the basic economic arrangements of Quebec in any drastic fashion but merely wish to see the economy run in French within a different political system. For the majority of Canadians the major divisions in the country are linguistic, ethnic, religious, and regional issues, not economic ones. The two major parties use these differences in ways which are designed to give them power, but only one, the Liberal Party, has been particularly successful. "Radical" groups, even "mild" ones like the New Democratic Party, find it difficult to establish a strong federal presence, particularly when their basic ideology is an economic one opposed to the *status quo*.

Canadians seem much more willing to argue and on rare occasions even compromise over traditional and easily comprehended "markers" than to come to terms with more abstract concepts having to do with the economy, social justice, and a national consciousness. It is the measure of Canadian political and economic life (and cynicism) that national and regional leaders do little or nothing to elevate the people's interest, but rather pander to those concerns which enable them to rule by continuing to divide. The result of this failure of leadership is that Canadians are generally quite unconcerned about foreign control over the economy and the media and are willing to ignore the wheelings and dealings of the corporate elite whose main interest is increased profit not increased national well being (which could reduce profits rather than increase them). On the other hand, they are easily stirred by bilingual cornflakes boxes, a statement by General de Gaulle about a "free" Quebec, or a proposal to establish another school in Ontario in which French is to be used as the language of instruction. Local skirmishes and battles are fought with passion over linguistic issues while the economic war is lost every day in the boardrooms of cities like Toronto and New York. Even the Quebecois do not care about this war, as was readily apparent when Premier Levesque hastened to New York shortly after his election to reassure Wall Street that nothing that concerned the financiers was really going to change in Quebec. But this is not so surprising. Traditionally, Quebec has been somewhat indifferent to the issue of increased foreign control over the Canadian economy when it exercises almost no control over its own. Having learned to survive in a very unfavorable set of circumstances it is difficult for the Quebecois to conceive that some other arrangement could be any worse and easy to believe it must be better.

In the 1980s, perhaps the most important question of survival in Canada is no longer that of the survival of the French in Quebec. That seems to be guaranteed either within Canada or in some other arrangement. The real question is one of the survival of Canada in North America as an entity neither part of nor dominated by the United States. Canada's fragile east-west axis is threatened by a series of north-south regional pulls. World War II saw a fairly dramatic shift in Canada's relationship to the United States. The war reduced quite drastically the old connection with the United Kingdom and produced a growing dependency on the U.S. The old fear of political domination left, but new kinds of domination emerged: social, cultural, and above all economic. Continentalism again became respectable and the development of the multinational corporation did nothing to increase the loyalty corporations owed to the nation when chances for even greater profits would result from going international.

While there was some opposition to the growing "Americanization" of Canada in the 1970s, it never got very far. It was never perceived to be as serious as Ottawa-Quebec or Ottawa-Alberta disputes. Certainly it was never perceived by the public as one of the possible causes of those disputes. But perhaps the most saddening observation is that while the English-French issue in Canada was kept in full public view throughout the 1970s, the whole country quietly slipped further and further under the economic and cultural domination of the United States.

There is a certain "colonial" mentality in Canada which is extremely influential in determining national behavior, particularly as Canadians have a love-hate relationship with the concept of colonialism itself. Economically, Canada was first a colony of France, then of England, and more recently it has become an economic colony of the United States. Politically, it remains a colony of the United Kingdom: in law until the British North America Act was patriated, and in practice even after patriation in 1982 through its system of government. The French of Quebec still look to France for cultural kinship as well as linguistic inspiration even after more than two centuries of separation. Within Canada the central provinces and those to the east and west seem to have an imperial-colonial relationship, and Canada's own "colonial" leaders, the provincial premiers, use this theme repeatedly to support their demands for greater regional autonomy. And permeating all this is a national emphasis on ethnicity, the attachment to the homelands elsewhere, with, of course, that attachment most strongly displayed through desires to preserve the various languages now spoken in Canada.

Canada's colonial status has become even more apparent recently. As multinational corporations have developed and capital has flowed freely from country to country in a quest to boost profits, the Canadian branch plant system has grown less profitable and a process called "de-industrialization" has begun. Large businesses such as the Massey-Ferguson farm implement manufacturers either collapsed or called for government subsidies so as to continue operating, and more and more the country has had to fall back on producing raw materials for others to process, a system well known to Canadians and other colonized people. The interesting fact about Canadians though is that they have always done this quite willingly and many of the most powerful people in the country have actually made their fortunes from managing the giveaway of Canada's resources. Canadians have even learned how to finance the takeover of their country by others, the supreme colonial gesture.

It is difficult to escape the conclusion that Canada is a most improbable country. Its constitution was until 1982 an Act of the British Parliament and its system of government and law, with the exception of Quebec Civil Law, is solidly based on that of the United Kingdom. It has a "nation" in its midst which looks to France for linguistic and cultural ties. Spread west of Quebec are millions of descendants of those who come neither from an English nor a French tradition, and these numbers have been considerably augmented by post-World War II immigrants. It contains an intractable group of native peoples. Geographically, the country lies east to west yet economically it functions north to south toward its giant North American partner. Culturally, the partner dominates Canada with considerable influence, even within Quebec. It is a country split every which way—linguistically, religiously, economically, culturally, socially—but a country that in spite of its improbability has lasted longer than most other modern states. It is therefore one which must still have considerable strengths in spite of all its problems. Perhaps it is linguistic and ethnic conflict which actually keeps Canada together, along with a reluctance to face other issues. Such a narrow definition might indeed comprise the whole of that mythic quality sought by many, "Canadian identity"!

# 2

# OFFICIAL BILINGUALISM

Since the English-French relationship in Canada, particularly the linguistic relationship, is perceived by many Canadians to be the country's central problem, it would be well to look at one of the major pieces of legislation which attempts to regulate that relationship, the Official Languages Act of 1969. This Act resulted from the work of the Royal Commission on Bilingualism and Biculturalism and was steered through Parliament by the Prime Minister himself, Pierre Elliott Trudeau. The resulting relationship has been of considerable significance to events in Canada.

The Royal Commission on Bilingualism and Biculturalism was born in an atmosphere perceived to be one of crisis, an atmosphere which, indeed, one of its co-chairmen, Andre Laurendeau, may have helped to create. Laurendeau, the editor-in-chief of the Montreal daily *Le Devoir*, had long sought equality for Quebec within Confederation although extracts from his diary published posthumously in that paper on June 1, 1978, showed how he had also nurtured separatist notions. Appointed on July 19, 1963, the Royal Commission was asked:

> to inquire into and report upon the existing state of bilingualism and biculturalism in Canada and to recommend what steps should be taken to develop the Canadian Confederation on the basis of an equal partnership between two founding races, taking into account the contribution made by the other ethnic groups to the cultural enrichment of

Canada and the measures that should be taken to safeguard that contribution.[1]

The Royal Commission worked in the same kind of atmosphere of crisis. Its preliminary report, published in 1965, said: "Canada, without being fully conscious of the fact, is passing through the greatest crisis in its history."[2] This view was reiterated in the Commission's eventual final report of October 8, 1967: "decisions must be taken and developments must occur leading either to [Canada's] break-up, or a new set of conditions for its future existence."[3] Such a view was generally accepted. To what extent the work of the Royal Commission helped create or validate a "crisis" one can only surmise. Certainly, the work of the Royal Commission was itself one of the "events" which ushered in a decade of great uncertainty about the future of Canada. How much of that uncertainty was created by opportunists of various persuasions and how much it reflected genuine popular concerns only the long historical perspective will reveal.

The Royal Commission was heavily committed to a bicultural view of Canada. Its report abounds with terms such as *equal partnership*, *cultural duality*, *two founding races*, and *cultural partnership*. To many critics, that was an initial basic flaw in both the terms of reference and in the Commission's perception, which no amount of good intention could redeem. As one critic later observed:

> By 1961, with 26 per cent of the Canadian population of other than British or French ethnic origin, with over two hundred newspapers published in languages other than French and English, with fairly well defined Italian, Jewish, Slavic, and Chinese neighbourhoods in large Canadian cities, and with visible rural concentrations of Ukrainians, Doukhobors, Hutterites, and Mennonites, how was it possible for a royal commission to speak of Canada as a *bi*cultural country?[4]

In their interpretation of the key words in the charge to them the commissioners did downplay the notion of "race" or "people" (when applied to the English and French charter groups) in favor of emphasizing linguistic and cultural criteria. They accepted the concept that patrilinearity was appropriate in matters of "ethnic origin," though not without some hesitation. Since official census figures were based on that concept, they really had little other choice.[5] They preferred, however, to play down ethnicity and give more importance to language than ethnic origin. They also decided that their terms of reference excluded the native peoples of Canada from their concern.[6] Not for the first time and not for the last either would the native peoples be thus excluded from consideration in matters of grave national concern.

"Bilingual" the commissioners defined as the use of the two official languages,[7] either individually or institutionally, but they added that institutional bilingualism depended on sufficiency of bilingual individuals. They recognized that "biculturalism" referred to the distinctive ways of life of the basically English and French populations of Canada. In doing so, they acknowledged the considerable diversity and variation in the first. They also declared that while language and culture are by no means inseparable components in group identification, attempts to preserve cultural equality are primarily attempts to perserve linguistic equality.[8]

In the general introduction to their report, the commissioners accepted without question the notion of "equal partnership" between the English and French in Canada, an equal partnership in which members of other ethnic groups could share freely and equally:

> ...we believe the place of the Quebecois in the French fact in Canada will in practice have to be recognized much more than it is today....All...facts combine to give Quebec a leading role in promoting the French language and culture in Canada....it is an obvious and incontrovertible fact that Quebec is not "a province like the others."[9]

The second chapter of Book I of the 1967 Report surveyed the basic demographic situation in Canada, using information from the various censuses, including that from the 1961 census. The commissioners concluded that "linguistic duality remains the basic characteristic and foundation of the Canadian community.[10] They noted the "pluralistic character" of each of the groups that made up the duality "even if assimilation to English is much stronger and more marked than assimilation to French." However, "neither demography nor the law of numbers is the sole factor governing bilingualism in Canada."

Chapter three of Book I of the Report dealt with the legal status of the English and French languages in Canada, focusing particularly on Section 133 of the British North America Act but also with matters such as the abrogation in 1890 of the provisions to protect French in the legislature and courts of the province of Manitoba, provisions which had been written into the Manitoba Act of 1870 and not restored until 1979. Among some level-headed remarks concerning the virtual elimination of French in the Prairie provinces was a reminder that the acts establishing those provinces were written in both English and French and "it is therefore not true to say that French has no official status on the Prairies."[11] What impressed the commissioners most about Section 133 was that it at best "represents embryonic concepts of cultural equality, and it cannot be expected to provide for the many complex situations that must now be faced,"[12] for example, the growth of quasi-judicial bodies and federal agencies, of a huge bureaucracy, and of a modern society. Custom and expediency in devising solutions were not enough; statutory provisions were apparently the only solution to the prevailing inconsistencies, inequalities, and disorder. Official bilingualism should replace an incomplete and unequal bilingualism.

So far as Section 93 of the British North America Act was concerned, the commissioners saw it as guaranteeing confessionality, that is, religious rights, rather than language rights, but pointed out that Quebec, in contrast to both Manitoba and Ontario, has always equated the two:

> The history of language privileges in the schools of the other provinces has been very different, and such opportunities as do exist have been achieved by the vigorous and persistent efforts of the French-speaking minority. Even though at times

there was co-operation or at least tacit consent from provincial officials, these efforts most often met with great financial hardship and administrative difficulties.[13]

One of the many studies conducted for the Royal Commission, Claude-Armand Sheppard's *The Law of Languages in Canada*,[14] had arrived at many of the same conclusions concerning inequities between the two languages in Canada:

> ...from the legal point of view there are only two jurisdictions in which there is no doubt that both languages [English and French] enjoy almost equal official status: the federal and Quebec jurisdictions.
>
> In most jurisdictions, this situation only reflects the distribution of population....It is also apparent...that no Canadian jurisdiction has yet had an overall approach to language rights and that most legislation is the result of an *ad hoc* attitude to the solution of specific problems. In some this may be due to the absence of any real necessity to deal with the subject in a general and comprehensive way, but most often it would seem that this situation stems from the failure, or refusal, to fill the obvious gaps in the constitution and to face the political and cultural significance of ensuring language rights. There may be many other explanations for this lack of a broad linguistic bill of rights or it may even have been the least perilous course of action in the past. Nevertheless it is clear to us that it will become increasingly difficult in the future to maintain this haphazard and piecemeal approach.[15]

After examining what is called the "territorial principle" and "personality principle" of bilingualism and looking at the situations in Finland, Belgium, Switzerland, and South Africa, the Royal Commission on Bilingualism and Biculturalism rejected territorial bilingualism for Canada, i.e., "official French unilingualism in Quebec and an English unilingualism in other provinces, with bilingual federal institutions in the centre."[16] The commissioners concluded that such a solution would oppress the official language minorities, the English in Quebec and French outside. Instead, the Royal Commission opted for *"the recognition of both official languages, in law and in practice, wherever the minority is numerous enough to be viable as a group."*[17] The personality principle was to mean that the federal government was to protect language minorities and deal to the best of its ability with all speakers of the official languages in the language of their choice. Federal institutions would be required to develop bilingual capability.

Although the Royal Commission opted for a policy of federal bilingualism, it wanted to see that policy extended to the provinces: "...we believe all the provinces should accept official bilingualism in their jurisdictions, though to degrees which in practice will vary according to the prevailing demographic conditions."[18] They proposed the extension of Quebec's "generous and coherent" system of bilingualism to other provinces and argued that Ontario and New Brunswick should become officially bilingual provinces. (To date only New Brunswick has done so.) They added that any other province whose official language minority reached 10 per cent should also become officially bilingual. Further proposals dealt with allowing the French language to be used in all provincial legislatures, the establishment of federal bilingual districts, the establishment of a right for all Canadian parents to have their children educated in the official language of their choice, numbers permitting, the passing of an Official Languages Act and the appointment of a Commissioner of Official Languages, and an outline of changes that would be necessary in the British North America Act as a result of all of these. In a separate statement appended to the Report, Commissioner J.B. Rudnyckyj pleaded the case of other languages and recommended that languages such as German, Ukrainian, and Italian should be given the status of "regional languages" in certain well-defined circumstances and that that status should entitle them to certain privileges. However, it would not put these languages on a par with French.

The third volume of the Report of the Royal Commission on Bilingualism and Biculturalism issued in 1969 pointed out how little attention was given to French in Quebec's business world and how economically disadvantaged the average French resident of Quebec was in relation to English counterparts. It recommended that French should become more and more the language of work in Quebec and that the French should assume greater control over the economy of the province. In this analysis and in its recommendation, the Royal Commission got nearer to the heart of the matter of English-French relationships in Canada so far as most Quebecois were concerned. Later Quebec legislation was to confirm this fact. Needless to say the Royal Commission's views on these issues were not particularly welcome in English Canada and the Official Languages Act and much of the national debate which led up to its passage virtually ignored this critical aspect of the Royal Commission's work. The language recommendations were largely implemented, but the critical issue of English-French relationships within Quebec was left untouched. Legislation to protect the French language in Quebec would have roused the country against the French. It might have indicated to the English that Quebec had a "special status" within Confederation. The Official Languages Act actually protected even further the English in Quebec, both their presence and their language, a protection which the Quebecois saw as quite unnecessary, indeed as a further threat to their own well being in their very homeland.

The Royal Commission on Bilingualism and Biculturalism undoubtedly failed in at least one crucial regard. Its recommendations addressed themselves only partially to the crisis that the commissioners perceived to exist in Canada. That crisis, if it existed, was largely constitutional in nature. A volume on the constitutional issues was clearly called for and was indeed promised. But it never materialized, proving too difficult to write after Laurendeau died in 1968. Consequently, what measures the federal government later brought forward were implemented in a constitutional vacuum: the new policy lacked the necessary constitutional cornerstone. Supported, however, by all parties in Parliament, the Official Languages Act became divisive when those outside saw its few baby teeth as fangs at their throats—they felt completely uninformed as to the nature of the animal that had been created and the bounds within which it would be allowed to roam.

The recommendations of the Royal Commission on Bilingualism and Biculturalism were also based on findings of the censuses up to and including that of 1961, a series of research studies the Royal Commission sponsored, and the various briefs and presentations made by interested groups. They were also seriously constrained by the make-up of the Commission itself and its terms of reference. Undoubtedly a different group of people given somewhat different terms of reference and the data from the 1971 census would have arrived at another set of conclusions and recommendations. Just what these might have been one can only speculate, but it is quite likely they would have been rather different from those which the Royal Commission did present to the government. They may also have been more palatable to just about everyone except, one suspects, Prime Minister Trudeau, who had long been committed to the majority of the views which the Royal Commission did express on the language situation in Canada.

Undoubtedly, too, some of the impetus for action in the late 1960s on such matters as language rights come from the example and successes of the Civil Rights movement in the United States. That movement had as its first goal the desegregation of the public school system so that schools could not draw their populations according to color and race (though, of course, the injustice of economic segregation was hardly ever questioned). The same kind of movement in Canada produced almost the opposite effect. In Canada very few school systems had practised racial segregation and the 1960s ended such practices. Equal rights in Canada actually meant the establishment of "separate but equal" facilities, not their abolition. In this case it led to the establishment of facilities on a linguistic basis, to protect the French language outside of Quebec. Indeed, bilingual schools, in which children would have a choice between English and French as a language of instruction, were resisted. (To the French in Canada, bilingualism is above all a measure of linguistic assimilation.) Only schools whose populations were segregated from each other according to the language of instruction were deemed suitable to guarantee rights which had long been denied. The consequences of the "rights" movements in the two countries were therefore almost diametrically opposite, a good indication of how interests served by a popular ideology can lead to very different consequences in different situations.

However, while the Official Languages Act encouraged the development of this kind of "separate but equal" institutional response, it did so in order to respond to what were regarded as individual rather than collective disabilities. Except in regard to the native peoples of Canada, Canadian law and practice have never favored guarantees of collective minority rights; instead they have emphasized the guaranteeing of individual rights within a system of majority rule. In this respect Quebec itself is no different from any other province. Discrimination against individuals for any of a variety of reasons is against various laws of the land (often ineffectively applied), but in general those laws do not provide relief for groups through establishing quotas of one kind or another. Individuals may stand together to ask for a French or English school, thereby asserting their individual rights collectively but one individual is rarely allowed to speak for a "class." In this respect Canada again differs from its neighbor to the south. In the United States class action suits and quota systems of various kinds are facts of everyday life and the courts actively intervene to decide who does what and who gets what in society. In contrast, until 1982, the Canadian system was one in which legislatures could decide what individuals were to do or to have and how social institutions would accommodate to these doings or havings. Legislatures rather than courts were supreme, a principle reiterated time and time again during the constitutional debates of 1980-82 by those who opposed any proposal to entrench a Charter of Rights into a patriated Canadian Constitution. One of the most controversial parts of the Constitution Act of 1982 is its Charter of Rights which, weak though it is when compared to the Bill of Rights in the Constitution of the United States, still profoundly affects the relationship of the individual citizen to various levels of government and allows the courts to intervene between the two.

Above all, the Official Languages Act of 1969 is a document which specifies how the central government must deal with Canadian citizens in the two official languages of Canada, English and French. The policy is designed to ensure that the federal government provide services in the official language which an individual prefers when there is an official language minority of some reasonable size in a particular location. The law obliges no individual to become bilingual, even though that is a common misinterpretation. It also tries to guarantee that neither the English nor French in Canada suffer discrimination because of the languages they speak in their daily lives and work. They should be free to move around the country and while doing so enjoy certain rights, particularly to have their children educated in the official language of their choice and to be able to use the mother tongue in their dealings with federal institutions and to hear it spoken on radio and television. Therefore, money has been provided to the provinces to support minority official language instruction; the Public Service, that is, the federal bureaucracy, has been given a bilingual capability; and separate national radio and television systems have been established to operate in English and French.

Under the Official Languages Act the Government of Canada appoints a Commissioner of Official Languages, a kind of language ombudsman for the nation. There have been two such commissioners, Keith Spicer for the first seven years of the Act's life, and currently Maxwell Yalden. Their literate and anything-but-stuffy annual reports to the Parliament of Canada make instructive reading. A number of themes recur: the foot-dragging slowness of the federal bureaucracy in introducing changes; the wastefulness of much of the language training within the Public Service; the key role of various translation services; the continued lack of co-operation in certain areas of government; and the widespread misunderstanding of government policy and the persistent failure of the government to provide explanations of that policy. A typical comment from the Fourth Annual Report on the government's slowness reads as follows:

> Bilingual signs, forms, plaques and panels fall in one sense into the area of tokenism. But when they remain unilingual five years after the Official Languages Act was passed, their conversion can resemble a dangerous contradiction of other,

more substantial, reforms. If these physical, and often simple, elements of linguistic char ye cannot be handled readily, one wonders indeed how ever the Government can cope with the infinitely more sensitive and complex problems of personnel management.[19]

Right from the beginning the majority of the public was either misinformed about, or deliberately did not want to understand the legislative intent of the new Act. As early as his second report, dated January, 1973, the Commissioner of Official Languages, Keith Spicer, found it necessary to say:

> . . . if there remains one disturbing setback in the slow march of Canada's federal administration toward equality for our two official languages, it is the scandalous misinformation that, in too many parts of Canada, still overshadows the Act's basic, civilized truths—its aim of institutional, not individual, bilingualism, its fundamental and long-overdue fairness, its almost limitlessly supple possibilities of adaptation to local human needs.[20]

In saying this, he found himself repeating remarks he had made in his initial report. Later reports were also to pick up the theme.

Since one major intent of the Official Languages Act was to require the government to deal, where numbers warranted, with taxpayers in the official language in which they paid their taxes, it is of interest to see how the Public Service responded to the requirement. First of all, it can be observed that at Confederation (i.e., in 1867) the French actually filled positions in the federal bureaucracy in excess of their proportion in the population of Canada. However, the next 80 years saw a considerable decrease in that proportion, accentuated by the deliberate anglophonization of the bureaucracy in the between-war period (the 1920s and 1930s) and by the cultivation of the "merit" principle which, because of the particular characteristics of Quebec's system of higher education, disfavored the French, whether unilingual or bilingual. In Quebec, government service as a career meant service with the provincial rather than federal government. Consequently, by the end of World War II the federal bureaucracy was nearly 90 per cent English and the Quebec bureaucracy almost 100 per cent French.

Even before the passage of the Official Languages Act, changes had been made to induce more French to join the federal bureaucracy. For example, the Civil Service Act of 1961 empowered the Civil Service Commission to determine the language requirements of positions in the Public Service and required certain offices to have a complement of bilinguals to serve the the public adequately. The coverage of the Act was later extended to allow the possession of bilingual skills to be used as an element in merit for promotion and to encourage government bureaucrats to acquire the necessary skills. The Official Languages Act was regarded as a further inducement to the French.

The 1979 Report of the Commissioner of Official Languages shows some of the results. Between 1965 and 1979 the percentage of francophones in the Public Service (that is, those government employees who are most at home in the French language) increased from 21.5 per cent to 26.4 per cent, a proportion approaching the proportion of those of French origin in Canada, 28.6 per cent in the 1971 census.[21] By 1981 the percentage had risen slightly to 27.2 per cent. In the officer categories (Executive, Scientific and Professional, Administrative and Foreign Service, and Technical) francophones increased their percentages from 13.4 per cent in 1971 to 22.7 per cent in 1978 and 23.7 per cent in 1981. However, certified bilingual federal employees in regions designated as "bilingual" by the Treasury Board (the National Capital Region, northern and eastern New Brunswick, northern and eastern Ontario, parts of Montreal, and certain other regions in Quebec) reported that English still dominated French as the language in which most certified bilingual anglophones do most of their work in such districts and in which many certified bilingual francophones actually find themselves working. Only in Quebec is this not the case.[22] Two further indications that English is still largely the language of work in federal affairs can be given. In his 1979 report, Commissioner Maxwell Yalden pointed out that the ratio of translation from English to translation from French is 12:1

within the Translation Bureau.[23] It was actually only in 1979, with the election of a short-lived Progressive Conservative government, that simultaneous translation was introduced into meetings of the Cabinet and Treasury Board, thus achieving working equality at the highest level of the federal government itself, and this ten years after the proclaiming of the Official Languages Act.

Of course, one intention of the Act is to ensure that government employees should be given the opportunity to work in their mother tongue if they wish, for no one is to be compelled to become bilingual—encouraged, but not compelled. However, Christopher Beattie's 1965 study, with a follow-up in 1973, of a number of middle federal civil servants showed quite clearly that it was disadvantageous to speak only French in the service of the federal government.[24] Francophones earned less and found promotion slower than their anglophone counterparts, and the Official Languages Act had actually done very little to improve their position. Beattie also pointed out that the Quebec Public Service is more attractive to Quebecois than the federal Public Service, a situation which results in the latter having to recruit its francophones from outside of Quebec. This recruitment necessity also has certain damaging consequences for those recruited: since educational provisions for the French outside Quebec are neglected by the provincial governments, French candidates do not necessarily measure up well with their English counterparts and may be held back for matters which are really beyond their control.

Over the years apparently much of the federal Public Service has been rather resistant to the attempt to give it institutional bilingual capability. The two Commissioners of Official Languages have had many harsh things to say about the reluctance of various departments and groups falling within the jurisdiction of the Act to conform to the institutional requirement. Language training programs to develop personal bilingualism within the Public Service have also been notoriously wasteful. Tens of thousands of bilingual positions were created, financial and promotional inducements to become "bilingual" were generously provided, money was spent in large amounts, but

English civil servants who did not like the idea of learning French were carefully protected in their positions, even when those positions required a genuine bilingual capability.

By 1975 it was apparent that the federal government's attempt to create a Public Service with considerable personal bilingual capabilities had seriously failed. However, one may well heed Raymond Breton's words on the subject of this "failure":

> Some people claim the bilingualism program has been a "failure." But what does failure mean? It could mean that many people who took the language training do not really know the language; that the results are not adequate for the level of expenditure. But I would hypothesize that the perception of "failure" refers either to the fact that the program did not alter the distribution of control over career lines and related advantages—as some were hoping it would do—or that it altered it in a way that disfavored certain categories of people—as some were fearing it would do.[25]

The Bibeau Report of that year on developments in the Public Service indicated that as many as 53,000 of the bilingual positions that existed in 1973-74 had been so classified without any thorough evaluation of the actual needs of the positions for a second language capability. It pointed out that fewer such positions were needed but that the actual level of bilingual skill required was greater than had been indicated. The 1974 Report of the Commissioner of Official Languages also confirmed that much of the expenditure on bilingual training had been wasted since the vast majority of civil servants who had received training were not in positions requiring much or any use of the newly acquired language. Millions of dollars were being wasted on providing training which was not put to use.

The Report of the Commissioner of Official Languages for 1977 declared that "the massive, shotgun approach to language training has not produced results that match the costs"[26] and reiterated earlier criticisms of the "bilingual bonus." By 1979 this bonus was costing the taxpayer $38 million a year and the federal government found itself unable to end it over the opposition of recipients. In 1981 it cost $40 million. Perhaps the wittiest summation of the ineffectiveness of the government's attempts to create a Public Service capable of carrying out the intent of the 1969 Act and, therefore, a comment on the continued disadvantages experienced by the French in that Public Service is the following statement from the Commissioner's Fourth Report:

> English-speaking mandarins may sign, and send to each other, a few more letters in French drafted by French-speaking subordinates. Cosy and colourful as this political dadaism may seem, it does little to ensure that French becomes a believable language of the upper administration previously, and not even scurrilously, known as the English Establishment.[27]

The situation in other parts of the federal system was generally not any better and often much worse. For example, by the mid-1970s within the Canadian Armed Forces only the army had made any really noticeable progress toward bilingualism. The navy and air force were still basically English in orientation. Within the Armed Forces as a whole two-thirds of the 17,000 bilingual personnel were actually of French origin. It was, however, possible for unilingual francophones, in the army at least, to serve in entirely French units and to achieve promotion within such units. But high level control of the Armed Forces as a whole remained firmly in the hands of the English.

The development of French units in an institution such as the Armed Forces shows one possible pattern for bilingual development in the country: a kind of separate but equal unilingualism. Personal, universal bilingualism is obviously impossible in a country such as Canada: one of the languages would be completely redundant and efforts to achieve that situation would be both linguistically absurd and financially ruinous. Institutional bilingualism is an entirely different matter; however, it has proved to be politically divisive and almost equally unappealing to the English and French alike and to members of other ethnic groups.

One important provision of the Official Languages Act has still to be implemented. The Act created a Bilingual Districts Advisory

Board to recommend areas in the country in which the federal government should provide full bilingual services to citizens. In 1971 the Board produced a report which aroused so much criticism that nothing came of it. A second report in 1975 by a reconstituted Board recommended that the government establish a number of specified bilingual districts including at least one in every province except British Columbia. For example, the whole province of New Brunswick was to be a bilingual district. However, Montreal was not to be one, the majority of the Board feeling that the English population of Montreal was sufficiently well protected and did not need the further support which being included within a bilingual district would provide. Hardly anything has come of the recommendations. Today only the National Capital Region is an official bilingual district. By 1975 the whole federal language policy had lost what initial appeal it had and any move to implement the Board's recommendation would have aroused hostility just about everywhere in the country.

One recurring theme of the reports by both commissioners is the neglect, or, if not neglect, the quite indifferent results of teaching French in the schools and universities outside of Quebec. Both commissioners have advocated the teaching of French as providing at least part of the solution to a misunderstanding of the policy of bilingualism and to encourage individual bilingualism in Canada. Both insist that there should be more teaching of French in the schools of English Canada and that movements to abolish French as a requirement for university entrance or graduation are not in the country's best interests. They ignore the fact that such instruction has almost always proved wasteful in imparting real language skills, and that often compulsory language instruction generates as much hostility toward the other group as empathy. This kind of short-sightedness is all the more remarkable in view of the severe criticisms meted out to the Public Service's richly supported attempts to teach French. One must ask how much less likely are the poorly supported efforts of the schools to succeed, and regard as a piece of "pie-in-the-sky" longing a statement from the 1979 Report that a policy which brings about a healthy bilingualism is one of the guarantees that the non-official languages will survive because of the linguistic climate such a policy creates.[28] To state the obvious, the Official Languages Act has hardly created a healthy linguistic climate in Canada!

Over the ten years in which it has been in force the Official Languages Act has cost Canadian taxpayers several billions of dollars in direct costs alone. The estimated direct costs for 1980-81 and 1981-82 were $416 million and $448 million respectively, which amounts to a charge of almost $20 a year for each person living in Canada. The heaviest proportion of these costs goes in formula payments to provinces ($148 million in each of the two years) in an attempt to encourage official language minority undertakings, but more than half of that goes to support English in Quebec. Language programs and training in the Armed Forces, in the various government departments and agencies, and in the Public Service take about an equal amount. The amount devoted to translation approached $67 million in the 1981-82 estimates. Altogether in 1981-82 the Official Languages Act generated 6,075 person-years of activity.[29] Canadians may legitimately ask what they are buying for all this time, effort, and money. The answer does not appear to be linguistic harmony.

A policy of official bilingualism means different things to different people in Canada. To the Government of Canada, it means the institutional capability to respond to citizens in either of the official languages. To many English, it represents a threat to what they see as basically an English-dominated Canada, and a fear that bilingual "control" of the country will be tantamount to French control since most English resist the notion of learning French. To those who are members of ethnic groups other than the English or French, official bilingualism means a struggle to preserve some other language or culture in the face of overwhelming odds. To the French of Quebec, bilingualism is a direct threat to their language, particularly the creation of a bilingual Quebec within a unilingual English Canada. Only if Quebec can be preserved as a unilingual French province can assimilation be resisted. Even someone like J.T. Thorson—a strong proponent of a strict interpretation of Section 133 of the British North America Act, a strong opponent of the Official Languages Act, which he sought to have voided, and counsel before the Supreme Court of Canada—felt that bilingualism did nothing to meet Quebec's real needs within Confederation.[30]

Outside Quebec, bilingualism remains the only hope of the French submerged in a sea of English, but a bilingualism backed by all the panoply of powers that the various provincial governments can be persuaded to display. Such an organization as the Federation des Francophones hors Quebec, founded in 1975, has tried to persuade the various governments to do just that but with little success so far. There is really no reason to believe that either the Official Languages Act itself or what direct federal and provincial support has been allotted for the teaching of French outside of Quebec has done much if anything to stop the decay of the French language there. Certainly no one has ever indicated that there has been a marked increase in the use of French nor has anyone claimed that the movement toward the use of English has been arrested or even that the rate of decline in the use of French has been significantly affected. It is difficult to see how this could be otherwise, since the trend to English appears to be almost irreversible in the political and social climate that exists in the country outside the province of Quebec.

The Official Languages Act has done nothing to please the French either inside or outside Quebec. Within Quebec it actually further entrenched the rights of the English, already well protected by the British North America Act. The Constitution Act of 1982 reaffirmed that protection. The Official Languages Act has tended to perpetuate a situation which many French deplore because of the inequities they know exist elsewhere in the country. Outside Quebec, partly because of hostility and misunderstanding, the official languages legislation has proved largely ineffective in preserving French minority rights: one cannot legislate a language back to life without massive public support. It has also angered other linguistic groups who felt neglected and suddenly cast as second-class citizens. In other words, the major beneficiaries in Canada were the English, the very group who did not need any help.

However, there is a widespread feeling in the English community that there have been too many negative consequences of the Official Languages Act to make it, in retrospect, a good piece of legislation. These range from the unnecessary costs involved in labelling, translating, training, and publicity, through the apparent replacement of "merit" by bilingualism, as a criterion for hiring and promotion in the Public Service, to a belief that the French are using the issue of bilingualism to take over the Government of Canada.

The extent of English paranoia and xenophobia in matters to do with language can be seen in the success of a tract published in 1977, *Bilingualism Today, French Tomorrow*, which went through printing after printing in a few months and which was serialized in Toronto's tabloid daily, the Toronto *Sun*, as a kind of public service.[31] That the book completely distorts the federal policy of bilingualism, shows scant respect for facts, retails a "conspiracy" theory, sets a Doomsday-like scenario, and is personally vindictive of Prime Minister Trudeau and others is sad in that so many people found in its pages chords to which they responded. When discussion of policies so important to the future of Canada descends to such a level, one can only regret what has happened. However, some of the blame for such distortions must be laid on those who so conspicuously failed to explain their policies and convince Canadians of their merits, in this case the federal government itself.

The government's language policy actually ran into trouble almost from the very beginning. The 1972 general election was a severe blow to the Liberals. The results clearly indicated considerable dissatisfaction with the policy, and the people of Quebec interpreted them as evidence of a strong backlash in English Canada against policies regarded as favorable to the French. Fortunately for the Liberals the economy became a critical issue and it was able to fight the 1974 election mainly on economics while keeping bilingualism out of the public attention.

Perhaps the most serious recent national dispute in the 1970s over English-French language relations occurred in 1976 when the predominantly anglophone Canadian Airline Pilots Association and Canadian Air Traffic Controllers Association struck over allowing French as well as English to be used in air traffic control in the province of Quebec, claiming "safety" as the reason. In fact safety was not the real issue, as bilingual air traffic control is quite

normal in many international airports. The real issue was the
government's insistence that the Official Languages Act should
apply in an area where the English felt specially privileged and
therefore specially threatened. The issue was exploited skilfully by
those who resisted bilingualism. English reactions were noted in
Quebec and undoubtedly helped the Parti Quebecois in its bid
for power in the election in Quebec in November of that year. The
dispute brought about the resignation of two Liberal cabinet
ministers for almost opposite reasons: Jean Marchand, a
Quebecois, to protest the growing hostility toward the French,
and James Richardson, a westerner, to whom bilingualism was
not really an acceptable policy at all, particularly within western
Canada. Eventually, safety was shown to be an irrelevant issue
and today bilingualism is the norm in air traffic control in
Quebec, as it is in Paris, Lisbon, Rome, etc.

The 1976 dispute indicated just how resistant English Canadians
were to the bilingual policy of the federal government. It also
indicated how determined Prime Minister Trudeau was to have
his own way with colleagues and public alike and, in that way, it
foreshadowed his role in the constitutional debates of 1980-82. One
direct result of that dispute and of the election of a separatist
government in Quebec was the publication in 1977 by the federal
government of a document entitled *A National Understanding*.[32]
In this document the government attempted to explain and justify
its language policy to a public confronted with a new separatist
government in Quebec and disenchanted with official bilingualism. The government insisted that its view of bilingualism was
correct:

> The federal government rejects the concepts of a Canada
> divided into two mutually exclusive unilingual separate coun-
> tries or two mutually exclusive unilingual regions within one
> country. While these two options have a superficial
> appearance of dissimilarity, they amount in practice to the
> same thing, a province or state of Quebec that is unilingual
> French speaking and the rest of Canada, or a truncated
> Canada, that is unilingual English speaking.

> The government rejects these concepts above all because

they entail a denial of the existence of the official language minority groups of Canada. . . . There is an official language minority group in every province and territory in the country. . . . It is hardly to be doubted that those who see a Canada divided on linguistic lines, or separated on a similar basis, envisage the gradual absorption of the minorities in the country as the solution to Canada's language problems.[33]

The policy statement also emphasized that personal bilingualism had never been the intention of the federal government, although, of course, personal bilingualism is a desirable attribute in individual citizens. It acknowledged that French Canadians tended to carry the burden of such bilingualism but that they have regarded it as a Trojan Horse leading to assimilation if English Canadians do not do their share. However, the mere fact that the statement had to deal as forcefully as it did with this issue and with such an issue as the labelling of goods shows one or both of two things: the government's failure to explain its policies adequately, and the public's misperception of the content of those policies, whether through lack of information, misinformation, or deliberate distortion.

The conclusion to *A National Understanding* proceeded to make a virtue of disunity, a typical "Canadian" response:

It is precisely the rejection of uniformity, the refusal to accept a homogeneous view of themselves and their country, that constitutes the most authentic and widely shared experience of Canadians. The affirmation and preservation of differences, personal, social, local, regional, cultural, linguistic, has consumed the minds and hearts of Canadians all through their history. It is the Canadian response to the question of identity. Our unity—and it is a real and profound unity if we will only bring ourselves to see it—arises from the determination to preserve the identity of each of us. And this is the root of the freedom, the very remarkable degree of freedom, that exists in this country.

Our two languages and our diversity of cultures in Canada are the expression of our spiritual values even as our vast

country is the reflection of our physical strength and variety. . . .

Our linguistic duality and cultural diversity are both the
condition and the safeguard of our continuing freedom and
our unity as a country. . . .

. . . Let us not permit our country to be divided by what can
so enrich us.[34]

This is strong rhetoric, but if actions speak louder than words,
rather empty.

Looking at the history of the last ten years or so, one must ask
how seriously has anyone other than the Commissioner of Official
Languages taken the federal policy of bilingualism and its
associated policy of multiculturalism, policies supported, in
principle at least, by all the federal political parties. A great deal
of money has been spent but not very wisely. Two unilingual
communities, one English and the other French, have become
further entrenched in Canada. The Public Service is a little
changed. The economic establishment and various other elites are
virtually untouched. The provinces are still as resistant as ever to
do anything which does not serve their own narrow interests. The
media are still almost as obtuse as before and the public perhaps
only slightly less. But folk dancing and ethnic restaurants have
flourished somewhat. Not a very surprising accounting for more
than a decade of a policy that was neither well conceived, capably
articulated, nor effectively implemented. Yet one designed
nevertheless to solve Canada's "crisis."

In retrospect, the Official Languages Act may be viewed as one
of the most controversial acts in Canada's Statute Book during the
1970s. Designed to increase the visibility of the French in Canada,
it at the same time denied them any special status. Because of
that denial the policy has had little effect in Quebec, where it was
largely regarded with indifference, being perceived as largely
irrelevant to the province's needs. However, that increase in
visibility was seen in many parts of Canada as the conferring of a
special status on the French at a time when citizens in various
regions outside of Quebec were also seeking special status because
of local needs and interests. The special status that bilingualism

appeared to give to the French seemed to many to be at the expense of the status of the people of almost every other province but Quebec, the possible exception being Ontario, usually regarded by all others as having too much anyway. In this respect the federal policy of bilingualism, independently of language policies adopted within Quebec, may have increased feelings of regionalism, even separatism, throughout Canada outside of Quebec. Status is often perceived to exist in fixed amounts. It can be gained only at someone else's expense. If Ontario's status is unchanged and Quebec's increases the other provinces must suffer a decline. If the French are to get something, it can only be gained at the expense of the English. It seems not to matter that another value system might show benefits accruing to all: the only thing that counts in a status-oriented system is who benefits more, who less, and who not at all. Such is the characteristic tenor of debates about language in Canada.

The Constitution Act of 1982 went even further than the Official Languages Act. Now Canada is bilingual constitutionally. That is, its fundamental bilingual nature is protected from action by the Parliament of Canada alone and must be recognized by the various legislatures according to the requirements of that constitution. The first victim of this new arrangement was that part of Quebec's Bill 101 which restricted the language rights of the English minority in Quebec. It is still far too early to see what the ultimate effect of a constitutional requirement for bilingualism will have on the country and how it will differ from the former purely legislative requirement. In the past, some of the constitutional requirements of the British North America Act went ignored; whether Canadian courts will prove in the future to be better guarantors of constitutional rights than the Canadian Parliament was in the past remains to be seen.

# 3

# FORTRESS QUEBEC

Confederation recognized the important role of the French in Canada. The British North America Act of 1867 ended the dominance the English had achieved through the earlier Act of Union. It gave Quebec to the French to govern and it allowed them to preserve their language and religion there. Nor was the rest of Canada seceded to the English: sizeable numbers of French could be found in Ontario, Nova Scotia, and New Brunswick. Lands to the west which were later to become part of Canada also had a considerable French presence, one recognized for example in the educational provisions of the Manitoba Act of 1870, which established a new province to the west of the Great Lakes. A real chance existed in 1867 for the French to expand their presence everywhere in the new country so as to make Canada a truly bilingual nation.

However, while Confederation was born in a spirit of tolerance and accommodation, it had to develop in an era of English superiority and bigotry and of British imperialism, a time in which the rights of the French outside Quebec were trampled on with impunity. Indeed, the English did not wait long after Confederation to assert their power over the French. Three years after Confederation the Manitoba Act created a new province, somewhat hurriedly to be sure but with a constitution that appeared to guarantee equality between the English and French there: Manitoba was not necessarily to be another Ontario. But by 1916 the last vestiges of equality for the French had disappeared and the English had imposed their will on everyone in Manitoba, the new European settlers and the old French population alike, in an attempt to make the province into a kind of Ontario. It was not until the end of World War II that this climate was modified to any significant extent. But such modification proceeded concurrent with strong moves by the central government to intervene in areas such as health and welfare, education, cultural activities, and resource development, areas which under the British North America Act were within provincial jurisdiction. The threat to the French remained; only the form it took had changed, and the Official Languages Act of 1969 was to seem largely irrelevant as a protective measure.

Looking back to the time of the Treaty of Paris, one finds that in 1763 the French outnumbered the English in what was eventually to become Canada. It was not until the mid-nineteenth century that they became a minority, and not until the 1871 census that they comprised only 31.1 per cent of the total population. Losing members by emigration and faced with the addition of new provinces and new immigrants to English Canada, the French after Confederation were able to maintain their proportion of population only through *la revanche des berceaux*. For a while indeed, until 1901, they actually managed to increase their proportion to 34.7 per cent. However, throughout most of the twentieth century the proportion stabilized at approximately 30 per cent even as the total country grew, for example through the acquisition of Newfoundland in 1949. A noticeable decline did begin though in the mid-twentieth century: to 31.6 per cent in 1951; to 30.4 per cent in 1961; and to 28.7 per cent in 1971. Moreover, numerous observers agreed that this initial slow decline showed every sign of becoming a more and more rapid one. The 1971 census figures also showed that those of English origin in Canada formed 44.6 per cent of the population (1871, 60.5 per cent), those of native origin 1.4 per cent (1871, 0.7 per cent), and those of "other" origins 25.3 per cent (1871, 7.7 per cent). The same census figures indicated that only the French proportion of the population had declined since 1961; all other groups had made small gains either through natural increase, immigration, or some combination, and all apparently at the expense of the French. Even if the 1971 census figures are corrected because of the bias that existed in the collection of data toward declaring an "English" ethnicity, the French part of the population still showed a decline (to 29.2 per cent) and the "other" origins groups an even greater increase (to over 27 per cent).

For the first time the 1971 census allowed investigators to look directly at relationships among three important characteristics of the Canadian population: ethnicity, mother tongue, and the language most often spoken at home. Although questions asked in a Canadian census concerning ethnicity yield somewhat dubious information, the responses from the other two requests are much more reliable. The mother-tongue question is one that has been asked since the 1941 census: it refers to the first language learned in childhood and still understood. The 1971 census added the question about language of the home. In both cases only a single response was recorded in tabulating the data (the most heavily marked response if there was more than one), so genuine cases of two languages learned concurrently were ignored. One might query whether a request for the language of everyday living or the language of work might not have been a better choice than a request for the language of the home, but the language of the home does offer some indication about the direction of language mobility in the following generation, an important demographic indicator.

When the 1971 figures for four possible groupings of the Canadian population are examined according to ethnicity, mother tongue, and the language of the home, one finds that the English in Canada exhibit a pattern distinctly different from all others.[1]

|         | Ethnic Origin | Mother Tongue | Language of the Home |
|---------|---------------|---------------|----------------------|
| English | 9,624,000     | 12,974,000    | 14,446,000           |
| French  | 6,180,000     | 5,794,000     | 5,546,000            |
| Native  | 313,000       | 180,000       | 137,000              |
| Other   | 5,451,000     | 2,620,000     | 1,439,000            |

Although only 44.6 per cent of Canada's population were of English origin, 60.1 per cent of the population used English as their mother tongue and two-thirds (67 per cent) used English as the language of the home. The particularly interesting difference is the one between the figures for mother-tongue use and language-of-the-home use, because these show shifts that individual speakers have made during the course of their lives rather than intergenerational shifts. The shifts may be even greater than those indicated because the mother-tongue measure is quite insensitive to the earliness of any change that could have occurred in language use. The shifts are likely therefore to be even more pronounced than the figures indicate. Preliminary figures from the 1981 census show that 61.3 per cent of the population have English as their mother tongue. Corresponding data on ethnic origin are not yet available.

When one examines the data for different groups within the "other" category, the figures always show a decrease from ethnic origin to mother-tongue use and a further decrease in language-of-the-home use. In some ethnic groups the decreases are more marked than others, the Scandinavians and Dutch in particular. For other groups, such as the Ukrainians, the slope is less steep, and for still others, for example the Italians, Portuguese, Chinese, and Greek, only the beginnings of a slope were detectable in 1971, a fact which attested not at all to the different language retention ability of these groups but rather to the recency of their arrival in Canada.

The language-of-the-home figures reveal quite clearly that 93 per cent of Canada's population use either English or French at home, 67 per cent and 26 per cent respectively. If no more than 7 per cent use other languages (2 per cent Italian, 1 per cent German, and all the rest comprising the remaining 4 per cent), then Canada is really a country of two languages rather than one of many languages, a country which exhibits a linguistic duality rather than a great linguistic diversity. This duality is further emphasized in the geographical distribution of the speakers of French, because in 1971 81 per cent of those speakers lived within Quebec and many of the rest near its borders in either New Brunswick or Ontario; the rest of Canada is therefore overwhelmingly English in its choice of language.

Post-World War II Canadian census figures have also showed

that for French Canadians Quebec is increasingly the motherland. As the French outside Quebec continue to be assimilated into the English community, censuses have shown that Canadians for whom French is the mother tongue are concentrating increasingly in Quebec: whereas only 82.3 per cent lived in Quebec in 1951, by 1971 84 per cent did, and the 1981 census indicated that the proportion was then close to 85 per cent, numerically more than 5.3 million people.

It might appear that with over five million people whose mother tongue is French Quebec should feel fairly secure about its linguistic future. However, within the overall population of Quebec, the period 1951-1976 showed an actual decline in the proportion of those who had French as their mother tongue, from 82.5 per cent in 1951 to 80.7 per cent in 1971 and 80.0 per cent in 1976. Moreover, the English-mother-tongue proportion also declined during the same period, from 13.8 per cent in 1951, to 13.1 per cent in 1971, and then to 12.8 per cent in 1976. It fell to 11.0 per cent in 1981. Both declines were in contrast to the proportion of those who had neither French nor English as the mother tongue. This proportion rose from 3.7 per cent in 1951, to 6.2 per cent in 1971, and to 7.2 per cent in 1976 (but declined to 6.6 per cent in 1981). With the French facing a declining birth rate, Quebec's crude birth rate having become the lowest in Canada by 1971, and with migratory patterns and behavior disfavoring the French even in Quebec, it seemed natural to many Quebecois that the first attempt to arrest any further decline in the 1970s should be directed toward this last group, those who spoke neither English nor French in the province, to francophonize it if at all possible. Or to place the emphasis more properly, the aim was to resist the anglophonization of this third group.

Demographers and commentators agreed on the urgency of the situation that existed in the 1960s and 1970s. For example, Jacques Henripin's 1974 study *Immigration and Language Imbalance* conducted for the Department of Manpower and Immigration contained ominous conclusions concerning the position of the French language in Canada.[2] Henripin indicated that about 95 per cent of immigrants to Canada who were not of either English or French origin would adopt English as their mother tongue and that by the year 2000, 66 per cent of the Canadian population would have English as the mother tongue and nearly 75 per cent would use it as the language of the home. On the other hand, the French language would decrease in use outside of Quebec and would even drop somewhat in use within Quebec if social and educational policies remained unchanged. A decline in the use of French in Montreal was also indicated: from 66 per cent to under 60 per cent by the year 2000. In Henripin's view the English language would gain everywhere in Canada at the expense of both the French language and other languages.

Another demographer, Richard Ares, concluded his assessment of what the 1971 census indicated for Quebec by declaring that the two principal elements which characterized and assured French Canadian life, the French language and the Roman Catholic Church, no longer offered the same protection as before. Outside Quebec the French were losing their language to the English and even within Quebec there were losses in both language and religion. But for Ares the biggest problem was not loss but "demographic stagnation." With the lowest birth rate in Canada and an inability to attract immigrants to use the French language, there was a real danger that the French would eventually lose even Quebec.[3]

The decline in religious power seemed to foreshadow a decline in the linguistic health of the French. The first decline was probably irreversible. It was almost certainly too late to stop either the flight from religious commitment or to arrest the decline in the influence the French once had on the Roman Catholic Church in Canada. In the first census after Confederation Roman Catholics constituted 43 per cent of Canada's population, a proportion which fell steadily to 30 per cent in 1921. By 1971, however, the proportion had risen to 46 per cent but with a profound change. In 1971 48 per cent of the Roman Catholics lived outside Quebec, whereas a century before only very few residents of English Canada had been anything but Protestant. The Roman Catholic Church in Canada is no longer exclusively a French church; outside of Quebec it is English in its orientation and French is no longer the language which protects the faith in Canada. It is worth remembering that the current linguistic polarization between the

English and French in Canada was accompanied for a long time by a religious polarization between Protestants and Catholics. The French made sure in the various enactments preceding and including the British North America Act that their religion was protected. There is no strict separation of the Church and State in Canada as there is in its neighbor to the south. The religious preference of the French was, of course, expressed through their language, and their language and faith came together in their hearts and minds as inseparable. Even outside Quebec the French language and Roman Catholicism went hand in hand until various provincial governments enacted a series of measures which effectively separated the two, sometimes, as in Ontario, with the help of English (in this case Irish) Roman Catholics. With the decline of the Church's power in Quebec after World War II and the emergence of a new Quebec in the Quiet Revolution of the 1960s, the French language rather than the Catholic faith became the centre of Quebec identity, and this at a time when the presence of the French language was acknowledged to be fading fast outside Quebec and to be dangerously threatened within.

The decline in influence of the Roman Catholic Church in Quebec turned out to be to the advantage of the state. It did not leave a vacuum—the Quebecois are still quite religious—but the traditional influence of the Church on daily social life gave way to that of state organizations. This new arrangement in turn reinforced the official position of the state in such secular matters as language and culture. Loyalty could be given to the state as well as to the Church. No longer is the traditional rallying cry of Quebecois "la foi, la race, et la langue." By the end of the 1960s the province had become secularized so that preservation of "la foi" had become largely irrelevant. "La race" outside of Quebec was almost completely abandoned, and, within Quebec, it seemed to be necessary to assimilate outsiders if continuity was to be guaranteed. Only "la langue" could be given a secure future through legislation. In giving "la langue" a secure future, the French would truly become "maitres chez nous": an effective language policy would enable them to exercise control over all aspects of Quebec's life including the economic one, about which they had long felt great resentment.

The late 1960s and early 1970s were obviously a time for action in Quebec if the French were to assure their future there. It was the time too of the federal government's Official Languages Act, but also the time of the publication of a book, which, though ignored on publication, far more accurately surveyed the linguistic situation in Canada than any other book. The year 1967 saw Canada celebrate 100 years of existence, but it also saw the publication, by the author himself, of Richard Joy's *Languages in Conflict*.[4] At a time when Canadians were puffed with pride at their collective endurance, Joy indicated in his book how the linguistic complexion of Canada was changing so far as its two founding peoples were concerned. However, the publication of *Languages in Conflict* was completely overshadowed in 1967 by the publication of the first volume of the report prepared by the Royal Commission on Bilingualism and Biculturalism. That book was to exert a profound influence on life in Canada; in retrospect, it is to be regretted that Joy's book went unnoticed or deliberately neglected by those who were to frame federal policy. Today, one can see how far that policy went against the tides of history, tides plotted and forecasted with considerable precision in *Languages in Conflict*.

From his analysis of the 1961 census data Joy concluded that 93 per cent of all Canadians of French mother tongue lived in an area extending east and north from Sault Ste. Marie (the "Soo") through Ottawa to Cornwall in Ontario, all of Quebec, and north of a line from Edmundston to Moncton in New Brunswick. The heartland of this area lay to the north and east of Montreal. Later, using information from the 1971 and 1976 censuses, Joy, in his 1978 updating of the linguistic situation, *Canada's Official-Language Minorities*, divided all of Canada into eight language regions.[5] One of these, the north and east of Quebec, has 82.7 per cent unilingual francophones and only 1.5 per cent unilingual anglophones. Four areas (Atlantic Canada, southern and western Ontario, the Prairies, and British Columbia) each have well under one half of 1 per cent francophones and a very small percentage of bilinguals. The other three areas have significant bilingual populations: the northern and eastern parts of Ontario with 28.1 per cent bilinguals and 64.7 per cent unilingual anglophones;

south and west Quebec with 35.3 per cent bilinguals and 46.9 per cent unilingual francophones; and northern New Brunswick with approximately one-third in each of the three categories. Over 60 per cent of Canadians claiming to be bilingual therefore live in a "bilingual belt" comprising northern New Brunswick, south and west Quebec, and north and east Ontario. This belt, which includes the cities of Ottawa, Montreal, and Moncton acts as a buffer between two overwhelmingly unilingual populations, francophone in north and east Quebec and anglophone in the rest of Canada.[6]

*Languages in Conflict* documented several important trends: an increasing unilingualism in the population of Canada, particularly noticeable in Quebec; the gradual loss of the French language outside the "Soo-Moncton" area in which French is still viable; the lack of replacement of francophones there through either immigration from Quebec or high birth rates; the paucity of francophone children in schools outside the Soo-Moncton area (only one francophone child for every 45 anglophones in 1961); the growing anglophone school population of Quebec increasing at a faster rate than the francophone population and outnumbering the francophone children of all other provinces combined, many of whom are required to attend English schools; the strong preference of immigrants to Quebec to learn English rather than French; the growing concentration in the Montreal area of the anglophone population of Quebec; the decline of the English populations of the Eastern Townships and Ottawa Valley region; the linguistic wall which divides Montreal along St. Lawrence Boulevard with English predominating to the west and French to the east; and, most important of all, the growing linguistic segregation of Canada with French the language of Quebec and English the language used everywhere else.

Joy's analysis is corroborated fully in maps contained in Bulletin 2.2 of the 1976 Census of Canada: these maps show very clearly the status of English, French, and other languages in Canada. One map displays the predominant mother tongues in Canada. French is shown to be predominant in just about all of Quebec with a few scattered exceptions. English predominates elsewhere in Canada, again with a few exceptions: parts of

Ontario and New Brunswick bordering Quebec and two census divisions in Manitoba (Divisions Two and Three, south of Winnipeg with a considerable German-speaking population). The Atlantic provinces (except for the French part of New Brunswick) and south central Ontario are shown to be almost completely English in language use, just as the area north and east of Quebec City extending along the St. Lawrence is almost completely French. A second map shows the distribution of official language minorities. The interesting phenomenon here is that the French minorities decrease in numbers as they are located further from Quebec, a trend particularly noticeable west of the Great Lakes. There are strong concentrations of French in southern Manitoba, fewer in Saskatchewan, a thin distribution through northern Alberta, but nowhere in British Columbia do the French comprise more than 5 per cent of a census division. The same trend is apparent within Ontario and the Maritimes. Within Quebec the thinnest distributions of the English are likely to be found in those areas in which the French are most heavily concentrated.

Joy's book contrasts noticeably with Stanley Lieberson's 1970 *Language and Ethnic Relations in Canada*, which, while full of interesting data, now has a curiously antiquated appearance.[7] Lieberson's major concern was the extent of bilingualism in the English and French populations of Canada. Language maintenance was a somewhat lesser concern and languages other than English and French were of no concern. While Lieberson has a number of interesting things to say about exactly who is bilingual and how the factors that influence bilingualism are different from those that encourage language maintenance, his work lacks the force and conviction of Richard Joy's. Joy's dramatic portrayal of a nation which is bilingual only in that there are two unilingual areas is far more convincing than Lieberson's detailed and somewhat pedantic account of personal bilingualism in Canada at a time when even official emphasis was on institutional bilingualism. The reality was neither; it was Joy's two unilingualisms, one English and the other French, with a small area of bilingualism between the two. Moreover, it was a French unilingualism that required measures of self-protection.

Lieberson, of course, was not blind to what was happening in

Quebec. In discussing the options available to a group of people who find themselves in a subordinate position within a multilingual society, he quite clearly perceived what was happening there. After discussing the options of assimilation and institutional reform, Lieberson mentions a third: "out migration, revolution, separatism or expulsion of the dominant language group." He adds, "The French in Canada, a conquered people who are subordinate in virtually all respects except their official political status of linguistic equality, are veering in recent years toward institutional reforms if not complete separation."[8] Institutional reform, linguistic protection, and eventually separatism were to become the defining characteristics of what came to be known in the 1960s as the "Quiet Revolution."

As has been indicated, the French in Quebec have always regarded themselves as a threatened people. The memory of defeat after defeat from the Plains of Abraham in 1759 to the air traffic control dispute of 1976 and the need to persevere and survive have been two persistent themes of French life in Canada. By the 1970s survival seemed reasonably assured if certain measures could be taken, linguistic ones definitely and certain political ones possibly. Before the Quiet Revolution the French protected themselves through isolation from the rest of Canada while at the same time maintaining what parity they had with the English through the revenge of the cradles. To a considerable extent the Quiet Revolution ended that isolation and Quebec emerged as an urbanizing, modernizing entity. It became a "modern" state with its educational system reformed, its managerial and technical skills developed, and its social programs well established. A new middle class leadership secular in composition replaced the old clerical and professional groups who had exercised social and political control. The state also ceased to be concerned only with narrow internal matters; instead the new leadership drew public attention to Quebec's rightful place in North America as a whole and even beyond. *Survivance* gave way to *epanouissement* as a motivating force. The new Quebec state was promoted as the only possible protector of the French in North America. The reforms of the educational and governmental system brought a new zest and purpose to the life of the province.

The Canadiens of the 1950s became the Quebecois of the 1960s and 1970s. As Canadiens they were a minority in Canada; as Quebecois they were a majority in Quebec. The resulting change had profound psychological effects: the Quebecois saw that their future lay in their own hands and they were determined to secure it. Since it was obvious that Quebec was faced with the prospect of a diminishing population, particularly of a diminishing francophone population, language appeared to be the key issue. The continuity of the French language and culture in Quebec could be guaranteed only by legislation. The right legislation could also force an entry into the economic sphere if French also became the language of work in Quebec. But it was to take nearly a decade for this solution to find its final realization in Bill 101 of 1977, and still today the courts have not said their last word on certain important language provisions of that Bill.

The Quiet Revolution in Quebec saw not only a new feeling of confidence in the French of the province, but it also forced the English in Quebec to adjust to changed circumstances and placed those who were neither English nor French in a somewhat precarious position between the two. The English were at first uncertain in their response to the French but education quickly became the battlefield on which the struggle for self-determination took place. The creation of a provincial Ministry of Education in 1964 threatened the laissez-faire system that had existed. Then, Premier Jean-Jacques Bertrand's 1969 proposal to establish regional boards of education for the Island of Montreal, rather than continue with boards chosen along linguistic and religious affiliations, became an even greater threat. The English thought that the existing arrangements satisfied both the English and French groups, allowing each to fulfil its historical role in Quebec society. The *status quo* which favored the English was visibly threatened by the government's move. The 1960s did see English schools in the province begin at last to take the teaching of French seriously with the aim of making the pupils in those schools bilingual, but in the absence of meaningful social contacts such teaching was not very successful.[9] The English population, which still wanted to maintain control of the economy, were prepared to learn enough French to do so. And those who either could not or would not learn French looked more and more to other parts of Canada for their future. But on the whole little was done to bring the communities together in a common purpose.

The closest relationship that is possible, of course, is that provided by intermarriage between the groups. However, the consequences are not generally what they are assumed to be. The result is usually not a relationship in which both parties maintain their language and cultural characteristics and produce a bilingual, bicultural setting for their children. A study of English-French marriages in Montreal showed such a result to be a rarity.[10] In practice, in the majority of cases the language and culture of one of the spouses completely predominated with the result a unilingual, unicultural household, nearly always anglophone English. Such a result is not really surprising: the French in Montreal were more likely to be bilingual than the English, and the English have traditionally been judged by both English and French to be somewhat superior in status to the French, so the pull to English language and culture was almost irresistible. Of course, the incidence of English-French marriage in Montreal is really quite small, persons in both groups overwhelmingly opting for marriage partners within their own group, thus consolidating language, religious, and cultural ties and maintaining the "two solitudes."

Between the two solitudes stood the immigrants to Quebec. Immigrants have always come to the province: indeed for great numbers of immigrants who come to Canada in the late nineteenth and the first half of the twentieth century, a Quebec port was the place of entry into Canada or a journey west from an Atlantic port took the immigrants through Quebec. Yet disproportionately few ever settled there and many who did initially, later moved on. Opportunities lay west, immigrants were oriented toward an "English" North American environment, the cultural and religious life of Quebec, apart from that of Montreal, seemed inhospitable, and even the French themselves were leaving, in what has been called Quebec's "fatal hemorrhage," for New England to the south, or for the north and east of Ontario and points west in Canada.

Unfortunately xenophobia has long been a characteristic of

Quebec society. Much of it is undoubtedly the result of the isolation of the Quebecois and the threats they have perceived to their continuation as a people. Consequently, the Quebecois have been rather inhospitable to immigrants, even to the extent of driving them into the camp of the English minority. They have also distrusted non-Catholics, feared secularization and urbanization, and attempted to draw boundaries around themselves, looking to their own natural growth for survival and cultural continuity. While the Quiet Revolution removed some of the real causes of the inferiority behind much of this feeling, it seemed to do little to ease the actual feeling itself. What it did was produce a series of governments willing to give expression to policies aimed at consolidating the Frenchness of Quebec, if necessary at the expense of the non-French in the province, a kind of xenophobia in a new form.

Quebec then has attracted neither immigrants nor their descendants. The only exception is Montreal with its sizeable "ethnic" population, but in the broader context of Canadian life Montreal is not really an exception. English interests have long dominated Montreal through control of the economy in Quebec. The English control economic opportunity in Canada. Immigrants quickly realize this fact about Canadian life wherever they chose to settle, and since economic mobility is one aspiration just about all ethnic groups share, a "wise" choice is to identify with and settle among the English. In Quebec this means choosing to identify with the English and to live in their English stronghold, Montreal.

Montreal is therefore often perceived to be the key to the ultimate survival of the French in North America. It is the largest North American French city by far but one with an economy long dominated by the English. The well entrenched elite minority is English; bilingualism symbolizes the way the less affluent majority has been forced to deal with the powerful unilingual minority. Newcomers to Montreal, particularly immigrants, but also those from rural Quebec, are attracted in various degrees to the language and values of that minority. The majority can no longer even be sure of maintaining their majority position through a superior birth rate. Given all these factors, plus the importance to the hinterland of what happens in the largest metropolitan area of Quebec, those concerned about the future of the French language are forced to give special attention to the linguistic situation in Montreal.

Within Montreal, when immigrants shift in language that shift has been toward English rather than French in the majority of cases: the 1961 census showed that about 70 per cent of the shifts were to English. Moreover, the more economic success an immigrant group has the more it shifts to English, often as an exclusive language. The same census revealed that the successful Jewish population showed a pattern of language use in which the majority were unilingually English and most of the remainder bilingual in English and French. However, among the recently arrived Italian population only 14 per cent used English exclusively, 35 per cent were bilingual in English and French, 27 per cent used French only, and the rest used neither English nor French. The greater incidence of French use in this population can be attributed to the socio-economic position of the Italians. They must work with the French so they learn French. The more successful Jewish worked with the English so they learned English. In Montreal in the 1970s an immigrant who spoke neither English nor French would learn English to increase chances of success; learning French would have been a poor choice if everything else were equal. Not unexpectedly many Quebecois regarded this result as intolerable, an insult to their own status and to all they held precious.

The 1971 census produced very similar figures. Information concerning which official language immigrants to the city of Montreal chose indicated that while more than 20 per cent of Italian and Portuguese immigrants chose French only, only 1 or 2 per cent of other groups such as Greeks, Germans, Jewish, Ukrainians, and Hungarians did likewise. For such groups 50 to 75 per cent chose to learn English only. Fewer also chose to become bilingual (12 to 30 per cent) than among the Italians and Portuguese (over 30 per cent). Such groups as the Jewish, Germans, Hungarians, and Ukrainians had also made significant strides in adopting English as the home language. French, on the other hand, was an infrequent choice as the language of the home.

Language of the home, however, is not necessarily a very good predictor of the language used outside the home for users of either English or French in an official language minority situation. Outside Quebec the pressure is always toward the use of English and inside toward the use of French, these being the languages which dominate the media and the various cultural institutions. The major exception in 1971 was Montreal. One study showed that among those who used English as the language of the home in Montreal, this fact only weakly predicted that English would be the language of work. In contrast, among those who used French as the language of the home, there was actually a negative relationship with French as the language of work; that is, there was a slightly better chance that members of this group would use English rather than French as the language of work.[11]

Even the French in Quebec, particularly those living in Montreal, have been subject to pressures to surrender French for English in order to increase chances of mobility. A study by Charles Castonguay of language transfers to and between the official languages showed that the 1971 census figures reveal just how important is the move toward English in Canada.[12] While 110,000 residents of Canada had moved to French, 1.6 million had moved to English. Even in Quebec the figures showed a movement of 100,000 to English in comparison with 75,000 to French. In areas in Quebec where the population was more than 4 per cent of English mother tongue, English better than held its own in a direct English-French pull and more than held its own in acquiring transfers from other languages. As the percentage of English mother-tongue users increased, the pull to English also increased. The pull was therefore considerable in Montreal. Only in Quebec City within the province were there substantial net gains to French at the expense of English.

Using the examples of the French population of Essex County in Ontario and the English populations of Quebec County and the Eastern Townships in Quebec, Joy has hypothesized that two entirely different processes are at work in Canada in reducing the official language minorities.[13] Outside Quebec, where French is in grave danger, loss occurs through assimilation: the French ethnic group remains and flourishes but the French language weakens and disappears. Inside Quebec, where English is under severe pressure, loss occurs through out-migration as the English leave the province. Those who stay tend to retain their English language. Successive censuses have shown fairly strong language retention but real declines in the population of English origin within Quebec. Whether Montreal will follow the pattern of Quebec City and the Eastern Townships and become almost entirely French through losing its population of English origin remains to be seen. Of course, Montreal is like neither of the other areas. Its special population mix and its economic pre-eminence in Quebec may prove more resistant to the effects of such legislation as Bill 101 and trends observed elsewhere than the political leaders of Quebec anticipate.

The economic dominance of the English in Quebec is one of the severest tests any attempt at linguistic engineering must face in the province. Typically, in Quebec a French-owned business is agricultural or service-oriented and relatively small, and has a predominantly Quebec market. However, large businesses are controlled either by English Canadians or a foreign interest and look beyond Quebec for their markets. At their upper managerial levels such businesses are almost certain to be controlled exclusively by anglophones, particularly if their corporate head offices are to be found outside the province, as many are. Only businesses of this kind with head offices in Quebec are likely to employ a significant number of francophones in high level positions.

It should not be surprising that English has dominated the language of the business economy of Quebec. That economy has been closely linked to the economy of the rest of Canada, particularly to that of Ontario, and to the economy of the United States, specifically in its generation of raw materials for processing elsewhere. Financing has come from Britain and the United States and the province has openly welcomed the large multinational corporations. Money has talked in the business and economic life of the province and its language has been English.

One of the studies conducted for the Royal Commission on Bilingualism and Biculturalism clearly showed the economic advantages to the French of assimilating to the English in Quebec.[14] Unilingual francophone employees of French origin earned less than bilinguals, who in turn earned less than those of French origin who were now unilingual anglophones, that is, those who had joined the successful minority. In contrast those of English origin who had become unilingual francophones earned least of all. English bilinguals, however, earned even more than unilingual anglophones of French origin. At the top in earnings were unilingual anglophones of English origin. In 1961 the pecking order was as follows from top to bottom:

1. unilingual anglophone English ($6049)
2. bilingual English ($5929)
3. unilingual anglophone French ($5775)
4. bilingual French ($4523)
5. unilingual francophone French ($3107)
6. unilingual francophone English ($2783)

Clearly the significant factor is language in this distribution. It was advantageous in the 1960s to know English and disadvantageous to know only French.

But not only did Canadians of French origin earn less per capita than Canadians of English origin, they earned even less than many Canadians of neither English nor French origin. Census figures have repeatedly shown French Canadians well behind the English, the North and East European, and the Jewish in average yearly income. What is particularly irritating to the French is that the same pattern is found in a city such as Montreal. In the 1971 census, for example, male Canadians of French origin in Montreal ranked behind males of Jewish, Scandinavian, English, Scottish, German, Irish, and East European origin, with some of the differences in income being quite considerable. When the incomes of all male workers in the city were averaged, the figures showed that the average income of a male of French origin was at least $400 below the city average for all workers.[15] Clearly, in Quebec not only control of the economy but also control of the language of work is an important issue.

Until recent linguistic changes in the province, even the educational policy of Quebec long contributed to increasing the amount of English spoken in a city such as Montreal at the expense of French. The schools were divided on a denominational basis rather than on a language basis: the French schools were Roman Catholic and the English schools were Protestant, with the latter designation interpreted broadly to mean non-Roman Catholic. Francophone Swiss Protestant children were required to attend schools which used English as the language of instruction, as were francophone Jewish children from North Africa. Until the provisions of Bill 101 came into effect the Protestant schools were often also the choice of francophone Roman Catholic parents, who wanted to provide their children greater social and economic mobility than seemed possible from attendance in the French Roman Catholic system. But it was the linguistic future of the children of immigrants rather than that of the relatively few who wanted to switch linguistic affiliation that seemed to require legislative intervention.

It is also not surprising that in recent years Quebec has claimed the rights it had under the British North America Act to regulate immigration to the province in association with the federal government. Since non-English-speaking immigrants to the province have long tended to identify with the English community of Quebec, some provincial control over immigration appeared to be necessary, and with it the development of language policies to deal with immigrants on arrival. Joint control of immigration with the federal government was the solution to the first issue and the language of schooling provisions of Bill 101 were the solution to the second.

Joint arrangements between the Government of Quebec and the federal government are, however, the exception rather than the rule. Disagreement is much more usual and much of it essentially focuses on the desire of the French in Quebec to safeguard their unique status in North America, particularly their language. Even the long-standing dispute between Ottawa and Quebec over the child allowance system is one that has a large language component. Constitutionally, Quebec has control over social services. But the Government of Canada also has certain responsibilities in these matters as well as considerably greater taxing powers. Quebec regards the federal child allowance system as a way of stimulating the growth of (or at least avoiding any fatal decline in) the French population of the province. Hence the Quebec government's insistence on tailoring the child allowance system to encourage a higher birth rate by paying progressively larger amounts for later born children in a family rather than progressively declining or equal amounts. Through their government, the people of Quebec have asserted the right to act in their own best self-interest whenever they feel the right and need to do so. But the stakes are high and victory is by no means assured.

In fact, the province of Quebec is not considered by its people to be a province like any of the other nine. To the Quebecois, Quebec is not merely a regional entity; it is the home of a nation. Moreover, it is the home of one of the two nations which founded Canada. Consequently, the government in Quebec City is considered to be an equal to the government in Ottawa. The latter is in no way the "senior" government; it might be so for the other provinces, but it cannot be so for Quebec. If it is the "national" government, it is only the national government of English Canada, since the national government of French Canada meets in Quebec City.[16] It is even called the National Assembly.

Quebec's dissatisfaction with its place in Confederation therefore has several dimensions to it. There is the linguistic-cultural dimension of the two nations conflict, with one nation feeling itself subjugated to the other. There is the economic dimension: the French feel that they are treated as colonials in an exploitative economic system within their own territory. There is also the national-regional issue, the feeling that particular parts of Canada have interests which are antithetical to those of other parts and to those of the central government. Moreover, there are few or no suitable mechanisms for resolving differences and plenty for making them worse.

One consequence is that Quebec has traditionally placed little emphasis on the outcome of meetings of first ministers, one of Canada's innovations in self-government. Such meetings hardly work to Quebec's advantage when the English provinces outnumber Quebec nine to one and when Ottawa is perceived as no ally and refuses to be acknowledged as an equal. The meetings do nothing to advance Quebec's claims for either a special status within Confederation or for a "two nations" concept of Canada. However, Quebec is not alone in its disenchantment with such meetings: unanimity is a rare occurrence at them and fundamental disagreement the rule. The result is that they have tended to become showcases, as was the 1980 meeting on the constitution; truly meaningful federal-provincial negotiations now tend to proceed on an issue-by-issue basis province-by-province in a kind of horse-trading system. And in 1982 Quebec was allowed to stand alone in its opposition to the Constitution Act, the country's new constitution.

New modes of consultation have had to be devised in dealings between the federal and Quebec bureaucracies. No longer does the federal government easily get its way in matters pertaining to Quebec: it is not a province like the others in the eyes of those who speak for it. Quebec's bureaucracy has its own mission and is much more assertive than it has ever been; consequently, more and more the initiative in federal-provincial matters, as these pertain to Quebec, has been wrested from the federal government and its servants. They are forced to react to initiatives taken by others rather than taking the initiative themselves. One interesting corollary is that this manner of dealing with the federal government has not gone unnoticed in other parts of the country. The whole tone of political argumentation has changed in Canada within the last twenty years or so and Quebec has led the way in forcing the change. Now there is even a Western "separatist" movement.

Even though the Quebecois have nearly always voted solidly to support the Liberal Party in Ottawa and the Liberals have formed most of the federal governments in recent history, they do not see the government in Ottawa as their government. Their government meets in Quebec City, conducts its business in French, seeks to meet their social and cultural needs, and provides them with the kinds of mobility that the world of industry and business does not. Deliberate attempts to alternate the Liberal Party leadership between anglophones and francophones, to ensure French representation in the federal Cabinet, and to award Quebec an adequate share of federal spending change little. The government in Ottawa remains alien even when it is a Liberal government voted into power largely on the strength of voters in the province of Quebec itself. It is perceived as essentially a creation of English Canada and therefore in its essential Englishness the government of the "other" nation.

Writing of the ambivalance of Quebec's political allegiance, Ramsay Cook has observed that it speaks well to the feelings of Quebecois about their place in Canada. They elect provincial governments which reflect their hopes for separate nationhood and members of a federal party which opposes that concept. Cook says this ambiguity reflects the shrewdness of a small, determined people who have discovered over the centuries that in the end survival depends on themselves, and that no single strategy is perfect.[17] What the people of Quebec do not lack though is a vision of what their "nation" is all about. This situation is in marked contrast to the rest of Canada, where there is very little agreement about what are the essential characteristics of a Canadian state, particularly one that is to include Quebec.

Other Canadians may reject the idea that Canada is a bicultural country, as the Quebecois claim it is. But they cannot reject the fact that Quebec is now a modern North American urbanized industrial society with distinctive French characteristics and a will of its own. Most Quebecois live very much like most other North Americans so far as material comforts are concerned. They are affected by most of the same social and economic forces and they are exposed to many of the same cultural influences. What they do is give a French flavor to much of the above in making use of it. The resentment the Quebecois feel owes more to a sense of powerlessness *within* Quebec than anything else. Non-Quebecois remain in control of much of the economy although the Quebecois themselves control the political system. The one aspect of Quebec life they can dominate is the language of the province. If the Quebecois succeed in making Quebec a thoroughly French province then everything will be filtered through that language; what will be unique about Quebec will be the fact that it alone will enjoy its variety of North American culture *in French*. The French language is therefore the key to political solidarity in Quebec. Although the exclusive use of French in the province cannot change the culture, it can serve as a unique screen to that culture.

In this way the French in Quebec will not only elevate themselves to be the equals of the English in Canada, but they will also become the equals of the English throughout the whole of North America. Such is the vision of the new Quebec.

# 4

# THE CHARTER
# OF THE FRENCH LANGUAGE

Although Richard Joy's *Languages in Conflict* remains one of the clearest statements concerning English-French language relationships in Canada, one prediction Joy made has proved to be quite wrong:

> From time to time, politicians, particularly of the more extreme splinter parties, demand that action be taken by the Quebec Legislature to abolish English-language schools or to otherwise harass the minority; it is quite unlikely that any provincial government would seriously consider introducing such measures.[1]

Successive Quebec governments not only considered such measures but actually passed them, with Bill 101 of 1977 being the ultimate refutation of Joy's prediction. In fact, in the period immediately following the publication of *Languages in Conflict*, language legislation preoccupied much of the political life of Quebec.

In the very year, 1969, that the federal government brought into law the Official Languages Act, which sought to make Canada bilingual, the Government of Quebec was going through the agonies of introducing and withdrawing Bill 85 and then passing Bill 63, an Act to Promote the French Language in Quebec, both pieces of language legislation. The major opposition to both bills came from Quebecois who wanted less bilingualism in Quebec and less freedom of choice than the bills guaranteed the non-French of the province. They were unsuccessful in that opposition, but it is significant that 1969 saw federal and provincial language policies begin to diverge quite drastically. At the very moment when enough Canadians aroused themselves to try to do something for the French in Canada, the Quebecois determined to move in the opposite direction in order to protect themselves within their own province. Again, at the very moment the English population of Montreal was discovering a certain need to become bilingual, the Government of Quebec was determined to make the province more and more unilingual. When school enrolments in bilingual and immersion programs in areas such as Montreal's Westmount were at an all-time high, governments in Quebec City of various political persuasions were drafting measures such as Bill 63, Bill 22, and Bill 101 with their intentions of promoting French, constraining or forbidding the enrolments of the children of immigrants in English-medium schools, and making French the language of the workplace. Many of the English in Montreal believed they were being dealt a low blow, particularly as they perceived a concurrent erosion of economic power and a growing social isolation in the province.

The linguistic conflict in Quebec was to be fought on two battlegrounds: the language of instruction in the schools and the language of the workplace, both areas in which the government of the province has clear jurisdiction. Section 93 of the British North America Act mandated that the province of Quebec provide schools for both Protestants and Roman Catholics; it said nothing about the language of instruction in those schools. Consequently, there was nothing in the law to prevent French being mandated as the language of instruction in all schools. Only the customary or acquired rights of the Protestant minority stood between a continuation of instruction in English and a change to French. But even the Parti Quebecois government of Quebec recognizes that such rights must be preserved for what it considers to be the genuine anglophone population of the province, defined as the children of those *who were themselves educated in English in the province.*

Just how far the schools are confessional in nature is indicated in the traditional treatment of the Jewish population of the province. Jewish children attend the Protestant schools, and the courts have repeatedly denied the Jewish community any right to tax-supported schools. Consequently, Jewish day schools are private schools, but those with some kind of "associate" relationship with the Protestant School Board of Greater Montreal receive subsidies for their secular instruction. The "confessional" rather than "linguistic" requirement of Section 93 obviously strengthens the hand of the Quebec government in legislating the language of instruction. Actually, in interpreting the original provisions of the British North America Act in this way the Quebec government is merely doing within Quebec to the English and others what other provincial governments have long done elsewhere to the French and others in denying instruction in the mother tongue.

Since the 1960s the demographic situation in Quebec, particularly in Montreal, has dictated that the French must somehow "capture" the immigrants to the province. These *Quebecois de nouvelle souche* are important to both the English and French. The English see them as people who will perpetuate their institutions: schools, hospitals, social agencies, and so on. The French see them as people who will eventually strengthen the French language in the province. In contrast to the English though, the French have had the political power to do something about their vision.

However, in the battles fought in Quebec over which language, English or French, the children of immigrants should learn in the schools, both the French and immigrants tended to regard the English rather than each other as the major cause of the problem. Both agreed that English Canadians and Americans dominated Quebec's economy and were reluctant to change this situation. Both also perceived the self-righteous stance of the English in defence of the immigrants' right to an education in English. Both were aware that the English needed the immigrants in order to maintain the viability of their institutions and that self-interest rather than altruism tended to motivate English support for the "rights of immigrants" to choose the educational system they preferred for their children.[2]

The French decided to compel the immigrants to join them in their linguistic and cultural battle against the English: that was the intent of various pieces of legislation leading up to and including Bill 101. Immigrant groups were reluctant to join forces with either side since they felt they would jeopardize their own futures if they did. Learning French would put them below the French on the economic and social scale in Quebec whereas learning English would give them the boost they needed to compete against the French and achieve some social mobility. However, immigrant groups also found little comfort from those Quebecois who wanted to change the whole social and economic system rather than just the linguistic and cultural one. They appreciated that any economic upheaval resulting from attempts to nationalize the whole or parts of the economy would inevitably hurt them, since they would almost surely be left unprotected. Essentially, then, many immigrants believed that they were in a no-win situation when they were either forced to take sides in the dispute over language or compelled to send their children to French schools.

To a considerable extent the immigrants to Quebec have become pawns in a battle of supremacy between the English and French in the province. It is a position which they do not relish since it is one which can bring them nothing but harm. The English seem to have as little desire as ever to share economic power and the French are no more eager to share political power. Many immigrants feel that their interests would be served best by learning both English and French: English is the language of North America, of economic opportunity, and of mobility; French is the language they need to get along with their fellow workers, though not necessarily the language guaranteeing acceptance in Quebec, where there still remains a traditional streak of xenophobia that is proving hard to eradicate. To speak French like a native is still not to be accepted as a native.

In 1970 the attitude of the typical Italian in Montreal toward English and French was summarized as follows by Jeremy Boissevain in *The Italians of Montreal*, one of the research studies conducted by the Royal Commission on Bilingualism and Biculturalism:

The Italian Canadian may have ambivalent attitudes towards the French and British, but he wishes above all else to be left alone. He does not wish to be forced into a public statement of why he chooses a French bride, or why he sends his children to an English school, or why he regards the British as gentlemen and the French as extravagant. Because he studies English and sends his children to study English, it does not mean that this language governs his complete social life. If language to the French Canadian is the symbol of his culture, its quintessence and the embodiment of his social and political status, for the Italian it is merely a socio-economic tool. He uses English to his boss, French to his workmates, Italian to his friends from other regions of Italy, and a local dialect to his closest kin and *paesani*.[3]

Undoubtedly many Canadians in the last decade have also had the same desire to be left out of the language wars, but, like the Italians of Montreal, they have been unsuccessful in avoiding the traditional national preoccupation with linguaphobia.

One trend in Quebec in the 1960s and 1970s saw immigrants sending their children to English schools even when the immigrants were Roman Catholic and might be expected to choose French Roman Catholic schools rather than English Roman Catholic schools. More surprisingly, a growing number of French parents were sending their children to schools in which English was the language of instruction. Admittedly, the opposite was true too: parents of English origin were sending their children to French schools in increasing numbers. But to the French it was the choice made by immigrant parents and the loss of their own children to the English language which determined them to act to reverse a situation in which, by the 1972-73 school year, nine out of ten new Canadian students in the Montreal Catholic schools were enrolled in its English schools and approximately one in ten students in all the English schools of Quebec had French as the mother tongue.

The first moves were very cautious. The 1966 Report of the Royal Commission of Inquiry on Education in the Province of

Quebec summed up the attitude of Quebecois toward immigrants as follows:

> Finally, the long continued isolation of French Canadians, the defence reflexes arising from their minority situation in Canada as a whole and their economic inferiority in Quebec have without doubt poorly prepared them to extend a generous welcome to new citizens whose ways of life and whose mentality differ from their own.[4]

However, the Commission favored improving education in the province so as to attract the children of immigrants to French schools. It did not want to see Quebec adopt the highly restrictive policies of the other provinces toward minority language groups.

Language policy at this time was somewhat ambivalent. While the French wanted to pull the other groups toward them, they were at the same time effectively pushing them away. Policies of traditional xenophobia were combined with deliberate moves to expand provincial support of English educational institutions to better accommodate immigrant children within them. It was the St. Leonard school crisis of 1968-69 which clearly demonstrated what was happening: the English educational systems had become multi-ethnic and attempts to curb further losses to the English and reverse the trend were likely to be contentious. But something had to be done if the battle for linguistic supremacy was not to be lost by default.

The St. Leonard school crisis, which actually began very late in 1967, was precipitated when school authorities in the northeast section of Montreal tried to compel the children of Italian immigrants to enter French schools and ceased offering them the choice of an education in English. The time had come to capture the immigrant population. The Italians resisted and sought to maintain the traditional freedom of choice that existed in Quebec. The dispute led to the setting up of the Commission of Inquiry on the Position of the French Language and on Language Rights in Quebec, the Gendron Commission.

This Commission produced a massive, three-volume, 1,423-page report in December, 1972, together with a set of studies comprising another 10,000 pages. In its report the Commission noted the inferior economic situation of the French people in Quebec, the negative attitude of the English economic elite toward the French, the unequal language burdens imposed on the many French who had to use English as the language of work, the propensity of immigrants to Quebec to learn and use English, and the shortage of a skilled French managerial group in the province. After revealing how immigrants to Quebec were educating their children and considering the reasons for their choice, the Gendron Commission concluded:

> ...it is quite clear that the problem of the integration of immigrants stems from causes quite beyond the mere fact that immigrants' children attend English-speaking schools. It is much more closely linked to the attitudes of the majority group, economic and denominational pressures, or the quality of the education dispensed, all of which are causes that have been and still constitute obstacles to the harmonious integration of immigrants' children into the schools.[5]

However, the Commission did not favor the introduction of coercive legislation to force immigrant children into French schools. Instead, it favored improving education in general and recommended that no changes be made to the existing system during a "cooling off" period of at least three to five years.

The Gendron Commission did, however, make the following observation about the privileged status of English in Quebec so far as the world of work was concerned:

> Our studies of the language use of the people of Quebec revealed that 84% of the Province's English-speaking population exists in a state of virtual unilingualism....60% of third group members are in either a unilingual English situation or in another unilingual situation which is neither English nor French....It is clear that a good portion of Quebec's population does not need to use French in the ordinary course of events. How can this be? The answer lies in the social

organization which serves as a framework for the everyday life of Quebecers. The Province has a double network of institutions and services....

The English-speaking population's lack of motivation to learn and use French is consequently understandable. There is not really any powerful inducement for them to do so....

Within the Quebec social framework, including the work world's existing ethno-linguistic structures, French is a useful and necessary language only for French-speaking people and a minority of members of the third group, but not for English-speaking people.[6]

The Commission's key recommendation was that the Government of Quebec should take measures to make French the language of work in the province, but essentially by inducement rather than by compulsion. So far as the law was concerned, no rights given to the English language in Quebec under the British North America Act should be infringed; however, the rights the French majority had under the Act should be asserted. The battle for the loyalty of the immigrants should be shifted from the schools to the workplace and French should be made the language of work in Quebec.

The 1972 Gendron Report provided Premier Robert Bourassa with the basis for the contents of Bill 22, the Official Language Act of 1974, a bill which by trying to satisfy all parties succeeded in satisfying none. In his later explanation of the Parti Quebecois government's policy on the French language, Camille Laurin, the Minister of State for Cultural Development, criticized the earlier Bill 22 of the Liberal government as follows:

Above all, Bill 22 was wrong in pursuing simultaneously two divergent aims—one, to make Quebec French-speaking; the other, institutional bilingualism. In short, Quebec was seen as an administrative division of a bilingual state (Canada), and at the same time as the national state of French Canadians.[7]

Bill 22 went too far for both the English and the immigrants but not far enough for the French. The English community, moreover, did itself no good when the Protestant School Board of Greater Montreal challenged the legality of the new act in the courts and lost on every point it raised. Bill 22 had been carefully drafted, and even though it was unpopular for different reasons with different people, such a challenge served to remind the French how reluctant the English were to consider any change at all in the *status quo*. By 1974 even the chairman of the 1972 Commission, Jean-Denis Gendron, had changed his mind about the major recommendations of the Commission that parents in Quebec should be allowed to have their children educated in the language of their choice and that French should be made the language of work in the province through a system of inducements. He now saw a need for more coercive measures to bring about francization, declaring that "it's only when the francophone majority of Quebec starts to behave like a majority—whereas it now acts like a minority—that these fears [of insecurity in Quebec] will be alleviated."[8]

The inadequacies of Bill 22 as a piece of legislation partly contributed to the defeat of the Liberal government in 1976 and its replacement by the Parti Quebecois, a party determined to take vigorous action in matters relating to language and culture. The result was the introduction and passage of Bill 101, The Charter of the French Language, in 1977. This new act severely restricted access to the English schools of the province and made French the language of work in Quebec through a mandatory program of francization. A further provision removed English as an official language of the legislature and courts, but this was ruled by the courts to be *ultra vires*, being a clear violation of the British North America Act. However, some legal experts had argued that such measures were not a violation since they were matters related to the constitution of the province which did not involve the office of the Lieutenant-Governor, the Queen's official representative in the province.

The Minister responsible for the 1977 act, Camille Laurin, was quite categorical about its intent:

There will no longer be any question of a bilingual Quebec.

> ...For the first time in Quebec, there will be a law which proclaims that every Quebecker has the right to work in French, to receive his education in French, to be informed and served in French, to express himself in French in any deliberative assembly, and to require that the public administration, health services and social services, professional corporations, employees' associations, and various enterprises communicate with him in French.[9]

In order to ensure these rights for the people of the province the Government of Quebec intended to francize the province:

> ...the francization of businesses will not be optional; it will be obligatory for all firms with fifty or more employees. It must be carried out at such a rate as to ensure that by 1983, all such firms have obtained their francization certificates.[10]

The educational provisions of Bill 101 mandated an education in French for all children except those who fell into certain distinct categories:

(a) any child one of whose parents has attended English elementary school in Quebec;
(b) any child, who is already receiving instruction in English, and his younger brothers and sisters;
(c) any child one of whose parents attended English elementary school outside Quebec, provided that the parent is domiciled in Quebec at the time the Charter is adopted.[11]

Two further groups of children qualified for instruction in English: the children of temporary residents of Quebec[12] and the children of the native peoples, who had a right, if they so wished, to instruction in their own language.[13] The freedom of choice provided by Bill 22 and the language testing provisions of that bill were replaced by a compulsory system which sought to increase the enrolment in French schools and decrease it in English schools.

Outside the educational system, French was made the language of work and even of all signs in the province, a highly symbolic move. *L'Office de la langue francaise* was established to supervise the francization of Quebec: its goal was not to give special favors to French people in the province but rather to ensure that the French language rather than the English language had privileged status. Direct pressure was placed on the English community to acquire the amount of French that would be needed in the new circumstances.

First, Bill 22, through its "language tests" provision, and then Bill 101, directly through compulsion, assaulted the English community's ability to sustain the losses it was already suffering through a combination of emigration and failure to draw new members from the immigrant community. Some attempt was made to subvert Bill 101 and many "illegal" students enrolled in the English schools of the Protestant School Board of Greater Montreal during the 1977-78 school year. But gradually the law was obeyed by almost everyone and the number of illegal students in the province was drastically reduced. A shift in the battleground occurred. Nothing prevented the Protestant School Board of Greater Montreal from opening French schools for immigrants and it was quite permissible to teach English in those schools though not to use English as the language of instruction. To some extent then the law left open a way for the immigrant population to have access to both languages but within an environment that would tend to favor the culture of the English community in Quebec. It was believed that such schools might even attract pupils from the French population, a number of whom had always enrolled in the English school system in Quebec. Bill 101 has been effective though in reducing the population base from the which the English schools draw. One estimate of the base for the Protestant School Board of Greater Montreal shows it to be shrinking at a 9 per cent annual rate, a rate which will very quickly produce drastic consequences for the English population of the province.

Moves to francize the workplace of Quebec have also drawn considerable attention. Sign legislation has proved contentious and there has been some reluctance to co-operate, particularly after the referendum defeat of 1980, when the people of Quebec voted against any move to seek an immediate agreement to separate from the rest of Canada. Proposals such as one to require all prints—except one—of English movies to be dubbed in French before they are shown in Quebec seem unnecessarily restrictive, almost a violation of a fundamental freedom of speech. But the move to francization continues; since both major political parties in Quebec believe in its justice, there appears to be no alternative course available to the English but to accept it, however reluctantly.

Even before the passage of Bill 101 the French language was being increasingly used as the language of work everywhere in the province, including Montreal. A comparison of figures for the 1931 and 1971 censuses showing the languages spoken by males in the 20 to 64 age group in Quebec shows that whereas 34 per cent spoke only French in 1931 that figure had increased to 45 per cent in 1971 and the corresponding figure for those who spoke only English had dropped from 16 per cent to 9 per cent. The proportion of bilinguals had also decreased over the same period, from 49 per cent to 40 per cent. Outside the three cities of Montreal, Quebec City, and Hull, 65 per cent of this population were unilingually French and only 3 per cent unilingually English. With 74 per cent of its male population of working age bilingual, Hull's position between the English and French populations of Canada is clearly documented. With less than 1 per cent of the adult male population of Quebec City unilingually English and 57 per cent unilingually French, the English language had virtually vanished as a possible language of work in the provincial capital by 1971. In contrast, in Montreal, with 16 per cent of its adult male population unilingually English and 57 per cent bilingual, it was obviously still possible to work in English with little difficulty in many occupations.[14]

In the 1970s both English and French were used as languages of work in Quebec. Outside Montreal, French was used in the vast majority of cases. Within Montreal and within specialized activities throughout the province, usage patterns were less clear. Professional, governmental, educational, social, and cultural activities were almost exclusively conducted in French except in certain linguistic enclaves such as McGill University and the Protestant schools. Higher level business and financial matters were most likely discussed in English, whereas low level floor management was almost exclusively conducted in French. Between the two there was a large middle ground under the control of bilingual brokers mainly of French origin. A 1973 study showed that almost two-thirds of both the English and French workers in Quebec actually worked in their own language exclusively and just under a third needed a bilingual capability.[15] Fewer than one in twenty were forced to work exclusively in the other language. Making French the language of work in the province worked greater hardship on those who were unilingually English and to a lesser extent on those who were neither of English nor French origin—a group in which nearly half worked in either English or a language other than English or French.

Quebec's move to make French the language of work in the province has already had some interesting repercussions for the English and for businesses which seek to adjust to the new linguistic conditions. Some have simply moved out of Quebec and ignored the effects of Bill 101 that way. Ten to fifteen years ago when the economy was booming such moves were easier; in difficult times it is much harder to make the move. Some firms have begun to insist that their unilingual employees acquire enough French to satisfy the law, whose aim is not to have those of French origin take over everything in Quebec but rather to make French the working language of the province. The difference between this latter expressed aim and the former perceived aim is enormous but one which the English community has been reluctant to recognize. It could mean the difference between the survival of the non-French ethnic groups in Quebec and their removal from economic influence—their removal from social and political influence having already been achieved. But the pressure on the English is considerable and dangerous, since as more English become bilingual, there will be less need for the French to do likewise, a situation which will ultimately jeopardize not the French language in Quebec, the traditional jeopardy, but the English language.

Whatever linguistic and social policies any government of Quebec may adopt, it is unlikely that the financial establishment that controls both Quebec and Canada will easily or gracefully yield its power over the Quebec economy; further, this establishment is most definitely not French in origin nor does it readily speak the language. With its membership more beholden to one another than to the country as a whole or to any one part of it, with governments at all levels regarded, publicly at least, as adversaries to be got around, and with interests which cross national boundaries at will, this group perhaps more than any other will control Quebec's destiny. Without continual infusions of capital Quebec cannot prosper, but the price it may be forced to pay for that capital is still unknown. If the people of Quebec decide to persist in the present policies and if the financial establishment acquiesces, then Quebec can only gain since its position either within Canada or as an independent political entity will be considerably stronger than it is today. At the moment with a few exceptions the two sides appear to be assessing their positions rather than acting definitively one way or the other. As Pierre Fournier has adequately documented in his book *The Quebec Establishment*, the province's successive governments of various political persuasions have managed very nicely to get along with Quebec's economic and business leaders and there is no real sign that the various cosy relationships are to be abruptly changed.[16] It is worth noting that those critics who have opposed the francization of the Quebec economy on the grounds that such a move would isolate Quebec from the rest of North America have overlooked the fact that Hydro Quebec, for example, has been francized throughout its entire existence. The use of French at all levels of Hydro Quebec has in no way impaired either its internal management, its relationship to other Quebec institutions, or its ability to function in the broader North American context. The Quebecois, rightly or wrongly, have long been able to separate linguistic and cultural issues from economic issues. One can note the following statement by Premier Robert Bourassa in *Le Monde* on August 6, 1970, shortly after his electoral victory:

> Definitely, Quebec must itself resolve the particular problem it has, that is of uniting French culture which is the most prestigious in the world, with North American technology which, in turn, is the most advanced in the world. This

synthesis, this marriage of French culture and of American technology, is the future of Quebec.[17]

To the majority of the Quebecois the oppressor is the English language and its associated culture rather than any technological or economic system.

Quebec no less than any other province finds itself influenced by the north-south economic pull which exists between the various Canadian regions and the corresponding regions of the United States and is fairly powerless to do anything about the overriding economic and financial framework. The 1972 Hydro Quebec agreement to export power to Consolidated Edison of New York during the period 1977-97 is but one example of how Quebec has responded to this traditional pull to supply materials and resources to United States industries directly to the south. Language is apparently no barrier to Quebec's interests in such matters no matter who is in power in Quebec City. Premier Levesque, for example, made it quite clear on several occasions soon after his election that Quebec in no way intended to reduce its co-operative endeavors with its southern neighbors. Nor would it do anything that would detract from its ability to draw capital from traditional sources of financing.

It is obviously much too early to assess the full results of Bill 101, but some consequences can be noted. The percentage of Quebec students attending English language elementary and secondary schools dropped from 16.7 per cent in 1975-76 to 13.8 per cent in 1980-81. The percentage of Quebec residents who have English as their mother tongue dropped from 13 per cent in 1976 to 10.9 per cent in 1981. Recent migration figures for Quebec also suggest that a significant part of the English population is either moving away or intends to do so, with the net loss to the province likely to be accentuated as the full effects of Bill 101 are realized. Montreal, however, continues to attract immigrants. In the past they have been either anglophone on arrival or have tended quite quickly to learn English rather than French. Recently, however, the numbers of Haitians, French North Africans, and Vietnamese admitted to Quebec have helped turn the tide toward French and away from English. The 1971 census clearly revealed that the foreign-born population of Quebec had increased its capability to speak French—to 53 per cent in 1971 from 43 per cent in 1961 and 38 per cent in 1951—mainly at the expense of those who spoke only English (57 per cent in 1951, 49 per cent in 1961, and 39 per cent in 1971).[18] Clearly a trend was underway before the passage of Bill 101, one which passage of that bill could only hasten.

Much as Bill 101 is an attempt to bring immigrants within the fold of French society, at the same time that society has little understanding of what is involved in the task. To newcomers to the province Quebec's policy appears to be one of assimilation, and not even the Italians, the immigrant group generally acknowledged to be "closest" to the French in Quebec, willingly accept assimilation. While English society outside Quebec has become increasingly pluralistic, French society within Quebec is almost as monolithic as it ever was. It is not even particularly sympathetic to certain francophone immigrants, as many Haitians have discovered.

Quebec still lags far behind a province like Ontario in its provisions for immigrants, for example in providing language classes, counselling, and the kinds of language and translation services newcomers so often require. The overstaffed and influential bureaucracy of the provincial government is virtually closed to anyone not of French origin: good job opportunities are almost non-existent and government bureaucracies are at best indifferent to the non-French community. In this respect the immigrant groups and English in Quebec find themselves in much the same position.

It will be particularly interesting to see what happens to the minorities centred in Montreal. How far will the various groups maintain their identities? Will a policy of multiculturalism evolve in Quebec as in some other parts of Canada? The Quebec government does not use the term *multiculturalism* in its statements nor in its policies, preferring the term *cultural pluralism* to describe its policies aimed at preserving some of the characteristics of ethnic groups in Quebec. However, there is a deliberate insistence in all statements made on the topic of cultural pluralism that the overall framework will be one of French language and culture. In this respect cultural pluralism in Quebec will be like multiculturalism in the rest of Canada, where the corresponding framework is one of English language and culture. To what extent will Quebec become a kind of microcosm of English Canada, the French doing to all others there what the English have done to all others in the rest of Canada? Within Quebec will the English retain their position only because of their charter group status guaranteed by the British North America Act and, in turn by the Constitution Act of 1982, even though the majority of Quebecois regard the situation as unjust? How will differences between the Constitution Act of 1982 and Bill 101 be resolved? Already the courts have decided that the provisions of Bill 101 which deny instruction in English to Canadian children of English parents are overruled by guarantees provided in the Constitution Act.

What happens to the French in the rest of Canada may well influence what happens to the English in Quebec. During the debate on Bill 101, Premier Levesque proposed that its terms could be modified through interprovincial agreements which would accord English parents moving to Quebec the same rights for their children in Quebec that French parents had for the education of their children in the originating province. His proposal that the other provinces sign reciprocal agreements with Quebec guaranteeing the educational rights of official language minorities met with resistance. The federal government saw any move toward signing a series of reciprocal agreements as a threat to national unity in that it would tend to reinforce Quebec's separatist position. The other premiers feared the move would create an unacceptable distinction between the French and all the other residents of their provinces. The English would be protected if they moved to Quebec but no other language group would be. Such a result would be divisive: it would certainly not be easily accepted by other language groups, who wished to see neither French nor English minorities given any greater advantage in Canada than they themselves enjoyed, which, of course, was usually no advantage at all. The premiers did however agree at the St. Andrews, New Brunswick, Conference in 1977 to provide instruction for students from the official minority group when numbers warranted, opting for this course of action rather than the one proposed by Prime Minister Trudeau, which would have entrenched such a right in the constitution. In 1982 Trudeau went ahead anyway with this provision in the new constitution. Where his decision will lead the country is hard to predict, particularly as it makes the courts of Canada rather than the legislatures the final arbiters in crucial matters, which is an entirely new position for Canadian judges to find themselves in.

Even that St. Andrews agreement shows a basic fact about language in Canada: the English and French are likely to have different views on language rights depending on where they live. The Quebecois are unlikely to be as concerned about the rights of the French outside Quebec as they themselves are. Above all, the Quebecois want to see French established as the language to be used throughout the whole of Quebec society. In this they are not unlike a majority of the English in the rest of Canada in their attitude toward the use of English. In contrast, the French outside Quebec and the English within are likely to share the view that bilingualism throughout the country as a whole is perhaps their only hope of maintaining their linguistic identity. But since each group is in a very weak minority position, and one which is constantly weakening, it is likely that the majorities will prevail. If present trends continue, the language situation in Canada must quickly become one of two quite separate linguistic communities held together through various systems of bilingual brokerage.

One of the interesting, even paradoxical, outcomes of Quebec's unilingual policies is that if they are successful, they will compel the English there to become bilingual while allowing the French to become unilingual. This result is paradoxical in that it is *federal* policy to support bilingualism, admittedly institutional bilingualism, but bilingualism mainly in English Canada to ensure that the French minority can be served there. There has been little real concern to do anything in Quebec where traditionally the English minority was well served in its language. But it was that very fact, along with the fact of the economic domination of the province by the English, which determined the Quebecois to become *maitres chez nous* in a French Quebec. There is some danger though to the French themselves if most Quebecois become unilingually French and only the elite remains bilingual and able to communicate with the rest of the North American continent: full social mobility within Quebec society might eventually require a knowledge of English.

The English in Canada really have themselves to blame for what has happened in modern Quebec. It was they who dealt harshly with the French in Manitoba, who virtually eliminated French as a language of instruction in the schools to the west of Quebec, and who resisted all moves to restore the rights that they had abrogated over the years. It was incidents and moves such as these which made Quebec's decision to become unilingually French ultimately the only viable one for its people. It was the failure of Canada outside Quebec to develop as a bilingual, bicultural nation and the too-little-of-the-wrong-thing-too-late response of such measures as the Official Languages Act which led to Quebec's language legislation of the late 1960s and the 1970s. Because Canada outside Quebec was determined to become unilingually English, Quebec's only real choice was to become unilingually French.

# 5

# THE FRENCH OUTSIDE QUEBEC

The French in Canada who live outside Quebec possibly experienced their best years in a brief period following immediately on the publication of the Report of the Royal Commission on Bilingualism and Biculturalism. Suddenly there was a climate of opinion favorable to them, grants to fund various organizations and programs became available, and the dark curtain drawn between the English and French in Canada was raised for a brief moment. However, the federal government declined to support both bilingualism and biculturalism, opting instead for a policy of "multiculturalism within a bilingual framework"; federal language policies were badly articulated and poorly executed, and the Official Languages policy quickly generated a strong English backlash. The French outside Quebec once again found themselves at loggerheads with the English and even officially in competition with various ethnic groups for support of their cultural activities.

There was also a basic conflict between federal and provincial views of bilingual rights themselves, a conflict that still persists. The federal view is that the Official Languages Act is a guarantee of an individual's right to use the maternal language anywhere in Canada, in certain circumstances. Territorial rights, that is, the exclusive right to use one language rather than another in a particular political jurisdiction, form no part of the policy. However, it is just such an emphasis on territorial rights which characterizes the provincial view. Outside Quebec, English, the majority language, has long prevailed and the minority has had few or no rights to use French, or have had their rights drastically abridged. Only in Quebec, sheltered by the British North America Act, did the minority English group preserve their rights. Bill 101 was basically a move to make Quebec just like the other provinces including even an abortive attempt to remove certain sheltering provisions of the British North America Act. The French outside Quebec must necessarily support the federal view in this matter, since any territorial principle dooms them to assimilation through the removal of some of the protections they need to survive.

The French outside Quebec do not necessarily view the resurgence of French nationalism within that province as a positive factor in their own relationships with the English in Canada. Indeed, many fear the opposite result. The Quebec government's move to restrict the rights of the English in Quebec has undoubtedly produced a "backlash" in English Canada. It has certainly made it more difficult to protect or advance the rights of the French there. An entirely francophone, possibly independent Quebec would leave the French everywhere else in Canada to fend for themselves. Although many are prepared to do this regardless of the moves Quebec makes to protect itself and how they feel about the propriety of those moves, what they fear is that the actions of the government of Quebec will make their own protection that much more difficult.

As the Quebecois have focused more and more of their attention on their own problems so have the French outside Quebec realized that they must look to their own resources if they are to survive linguistically. Certain moves by the Quebec government may even be to their long term disadvantage. As the province becomes more unilingually French and more attractive as a place of work, there are signs that the French elsewhere in Canada are being tempted to desert their outposts and return to their "patrie." Likewise, if French immigrants to Canada go only to Quebec, a possible source of renewal for the French outside the province will dry up. Indeed, there is plenty of evidence that the French outside Quebec now see a more natural ally in the federal government than they do in the Quebec government. Like the English within Quebec, the French outside are likely to be enthusiastic supporters of the Official Languages Act, deploring only the lack of enthusiasm and support that others have for it.

The 1971 census showed that nearly 1.42 million Canadians who claimed to be of French ethnic origin lived outside Quebec. Of these 926,000 gave French as their mother tongue but only 676,000 said it was the language of the home. In contrast, there were 640,000 residents of Quebec who were of English origin, but 789,000 residents of that province said that English was their mother tongue and even more (888,000) said that English was the language of the home. Such figures clearly demonstrate the strength of the English language within Quebec and the weakness of the French language outside.

To further emphasize the increasingly dualistic nature of Canada's official language make-up and the language split which is above all geographic, in 1951 outside of Quebec 77.6 per cent of Canada's population gave English as the mother tongue but that proportion had increased to 78.4 per cent in 1971. During the same period the French mother tongue population declined outside Quebec from 7.2 per cent to 6 per cent, and those who had neither English nor French as the mother tongue increased from 15.2 per cent to 15.6 per cent, largely the result of the considerable immigration to Canada in the 1950s and 1960s. Preliminary figures from the 1981 census show a further increase in the English proportion (to 79.4 per cent) at the expense of both the others: 5.2 per cent French and 15.4 per cent neither. These figures clearly indicate the continued lack of viability of languages other than English in English Canada, a situation deplored by the French and others alike.

The decline of French outside Quebec can also be seen if one compares the 1961 and 1971 census figures and percentages of those who declared French as their mother tongue with the data provided by the question asked in the 1971 census concerning the language used most frequently in the home. Although between 1961 and 1971 everywhere outside Quebec the number of those who gave French as their mother tongue increased (New Brunswick from 211,000 to 216,000; Ontario from 425,000 to 482,000; and elsewhere from 218,000 to 229,000), the general population increase was greater so that the actual proportions fell (from 35.2 per cent to 34 per cent, 6.8 per cent to 6.3 per cent, and 3.5 per cent to 3.2 per cent respectively). The extent of language loss can be shown by comparing the figures for French as the mother tongue with French as the language of the home. Whereas in 1971, 34 per cent of the population of New Brunswick had French as the mother tongue, only 31.4 per cent used it in the home. The corresponding figures for Ontario were 6.3 per cent and 4.6 per cent and for elsewhere outside Quebec 3.2 per cent and 1.7 per cent. The greater the distance from Quebec the greater is the extent of the language loss.

Exogamous marriage, that is, marriage outside the group, is increasing rapidly for the French outside Quebec, having as much as doubled in the last 30 years or so, and it again is found more frequently the further one travels from Quebec. In such marriages there is a probability of more than 90 per cent that English is the language of the home. Moreover, outside Quebec many couples of French origin also use English as the language of the home, with the incidence of such use increasing as does the distance from Quebec, the highest rates being found in the westernmost province, British Columbia. As Canada, particularly English Canada, becomes even more urbanized, more pluralistic in its ethnic and religious composition, more secular and less influenced by religious groups, and in certain ways more homogeneous through the uniformities which the mass media encourage, the French outside Quebec will experience increasing difficulty in maintaining their linguistic and cultural distinctiveness. As the Pepin-Robarts Report of 1979 observed:

> The rate of linguistic assimilation of French-speaking minorities is quite high, and appears to be accelerating in all English-speaking provinces other than New Brunswick. The French-speaking minorities, even more than Canadians generally, are becoming older and their school-age populations are in relatively sharp decline. Between 1961 and 1971, the number of children of French mother tongue four years of age and under dropped from 29,000 to 19,000 in New Brunswick, from 48,000 to 35,000 in Ontario and from

19,000 to 13,000 in the other English-speaking provinces. Due, among other things, to increasing urbanization (which brings with it greater contact with linguistic majorities), there is a relatively high rate of marriage to non-francophones. Among all the French-language minorities, except the Acadians of New Brunswick, this rate ranges between 30 per cent and 60 per cent and is accompanied by a shift to English as the language spoken at home in approximately 90 per cent of cases.[1]

No objective assessment of the situation of the French outside Quebec can escape the conclusion that almost everywhere they face the danger of linguistic and cultural extinction.

According to the 1971 census figures, the French outside Quebec maintain their language best in New Brunswick. The figures suggest that they should continue to do so if they can maintain their institutions and their proportion of the provincial population. West of Manitoba and in the north there is a very strong likelihood that the French language cannot be maintained even at the present low levels in the absence of French immigration to compensate for the shifts to English that have already occurred and the lack of institutional support. Elsewhere, particularly in Ontario and Manitoba, only a very high birth rate, possibly as high as 3.5 to 4 children per family, or steady French immigration, or some combination, can preserve what is even now a precarious situation in which as many as 40 per cent of those who have French as their mother tongue use English as the language of the home.

Traditional patterns of French migration do not, however, indicate that a sudden influx of new French immigrants will provide the help the French need almost everywhere to survive. In the traditional pattern of French migration the migrants would tend to be from Quebec and would show a strong and increasing preference to settle in the francophone parts of Ontario and New Brunswick which lie adjacent to Quebec. Migration from francophone countries has always been a somewhat insignificant factor in maintaining the French language in Canada and it has not always been helpful either to Quebec or the French elsewhere.

As well, migration of French from Quebec to other parts of Canada is unlikely to increase at a time when the linguistic situation outside Quebec is far less stable than the linguistic situation within the province. In fact, migration is very likely to decrease as Quebec comes to be regarded more and more as the homeland of the French; indeed, Quebec may attract French migrants from elsewhere in Canada rather than lose part of its French population to other parts no matter how desirable French emigration from Quebec might be for the total French presence in Canada.

Increasingly the French outside Quebec have been compelled to look to their own resources if they are to survive. For example, *Les Heritiers de Lord Durham*, a 1977 publication of La Federation des Francophones hors Quebec, presents a wide variety of data on how disadvantaged francophones outside Quebec are legally, educationally, and economically.[2] In addition, it clearly indicates how the Official Languages Act of 1969 has served the group poorly in that its efforts to promote institutional bilingualism and support minority official language instruction have proved wasteful, largely ineffective, and often divisive. While the document is a plea for help to remedy the situation, it also acknowledges that determined efforts by the French themselves will be required whether or not such help is forthcoming from the various levels of government.

In their earlier struggles for language rights at the beginning of the twentieth century, the French saw the ethnic groups in Canada as natural allies. They were trying to do the same things: preserve their languages and cultures and resist assimilation into the dominant English culture. Indeed the French often carried the battle, having behind them the support of an organized church and the encouragement of a province, Quebec. But after 1920 the French and other groups tended to grow apart as the others developed their own institutions and found shelter in their own communities. The French realized more and more that they would have to rely on themselves alone to preserve their language and culture.

The French have also refused to acknowledge the official view of the federal government that Canada is a multicultural country.

To the French outside Quebec multiculturalism must result in the death of bilingualism. It will lead only to preservation of shallow characteristics and make deep ones, such as the maintenance of a distinctive language, more vulnerable than before. The French view is that to be successful multiculturalism must be based solidly on a flourishing bilingualism, which alone can provide a solid base for cultural differences in society. The French believe that the ethnic groups should therefore support them in their efforts to preserve French language and culture everywhere in Canada since the preservation of French is the only real guarantee they have that they will be able to preserve their own languages and cultures. Without the French outside Quebec all will go into the melting pot or the English stew.

However, many ethnic groups are quite unsympathetic to claims for special treatment of the French language in Canada. This attitude is especially prevalent in the Prairie provinces, where speakers of French are outnumbered in many places by speakers of other languages. They tend to feel discriminatory threats from federal proposals to give a kind of "preferential" treatment to the French, provincial regulations which would allow education in French, and even the remote (by now) prospect of establishing federal bilingual districts. Opponents argue that other widely spoken languages deserve at least the same rights and that French should have no better status. This anti-French sentiment is not without its critics outside the French community. For example, the first Commissioner of Official Languages, Keith Spicer, warned that only if the approximately 26 per cent of Canadians who speak French have their linguistic rights protected would there appear to be some chance that minority languages spoken by 1, 2, or 3 per cent of the population might survive. If bilingualism fails, so will multiculturalism.[3] In this view, it is in the interest of "third force" groups to support the French in their endeavors to preserve their language outside Quebec.

As the French outside Quebec have had to fall back more and more on their own resources, a new phenomenon has arisen: the development of regional loyalty. Such regional loyalty has for a long time been important in English Canada. Being from British Columbia, Alberta, Ontario, or Newfoundland is quite often regarded as an important identifying characteristic. With the obvious exception of Quebec itself, until recently there has been little such regional identification in French Canada, except for people in the Acadian community. But it is now more and more important for a francophone to be seen as a Quebecois, a Franco-Ontarian, or a Franco-Manitoban than simply as a French Canadian. Moreover, whereas Franco-Ontarians may regard Quebec as their homeland, they will be particularly moved by the uniqueness of their own plight as French people living in Ontario, a situation quite different from that of their kin in either Quebec, Manitoba, or New Brunswick. The Council for Franco-Ontarian Affairs actually defines a Franco-Ontarian as "a Canadian whose mother tongue is French and whose permanent place of residence is in Ontario." By this definition, in 1976 there were 462,500 Franco-Ontarians even though more than 750,000 residents of Ontario claimed to be of French ethnic origin. The definition is therefore a somewhat restricted one based on language rather than ethnicity, because it is language issues rather than ethnic ones which provide the motivating force for action.

The 1971 census figures indicated that Ontario had just over 350,000 residents for whom French was the language of the home, approximately 4 per cent of the province's population. But only in the five counties of northern Ontario and the five nearest the southwest border of Quebec did the proportion approximate 25 per cent of the population of those counties. Even when those persons capable of speaking some French in each area are added to the numbers, the total capacity to speak French in the ten counties does not exceed 40 per cent. Elsewhere, only in the southwest part of the province, in Kent and Essex counties, does that total capacity exceed 10 per cent. Everywhere else in Ontario the figures for French are much worse. Richard Joy has estimated that in the south of the province, the area which includes Toronto, Hamilton, London, and Kitchener, only one person in 135 uses French as the language of the home.[4] Most of Ontario lacks the institutions such as parishes, schools, and cultural activities that tend to encourage language maintenance; instead the French in Ontario are almost overwhelmingly dominated by the English and their institutions.

Whereas in the extreme north and east of Ontario more than 70 per cent of those of French origin speak French in the home, the corresponding percentage for the province as a whole is only 48 per cent and in no other area does it exceed 40 per cent. The usual percentage is actually about 20 per cent. That is, outside the extreme north and east of Ontario, for every five people who declare themselves of French origin only one can be found who uses French as the language of the home! In Quebec of course, the opposite is true: more speakers of French exist than people of French origin. The same situation also exists everywhere in Canada regarding use of English and actual English origin. The effect, however, is much stronger: in Canada as a whole for every two people of English origin there are approximately three who use English as the home language. This result has been brought about by language mobility from the other ethnic groups, the French charter group, and the native peoples.

Joy's county-by-county analysis in Ontario of French language retention also reveals a clear correlation between the density of the French population of a particular county and the incidence of French language maintenance.[5] As would be expected, where those of French origin are very thinly spread, French as a home language is a rare phenomenon. When a county's French population is less than 20 per cent of its overall population, only about 20 per cent of the French population use French as the language of the home. With a quarter to half the population of a county of French origin, a dramatic increase is noticeable and more than two-thirds of those of French origin are likely to speak French at home. With over 80 per cent of French origin there is almost complete maintenance of French as the home language. The larger the proportion of French people the stronger the institutional structure that exists to support French and the wider its possible uses. There is a critical point below which suitable institutions cannot be supported nor opportunities for use created. Where that point is has been a matter of much controversy in Ontario over the generations.

The rapid urbanization of Canada during and following World War II has also hurt the French in Ontario. The industrial south has tended to attract not only native-born Ontarians, newly arrived immigrants, and those from other parts of Canada, particularly the Maritimes, but it has also attracted Franco-Ontarians. Just over a quarter of all Franco-Ontarians now live in this region. In 1971 of the 4.5 million residents of the region 166,000 were of French origin, less than 4 per cent of the total population. Since fewer than half of these had French as the mother tongue and no more than 33,000 used French as the home language, they were very much a linguistically invisible minority.[6]

Thomas Maxwell's study of the French population of Metropolitan Toronto led to several interesting conclusions.[7] The majority of the approximately 100,000 French in Toronto (out of a total population of approximately three million) participate willingly in a host society in which English is the dominant language. They are thinly spread throughout the area and tend to be more concerned with economic, occupational, and class issues than with linguistic ones. Religion is not a uniting factor nor, necessarily, is the French language since so many different French origins are included in the population. The heterogeneous, dispersed, French population has few institutions, a history of conflict and rivalries, and exhibits a greater concern with interests related to class differentiation than to ethnic unity. Many French therefore find it easier to identify with English friends and acquaintances than with other French people in Toronto. Not even the very significant advances achieved in public support of the French language since the passing of the Official Languages Act have done much to change this basic situation. The French remain almost as "invisible" as ever.[8]

No government of Ontario has ever been particularly sympathetic to the aspirations of the French in the province and none seems to have lost many votes in taking such a position. In the late nineteenth century various governments did nothing to encourage and much to discourage the development of a strong system of education for French residents of the province, who by the 1911 census comprised approximately 10 per cent of the population. Dissatisfied with the educational opportunities provided for them, the French sought more and better schools. While they were quite willing to allow their children to learn

English, they did not want such learning to be at the expense of their mother tongue. What they wanted was a genuine bilingual province, but this desire found little support among the English of the province nor even among English Roman Catholics. Once Roman Catholics of non-French origin began to settle in Canada in large numbers, particularly at first from Ireland, the French language no longer was the sole defender of the faith nor did the faith necessarily defend the French language outside Quebec. In the controversies over bilingual schools in Ontario many Irish Roman Catholics actively supported Protestants in their efforts to eliminate French almost completely as a language of instruction in the separate schools of the province. Possibly fearing a Protestant attack on the separate schools themselves, they were quite prepared to sacrifice the French language in those schools to preserve their religious distinctiveness.[9]

Persistent English opposition, chronic shortages of funds, poor teacher training, and lack of resources contributed to bring about a situation which the Government of Ontario through its Ministry of Education proceeded to "remedy." In 1912 Regulation 17 established the requirement that English be the language of instruction in the schools of Ontario, with only one provision for any other language: if a pupil did not understand English, at the request of the parents a school board could offer instruction in French for up to two or three years of elementary school. French as a subject could be taught if requested, but for no more than an hour a day. Regulation 17 restricted rather than enlarged the rights of the French in Ontario. They were reminded that the British North America Act protected only their confessional rights in the province and gave them no language rights there. The new regulation was regarded as no more than a codification of existing practices entirely permissible within the provisions of the Act. The Judicial Committee of the Privy Council of the United Kingdom, then Canada's highest court of appeal, upheld Regulation 17 on appeal in 1916 but the residue was bitterness. In 1916 the British House of Commons condemned the Ontario government for its treatment of the French, but the Canadian government refused to invoke Section 93 of the British North America Act and pass remedial legislation. The French in Ontario were abandoned. Other assaults on language rights in New Brunswick, Manitoba, and Saskatchewan also fanned the flames of French discontent with the English and their willingness and ability to dominate the French, a discontent which reached its height in the conscription crisis of 1917 when French Canadians resisted enlisting to fight in an "English" war in Europe.

What French presence there is in the schools of Ontario today has been gained gradually and grudgingly, beginning with the amendment of Regulation 17 in 1927 and continuing through changes such as the one made in 1968 to allow for French language secondary schools within the public school system and the funding of bilingual colleges and universities. Therefore, it was not until 1968 that Ontario finally gave full approval to the idea of French elementary and secondary schools. But even then the French experienced considerable difficulty in exercising the rights given them in 1968, particularly insofar as secondary education was concerned. They met with resistance in districts like Toronto, Ottawa, Sturgeon Falls, Cornwall, Essex County, and Penetanguishene, and direct government and ministerial intervention and support had often to be sought. The Ontario government tended to give its support reluctantly and slowly, doubtless because of fears of an ever-present English "backlash." Franco-Ontarians know that the French language can be maintained in Ontario only if a range of French institutions flourishes within their community. They believe that French-only schools rather than bilingual schools are one of the key institutions. They are also quite aware of how reluctant the English will be to grant them what is now their right in law, by the Constitution Act of 1982, to have their children taught in French where numbers warrant. The French in Ontario will be most interested to see what changes will result from the promise made by the Ontario government in 1983 to grant them the full opportunity to be educated in French. Some 75,000 pupils now attend over 300 French-language elementary schools in Ontario and another 32,000 attend the approximately two dozen French-language secondary schools or three dozen "mixed" (that is, French and English) secondary schools. It is not the happiest situation for the French but it does show considerable improvement from the situation that existed as recently as twenty years ago. It is still far from the "adequate system of education for the Francophone minority" which the Royal Commission on Bilingualism and Biculturalism deemed necessary for Ontario.[10]

While New Brunswick finally made itself officially a bilingual province in 1977 and Premier Richard Hatfield has repeatedly challenged Ontario to follow his lead, the Ontario government is very reluctant to budge. The Conservative government of Premier William Davis sees the possibility of a considerable backlash among the very people who have provided its electoral support if French is given official or constitutional status in the province. So while New Brunswick became a constitutionally bilingual province by the Constitution Act of 1982, Ontario did not. Instead the Ontario government's policy is to proceed as quietly, cautiously, and slowly as possible to provide educational opportunities in French when numbers warrant and if strong requests make no other course possible. This somewhat cynical but politically expedient policy offends many French in Ontario but allows the government to retain its strong political base among the English. The policy allows French to be used in schools when numbers warrant, permits any Member of the Provincial Parliament to speak in the Legislature in either language and have his or her remarks recorded in that language in Hansard, allows anyone to communicate with the government in writing in the French language, and grants trials and court proceedings in French in certain circumstances and in certain areas. But, except for the provision concerning French as a language of instruction, none of the above exists as a matter of right guaranteed by laws which cannot easily be abrogated. Premier Davis has refused to provide such legal status to provincial practice, and as recently as June 1, 1978, refused to allow passage to a private member's bill which would have enshrined French language rights into law within the province. Somewhat surprisingly perhaps, L'Association Canadienne-Francaise de l'Ontario apparently supports Premier Davis in his cautious approach to the matter, preferring consultation and agreement to confrontation and the backlash it might bring. An alternative interpretation of Davis' actions sees him keeping the language issue out of focus so as not to arouse old antagonisms in the province. His refusal to respond to the challenges of both the Prime Minister and other premiers could be construed as an act of pro-Canadian statesmanship rather than one of traditional Ontarian francophobia.

The French community in Ontario continues to seek public support for the institutions which it has been compelled to support privately, believing that they deserve access to their proper share of public monies in the province. Their largest success has been in the areas of public education, social service, and access to the media. Their economic success has been unremarkable. A statement in a Franco-Ontarian publication on this topic reads as follows:

> An important element in the vulnerability of French-speaking Ontarians today is their lack of economic power. In some areas of the world, minorities often succeed in not only maintaining their identity but even growing by seizing the reigns [sic] of power in commerce and industry. The world of business in Canada has been graced by such Franco-Ontarian luminaries as Paul Desmarais and Robert Campeau, but the Franco-Ontarian has not yet succeeded in truly gaining control of his own economic life.[11]

The two individuals named seem to epitomize what it means to succeed in Canada: to make many millions of dollars and gain control of a multinational corporation. In one sense that is success, for it is just such individuals who control the destiny of the country out of all proportion to their numbers. What is particularly interesting about the two individuals mentioned is the extent to which they actually have managed to join the "club" that runs the country. Some of their efforts met with considerable resistance: for example, Desmarais' failure to win control of the giant Argus Corporation and Campeau's failure in 1980 to take over Royal Trustco, another large holding company, have been seen by some observers as obvious attempts by the establishment to keep outsiders in their proper place in the order of things in Canada.

Any analysis of the legal status of the French language in English Canada outside the province of Ontario reveals that it is generally even lower than it is within Ontario. Only New Brunswick currently gives equal constitutional status to both languages, but Manitoba will soon emulate that province. The courts of the Prairie provinces operate in English, except in certain limited circumstances in Manitoba and Alberta. In the Atlantic provinces outside of New Brunswick provincial legal matters proceed in English. Throughout English Canada, French is from time to time used in the different legislatures, without apparent challenge but not always "officially"; the French sometimes appears only in an English translation in the provincial Hansard. French can be used as a language of instruction in schools in New Brunswick, in Manitoba when numbers warrant, in Saskatchewan by government dispensation, in Alberta in bilingual settings, and in the other Atlantic provinces on a discretionary basis. French can be used as a language of instruction in British Columbia only with ministerial permission. The majority of schools in which French is used as a language of instruction are located in Ontario and New Brunswick and these are usually schools in which French alone is used—about 500 altogether as compared to about 60 which are bilingual. Elsewhere bilingual settings for instruction are the usual pattern but the number of such schools does not appear to reach 100.[12] British Columbia has no representation in these figures, being quite unsympathetic to most initiatives to improve the situation of the French there.

The foot-dragging slowness to recognize that the French outside Quebec have any language rights at all is even apparent in New Brunswick, the only officially bilingual province. For example, as recently as 1975 there was opposition to any further extension of the use of French in the province. In that year certain English residents objected to the installation of a new sign for the City Hall in Moncton: it was, they insisted, the "City Hall" not "Hotel de Ville de Moncton." In fact, Moncton was a centre of English resistance to the French language in New Brunswick; neither bilingualism as an official policy nor the teaching of French in the schools met with the approval of the majority of the English. This situation is all the more noteworthy in that New Brunswick, above all others, must be considered the province in which almost any kind of bilingual policy could be expected to have its best chances of success. But even the path of slow implementation chosen by the provincial government has proved at times to be a rocky one.

Of course, any move to give any status at all to French outside Quebec must first confront the task of undoing history and reversing strong historical trends. When Manitoba, for example, was founded in 1870, there was no threat to the French in the new province: their linguistic and confessional rights were apparently guaranteed. But within a very few years much of the tolerance for the French language and for Roman Catholicism that had existed at the time of Confederation and the passing of the Manitoba Act in 1870 had been replaced by a desire to make the West conform to "English" traditions. The provisions of the British North America Act were given their most limited interpretation: there would be conformity to its letter rather than its spirit. Provincial legislation which changed language laws went unchallenged by the federal government, secular English schools became the model almost everywhere, and an attempt was made to fashion Canada outside Quebec in the image of Ontario. The English majority asserted its rights over the various minorities, all the while proclaiming that its actions were quite democratic in that everyone was being treated alike, that is, like the English. In the words of the infamous Equal Rights Association of the day, there was to be "equal rights to all, special privileges to none."

The most significant move against the French in western Canada was the decision of the Manitoba Legislature in 1890 to remove state support from the Roman Catholic schools of the province. English Manitobans, led by an Ontarian, D'Alton McCarthy of the Equal Rights Association, easily convinced the Manitoba government that the privileges of the French were undeserved and stood in the way of building a province united in the English Protestant tradition. That those privileges had been granted under the Manitoba Act of 1870 was of no consequence. Since they pertained to education, a provincial responsibility, they could be removed, or so the argument went.

The English voices raised in opposition to the proposed changes were few. The editorial writer of the *Manitoba Free Press* who wrote in 1889 that "separate schools themselves are a privilege conceded to Roman Catholics by the constitution, confirmed by years of possession, and which now cannot be taken away without a gross violation of faith, a cowardly exercise of accidental power, and a serious menace to the whole fabric of Confederation" found himself in a minority, even though history has come to recognize his prescience.[13]

The 1890 Act gave Manitoba an educational system modelled on that of Ontario with one notable exception: there was to be no public funding of separate schools. In this respect the schools of Manitoba were to be modelled on the nationalist non-sectarian schools of the mid-western American states to the south. The French language itself was not directly attacked but the imposition of a double burden on parents wishing to send their children to French Catholic schools was a formidable obstacle to continued instruction in French.

Beyond the sphere of education, attacks on the French language were quite direct. For example, the Manitoba government abolished the special linguistic rights given to the French in the Legislature and courts under Section 23 of the Manitoba Act, rights not returned until 1979 by a decision of the Supreme Court of Canada. After 1890 the French in Manitoba were to be a minority just like all other newly arrived immigrant groups. They had no special status; it had not been enough to hang Riel after his abortive insurrection.

The mid years of the 1890s saw the Roman Catholics in Manitoba take their case to the Privy Council in London where they ultimately gained support for their claim that their rights had been infringed and that their grievance was legitimate. The remedy, though, lay with the Government of Canada. But the federal government found it difficult to act in a matter which was clearly indicated to be entirely within its jurisdiction. The outcome of a series of acrimonious provincial and federal elections gained only a compromise solution, the Laurier-Greenway compromise of 1896, enacted into Manitoba law the following year. Under that compromise one half-hour of religious instruction would be permitted each day in the schools, a certain proportion of Roman Catholic teachers would be employed, and, when numbers warranted, French or another language could be used as a language of instruction. Needless to say the compromise did little to assuage the bad feelings that had arisen on both sides in the previous half dozen years. Although it signalled defeat for the French, it nevertheless left open certain possibilities for a variety of bilingual schools, possibilities that many groups in addition to the French took advantage of at the turn of the century. However, the outbreak of World War I brought an end to this flirtation with multiculturalism and multilingualism. Such a policy was felt not to be in the best interests of a country committed, outside of Quebec at least, to a defence of King and Empire. Bilingual education was suppressed and the Manitoba French had to wait until 1970 for the restoration of their right to have their children educated in French.

The French outside Quebec have had to travel a long and weary road in the twentieth century. That they are still so journeying is a testimony to both their resilience and the intent of the English almost everywhere to continue throwing up obstacles. How difficult those goals are to achieve can be seen in the outcome of the St. Andrews Conference held in August, 1977. At this conference the provincial premiers agreed to do their best to provide instruction in English and French whenever the numbers of official language minority pupils in their schools justified such instruction. The agreement was not uncontroversial in that it followed hard on the heels of Bill 101, which very effectively limited access to English instruction in Quebec. It was also left up to each province to decide what exactly "justified" the provision of instruction. At a further meeting in Montreal in February, 1978, the premiers reaffirmed their commitment to the rights of each child of the French-speaking or English-speaking minority to achieve an education in his or her official language, whenever numbers warranted, and instructed their Council of Ministers of Education to make appropriate suggestions. But even though that Council issued a report, "The State of Minority Language Education in the Ten Provinces of Canada," showing what had been done and what remained to be done, there has been little further improvement.[14] Only Quebec has a comprehensive program of instruction for its official language minority, one which it has actually sought to limit through Bill 101. English

Canadians still exhibit their traditional reluctance to do anything to preserve the French language outside Quebec. In the western provinces implementation of any policy to help the French faces the additional problem of resistance from several ethnic groups, the Ukrainian being the most vocal. Such groups grant no privileged "charter" status to the French there, seeking instead "equal" recognition for all minorities. Implementing the clause in the Constitution Act of 1982 that requires the provinces to provide school instruction in French (or English) where numbers warrant will not be without its difficulties.

One can in no way be sanguine about the future of the French language outside Quebec, except in those areas adjacent to the province, the "bilingual belt." English Canada is only slightly less reluctant than it has ever been to grant support to the maintenance of French language and culture, and now the English find allies among members of the so-called "third force" in Canada. Even the best ally of the French outside Quebec, the federal government, seems less interested than it was a few brief years ago in providing support. Its Official Languages Act has produced confusion and opposition rather than harmony and enthusiasm. Certainly the funds to support the official language minorities through "bilingual" education programs have declined through the spending "freeze" imposed in 1979 and its attendant devaluating effect. Canada appears to be inevitably committed to becoming a country of two unilingualisms as French continues to erode outside Quebec and English to be forcibly diminished within.

# 6

# CANADA'S ABSORPTIVE CAPACITY

No discussion of the English-French relationship in Canada, particularly with linguistic matters as a focus, can avoid the effects that immigration has had on that relationship. The English population of Canada has increased through a combination of immigration and natural growth, whereas the French increase has resulted almost entirely from natural growth alone. But the resulting "English" population is a somewhat heterogeneous one, containing within it peoples of all kinds. Attempts, successful and otherwise, to make immigrants fit into a pattern shaped by the English have had important consequences for everyone alike: the English, the French, and those of other origins.

The period 1951 to 1981 showed a remarkable growth in Canada's population, which expanded from fourteen million to over 24 million, a huge increase. The annual rate of growth was as high as 2.8 per cent in the early 1950s but fell to approximately 1 per cent in the late 1970s. Much of the increase can be ascribed to natural growth, the "baby boom" after World War II being an important component, but immigration contributed a significant share. Since World War II Canada has admitted more than four million immigrants.

Whereas Canada's foreign-born population comprised about 22 per cent of its total population in the first 30 years of the twentieth century, since then that proportion has fallen to about 15 per cent. These percentages are considerably larger than those found in the United States, where the corresponding proportions are 13 per cent and 5 per cent. Canada has proportionally many more recent immigrants in its population than does the United States and it appears to allow them to maintain their "ethnic" identifications in a more liberal fashion. One consequence, of course, may be that any move to create a national identity is thereby weakened, and, since such a move cannot be strong in any case because of the basic English-French polarization of the country and the necessity to downplay policies of "Anglo-conformity," a "Canadian identity" tends to be defined negatively ("to be Canadian is not to be American") rather than positively. One other major effect of immigration on the Canadian population has been to turn over that population periodically, so keeping it in a state of flux and making the development of any kind of national consciousness that much more difficult.

Immigration has its counterpart, of course, in emigration. Until 1901 Canada actually lost population through emigration. Quebec's "fatal hemorrhage," the exodous south of a significant minority of its population, is an obvious example of the importance of population movement away from Canada. Even in the twentieth century, only in the post-World War II period was Canada's net gain from migration a really important factor in its overall population growth. In the best intercensus period for immigration, the period 1951-61, the gain was only slightly over 100,000 a year whereas the gain from natural increase was three times as great. In the 1960s while Canada gained just under 1.5 million people through immigration, it lost nearly one million through emigration; a significant number of these—about 600,000—were themselves previous immigrants and the rest Canadian-born. In such circumstances then it is not difficult to understand how the main growth in Canada's population comes from within, through natural increase among those already living in Canada, rather than directly from immigration. Invariably, population gains from natural increase have been proportionally much greater than those from immigration: four times as great in 1961-71 and eleven times in 1941-51. Immigration does affect population growth indirectly: those admitted bear children who in turn bear children, and so on, but all those offspring are *Canadians*.

The Canadian government estimates that 75,000 people currently leave the country each year, so total immigration must exceed that figure if Canada's population is to achieve any growth at all through net migration. The 1980 Annual Report to Parliament on Immigration Levels from Employment and Immigration Canada gave a net migration gain for the calendar year 1978 of only 14,873: total immigration of 86,313 less an estimated emigration of 71,440. In that period Canada's population increased by 0.86 per cent or 203,500 people; consequently, only 7 per cent of the increase could be attributed to immigration and 93 per cent had to be attributed to the excess of births over deaths. 1978 was a year of extremely slow population growth, so slow in fact that if the same situation kept repeating itself it would not be until 2058 that the population of Canada would double again, and that growth would be almost entirely attributable to natural increase.

Every census shows that a significant proportion of Canada's population has an "ethnic" origin other than English or French. However, there are inherent problems in dealing with the concept of ethnicity and specifically with the Canadian variety. But an inescapable fact is that more than one Canadian in four is regarded as being of neither English nor French origin for certain statistical and other purposes. The 1971 census figures showed that 5.8 million (or 26.7 per cent) of the Canadian population attributed to themselves an ethnic origin other than English or French. The English constituted 44.6 per cent of the population and the French 28.6 per cent, with the vast majority of the latter located in Quebec. Outside Quebec the so-called "ethnics," taken together, rather than the French, constituted the second largest group after the English. In Manitoba, Saskatchewan, and Alberta they actually outnumbered the English: Manitoba 49.3 per cent to 41.9 per cent; Saskatchewan 51.8 per cent to 42.1 per cent; and Alberta 47.4 per cent to 46.8 per cent.[1] Immigration has provided the life-sustaining ability of much of this population just as it has been a force in maintaining the English population. However, while the latter population is quite viable without the new transfusions provided by continuous replenishment from the source, it may be critical for many ethnic groups to have such continuous replenishment.

Canada's population is an increasingly urban one and newcomers have actively participated in the trend toward urbanization. In fact, Canadians have not only moved off the farms and into towns, but the towns themselves have grown, many into large metropolitan areas. These metropolises have proved very attractive to everyone, native-born and newcomers alike. The 1976 census designated 23 Census Metropolitan Areas for Canada: altogether these contained nearly 60 per cent of the country's total population, with the two largest, Toronto and Montreal, containing over 12 per cent each and Vancouver over 4 per cent. However, there are signs that the trend toward urbanization slowed considerably after the mid-1960s and may now have stopped altogether, possibly having gone as far as it could in the social and economic climate of the times. Immigrants, however, still prefer urban Canada to rural Canada and have long exhibited stronger tendencies toward urbanization than have native-born Canadians.[2] In 1921 56.4 per cent of the foreign-born lived in urban areas in contrast to 47.5 per cent of the native-born. By 1951 the corresponding percentages were 71 per cent and 60 per cent, and by 1971 they had increased again to 87.8 per cent and 74.1 per cent. These figures do not indicate that all the foreign-born are of urban origin in their originating countries: many are actually of rural origin, e.g., Italians, Greeks, and Portuguese. What the figures do indicate is that the Canadian "urban village" has proved more attractive than Canadian rural life to such immigrants and that the transition from rural to urban life is being made quite often in a giant step from quite small villages to large metropolitan areas, such as Toronto and Montreal.

Many Canadians have regarded this strong tendency on the part of immigrants to urbanize as creating a social problem for Canada. However, the Special Joint Committee of the Senate and of the House of Commons on Immigration Policy in its Report to Parliament in 1975 dismissed the idea that it was immigrants who, by crowding into Canada's cities, exacerbate housing shortages, increase the crime rate, bring infectious diseases, tax the welfare roles and government services, and cause unemployment by taking jobs away from Canadians. On the contrary, the Committee stated, urbanization is very much a phenomenon within Canadian society as a whole, and within that pattern immigrants tend to underuse social services, their employability is good, and they are considerably more law abiding than native-born Canadians. But myths die hard!

When immigrants do come to Canada, they settle in Ontario (mainly Toronto), in British Columbia, and in Montreal. They studiously avoid the Atlantic provinces and settle in the Prairie provinces somewhat thinly. The 1971 Census showed that 51.8 per cent of the foreign-born lived in Ontario (27 per cent in Toronto), 15.1 per cent in British Columbia (8.7 per cent in Vancouver), and 14.2 per cent in Quebec (12.3 per cent in Montreal). Scarcely more than 2 per cent were located in the Atlantic provinces. The remaining 16.7 per cent were located in the Prairie provinces or in the Yukon and Northwest Territories.

However, even the regional preferences of immigrants within Canada affect the internal distribution of the Canadian population less than do the internal migrations of that population. The 1971 census showed considerable population redistribution of the Canadian-born population. Canadians born in the four Atlantic provinces showed a strong tendency to migrate to Ontario, with British Columbia an attractive alternative. Quebecois tended not to move a great deal although there was a considerable exchange between Quebec and Ontario, but one favoring Ontario. Ontario's main population loss was to the West, with British Columbia the principal beneficiary. West of Ontario the direction of movement was quite clearly toward the west coast. Consequently, the greatest beneficiary was British Columbia. The net effect of all this movement of Canadian-born population was that if only this segment of the population is considered (approximately 85 per cent of the total population), the Atlantic provinces, Manitoba, and Saskatchewan lost significant numbers of people to other provinces, mainly those to the west. Ontario, Alberta, and British Columbia made significant gains, with the last the largest gainer in that over 37 per cent of its Canadian-born population was born outside the province. On the other hand, Newfoundland and Quebec held least attraction to Canadians born in other provinces, and people born in Ontario and Quebec were the least inclined of any to move elsewhere. Quebec, therefore, exhibited the most stable population pattern, being least affected by interprovincial migration.[3]

Overall, in the 30 or so years after 1951, the Atlantic provinces and the Prairie provinces showed fairly sharp declines in population. In 1951, 11.6 per cent of Canadians lived in the Atlantic provinces and 18.1 per cent in the Prairie provinces; by 1976 the proportions had fallen to 9.5 per cent and 16.4 per cent respectively. Quebec's proportion of the population also declined from 29.0 per cent to 27.1 per cent. The 1981 census figures showed a further decline to 26.4 per cent. In contrast, both Ontario and British Columbia gained, with Ontario's share of the total Canadian population increasing from 32.8 per cent in 1951 to 35.4 per cent in 1981 and British Columbia's from 8.3 per cent in 1951 to 11.3 per cent in 1981.[4] There is every reason to believe that recent population movements continue to be favorable to British Columbia and Alberta, that the erosion of the population of the Atlantic provinces has ceased, and that the situation in Quebec is less stable than seemed previously indicated.[5] However, unforeseen changes in regional economies might spur new patterns in internal migration during the coming decades.

To summarize then, since World War II immigration has contributed to Canada's population growth but emigration has taken its toll too. However, the net gains from migration are calculated as less than one-quarter of the population growth between 1951 and 1976. The excess of births over deaths in the Canadian population remains the major direct cause of the population increase; immigraton is a minor cause, but, insofar as children are born to immigrants in Canada, the indirect results are somewhat greater than indicated above.[6] Urbanization and internal migration are indigenous Canadian phenomena: the immigrant population has participated actively in both kinds of movement, but the foreign-born have actually played a minor role in each compared with that of native-born Canadians.

Whatever the effect immigration has had on Canada's population growth and distribution, the movement of people to

Canada has been strongly influenced by certain ideas the people of the host country have had about their land. Immigration policy has varied over the years but certain distinctive themes quickly become apparent in any survey. Paramount among these has been the attempt to mould those who arrived, and their descendants, within a particular pattern. There has been a conscious pressure applied to almost all immigrants at all times to make them fit into a Canada dominated by the English. Not thoroughly assimilationist, this policy of "Anglo-conformity" nevertheless has elevated a certain "Englishness" as the goal all Canadians should aspire to. At the same time, though, every arriving group—together with, of course, the native peoples—is somehow to be slotted into its "rightfully" inferior station.

The history of immigration to Canada is not one that shows, at least until recently, any great respect for cultural pluralism. Immigrants have always been admitted to Canada to perform fairly specific tasks, to be unobtrusive, and to conform. Notions of racial superiority and purity have been endemic in government policy. Immigrants from Britain were to be preferred above all others, and English Canada expected conformity to the English Canadian model, however that was defined. One characterization of the spirit of Anglo-conformity that has persisted over the years is as follows:

> ...the argument for anglo-conformity also requires the assumption that in a democracy the minority should conform to the wishes of the majority. The anglo-conformist further assumes that the majority is identifiable and unchanging, it is basically good, and it will use its power well, even if faced with a minority which does not. Some anglo-conformists make their case on "practical considerations": it would save time, money and effort if communication were always conducted through the language and culture of the numerically larger group.... Some anglophones believe that the maintenance of distinctive languages and cultures militates against national unity; and that minorities should sacrifice their distinctive features to unify Canada and increase its chances of surviving as a British country.[7]

But perhaps no one has stated more succinctly and bitingly the consequences of such a philosophy for immigrants and for the French throughout Canada than Prime Minister Trudeau himself:

> ...tremendous reserves of nationalism were expended, in order to make everyone good, clean, unhyphenated Canadians. Riel was neatly hanged, as an example to all who exploit petty regional differences. The Boer War was fought, as proof that Canadians could overlook their narrow provincialisms when the fate of the Empire was at stake. Conscription was imposed in two world wars, to show that in the face of death all Canadians were on an equal footing. And lest nationalism be in danger of waning, during the intervals between the above events Union Jacks were waved, Royalty was shown around, and immigration laws were loaded in favour of the British Isles.[8]

The French in Canada felt threatened by federal immigration policies and their attendant philosophy. They tended not to want any immigration to Canada at all since the arrival of significant numbers of newcomers to the country would further diminish French influence. The growth of the French population depended almost entirely on a high birth rate, which even compensated for the considerable emigration to the south. Consequently, they successfully resisted English expansion and Anglo-conformity through natural increase in Quebec, but this stood in contrast to what happened to them in all provinces to the west.

In the early years after Confederation in 1867 Canada actually had a rather laissez-faire immigration policy, but one which worked in favor of immigrants from Britain and the United States and discriminated actively against no group except the Chinese, who after 1885 had to pay a $50 "head tax." Sir Clifford Sifton, the responsible minister, initiated new policies after 1895 in his determination to populate the west. To the British and Americans were added peoples from eastern and southern Europe, particularly in the first decade of the twentieth century. But the Chinese were even further excluded by a raise in the head tax (to $500 in 1903), other Asians were discouraged by the imposition of "landing fees," "continuous journey" regulations, and direct international agreements, as with the Japanese government. By 1910 the policy was explicitly one of settling farmlands, preferring northern Europeans, keeping out Asians as far as possible, and resisting urbanization. The years 1910 to 1913 were the heaviest period of immigration to Canada.

These policies developed during an era in which the British Empire dominated much of the world and British commerce spread itself everywhere. Since Canadian leaders prided themselves on the country's connections with Britain, it was "natural" that British immigrants would be given preference. Somewhat surprisingly Americans were held in equally high esteem. That both groups were regarded as biologically superior to all others was also a product of the Social Darwinism that currently prevailed. If other, "biologically inferior," people were admitted, this course was adopted only as a matter of necessity: to farm lands unsuited to the others, to build railroads, and to perform other menial but nonetheless essential tasks in a rapidly developing nation. Some should not be admitted at all. So, after those of British and American ancestry, the residents of certain northern European countries such as the Scandinavian countries, Germany, Belgium, Holland, and Switzerland were next favored as immigrants. People from France found themselves in this group, a comment on how Canadian leaders viewed immigration from France during most of the period and, of course, how they viewed the French in Quebec. Eastern and southern Europeans could come if they were needed and if not enough of the "better" kinds of immigrants were available. For a long time no "non-Whites," that is, Blacks, Asians, or Orientals, were welcome. Canada wanted immigrants it could assimilate: groups with a pronounced difference in skin color, religion, or culture would be "unassimilable" and therefore not good for Canada. The exceptions were few: some Black groups from Oklahoma and some religious groups, particularly Mennonites, Hutterites, and Doukhobors from Europe, who could isolate themselves on the vast western plains. Thus, a Canadian ethnic hierarchy that also replicated certain aspects of English social-class structure was developed with groups assigned their "proper" places in it according to ethnic origin. The French in Quebec were also fitted into this scheme of things as were the native peoples, assignments which today neither party is any longer willing to accept.

Not everyone readily accepted these policies: they were too liberal for many and there was also a strong racist element in the country, stronger even than the racist underpinnings of the policies. Perhaps the fiercest resistance came from those with the strongest British and Imperial connections, particularly Conservative political leaders. Labor leaders and workers in the new industries also saw immigration as a threat since it would provide cheap labor to undercut what few improvements they had achieved. A strong Protestant sentiment also feared the spread of Roman Catholicism. And, ever present, of course, was the feeling of the French themselves: any large scale immigration to English Canada would reduce French power within the country as a whole. If it were impossible to stem immigration however, measures could be taken to mitigate its consequences. Immigrants could be remade to fit the vision of Canada held by the Loyalists and Imperialists of the day:

> Canadian imperialism, then, had in common with all nationalist ideologies a definite conception of what the national character encompassed and what its destiny would be. According to this view, Canadians were British in their historical associations, political ideals, their preference for law and order, and their capacity for self-government. They were, French and English alike, a tough and masterful people, inured to the stern climate of a northern nation whose population would in time exceed that of Britain. While the French Canadians were recognized as having exhibited an unchanging loyalty to the Empire and added distinctive charm to the Canadian character, they were also understood to be least enthusiastic for imperial unity. Their opposition to imperialism, however, was of small consequence and could only be significant temporarily because the rapid growth of the English-speaking section of the population, including the "foreigners" who would be assimilated to the prevailing ideals, would in the end exert a total dominance over the

Canadian nationality.[9]

Not all Canadians took such an "imperialist" view of the immigrants. Some were more humane in their motives, but the results for the immigrants were likely to be much the same. As Marilyn Barber says in her introduction to a reprint of J.S. Woodsworth's *Strangers Within Our Gates*, originally published in 1909, he

> ...accepted neither the pessimistic belief that Canadian standards would be destroyed by immigration nor the optimistic assurance that assimilation was inevitable. His was the middle position of concerned Canadians who feared that there would be serious problems unless care was taken to ensure that the new immigrants were assimilated. For these Canadians, assimilation was not a natural and inevitable process, but one which required assistance and direction.[10]

Woodsworth was a humanist who saw the poverty and misery of immigrant life in Winnipeg and had some kind of vision about what life in Canada could be. Needless to say that vision had a certain "English" quality to it. He did not question the "natural superiority" of English ways; rather he was concerned with passing on their benefits to as many as possible and as quickly and painlessly as possible.

Whatever their political persuasion or whatever their motives, many English Canadians were concerned with what they saw as the west was opened up to immigration at the turn of the century. The ethnic mix was new and its effect on the rest of Canada unpredictable. Americans, Germans, and Ukrainians certainly reduced the influence of the French in the new provinces but seemed in turn to resist the attempts of the English to assimilate or melt them. If the new provinces were to look anything like Ontario, and there was fear that they would not, the public schools would have to perform a heroic task of making one people out of many. The key was language. Consequently, many of the most keenly fought political battles during the first two decades of the new century were to be fought over language rights. It is also the measure of the determination of the English that theirs was the victory, sealed, of course, by the events of World War I.

One can view the legislation to restrict the rights of the various groups outside Quebec as an attempt to do two things concurrently: develop the country economically and keep it English in its orientation. Large numbers of settlers were required to populate the newly opened lands of the west, but these lands had to be opened in a way compatible with a vision of Canada as a kind of extension of English, spared some of the disadvantages seen in the "old country." The model was to be Ontario. As much as anything else it was the vast numbers of new immigrants required to populate these lands that seemed to make restrictive legislation necessary; nothing could be left to chance if the goal of Anglo-conformity was to succeed. Consequently, "unassimilable" groups were to be restricted from admission, and later certain aliens were to be disenfranchised or even deported (as were "Bolsheviks"), the protest of the dissidents and unemployed were to be ignored or beaten down, and the English language was to be made the cutting instrument of acculturation.

In the early century the goals of the schools in the new Prairie provinces were clear and explicit. The newcomers were to be taught English. They were also to become good citizens, which meant developing a loyalty to both Canada and the British Empire. They were also expected to learn certain English-style values such as a respect for British law and democracy. And if they could be converted to Protestantism so much the better. The educational model was to be found in Ontario, which itself looked back to Britain, and the whole approach was unequivocally assimilative.

It was difficult to enfore such policies before 1914: teachers were in short supply, enforcement of regulations was difficult, and local opposition was sometimes almost insuperable, particularly in Manitoba and to a lesser extent in Saskatchewan. It was the events surrounding World War I which finally succeeded in establishing Anglo-conformity in the Prairie schools. The war proved to be a severe test for many immigrants, particularly those in the Prairie provinces. Language rights, pacifist beliefs, conscription, political and religious values, and even notions about how land was to be owned all became sources of conflict between the English and other groups. The various immigrant groups reacted differently and often a group would split in its reaction. The Doukhobors in Canada kept on moving and protesting in an attempt to live the kind of life they considered they had been promised in Canada, particularly a life of pacifism. The German Catholics hid their Germanness and adopted a low profile. The Mennonites split: some conformed as far as possible to society's norms; others made fewer compromises; and still others left for Mexico and Paraguay. The Ukrainians, many of whom founded or joined left wing organizations, resisted discriminatory measures and resolved to do what they could with what means they had. Different strategies were evolved to meet the different impositions and their success varied, but nowhere was it complete.

Some of the laws and regulations made in the period of World War I were to stay in force for over half a century: for example, the 1919 Saskatchewan amendment to the provincial Education Act prohibiting the use of any language other than English as a language of instruction was not repealed until 1974. What World War I did above all was accentuate trends and give a marked impetus to moves that were well under way before 1914. The 1920s only continued what had begun, and it was to be a long time before the requirements of Anglo-conformity were to be relaxed significantly by those who had felt so threatened by the pre-1914 influx of new settlers.[11]

The end of the war saw a succession of restrictions on further immigration, involving categories such as enemy aliens, various religious groups, and non-Whites. After 1921 only those who were either British subjects from the British Isles or American citizens were allowed into Canada without immigration visas. The early 1920s did see a slight relaxation of the 1918 restrictions, except for the Chinese who found themselves virtually prohibited from Canada. The Depression and the turmoils of World War II made the 1930s and first half of the 1940s again years when immigration was neither encouraged nor very feasible. The next important period for immigration was the period after World War II, when a succession of changes in the Immigration Act, a policy of accepting refugees, and a gradually evolving, more tolerant, and less discriminatory policy brought many hundreds of thousands of immigrants to Canada in very few years.

Immigration policy following World War II has been guided by the principle of "absorptive capacity" enunciated by Prime Minister Mackenzie King in 1947. It was not really a new principle. There had always been concern about the absorptive capacity of both the land and the economy to put immigrants to work for the betterment of the country. Similarly, there had also been concern with the racial and cultural implications of the principle as the absorption of various groups at one time or another was deemed impossible or dangerous. King himself was quite explicit: "the people of Canada do not wish, as a result of mass immigration, to make a fundamental alteration in the character of our population."[12] The main result of King's restatement of policy was that Canada opened her gates to immigration once more, but the new cycle set certain events into motion with consequences that seem scarcely to have been intended at the time.

Freda Hawkins has described the development of Canada's immigration policy in the quarter century following the end of World War II, years which saw a large movement of population to Canada.[13] She points out that in retrospect what seems important about this movement was its rather haphazard nature in the first half of the period, the mounting pressures for changes in policy, and the gradual shift toward measures which combined some form of restriction with non-discrimination. The result was that by 1970 the typical immigrant arriving in Canada was quite different in background from the one who had arrived ten or twenty years previously. By the same year too, Quebec was beginning to exert itself over matters of immigration in an attempt to use the powers it had under the British North America Act to safeguard, so far as it could, the position of the French language and people in Canada.

This is not to deny that the English were at all deprived of a kind of "most favored" status as immigrants in this post-war period. Indeed, Anthony Richmond's study of post-war immigrants to Canada shows how favorably the British were treated so far as encouragement to immigrate was concerned.[14] Yet, like American immigrants, the British showed high rates of return and low rates of application for citizenship. They also often tended to be very vocal in their criticisms of Canadian society. Nor were the returnees to Britain those who had failed in Canada; they were probably more successful on the average than those who stayed. To Richmond many were *transilients*, a group of people with "an international market for their occupational skills," who therefore move from opportunity to opportunity. Consequently, "transilience would appear to be positively functional in urban industrial societies whose populations are increasingly mobile, both geographically and socially."[15] English Canada continued to grow through immigration from the "old country," but even the patterns of that immigration began to reflect characteristics of immigration in general as Canadian policy in the area evolved.

By 1960 it seemed that a satisfactory immigration policy would define Canada's absorptive capacity solely on economic grounds, that controls were necessary, and that the various discriminatory practices in effect were no longer tolerable. In 1962 the regulations of the 1952 Immigration Act were made somewhat less discriminatory when racial preferences were removed and when a system of "points" was introduced to decide who received immigration visas and who did not. Family reunification through sponsorship was also encouraged. The years 1967 and 1976 saw further changes made to reflect the different economic and social conditions in the country and what was perceived to be public opinion. While by no means entirely free of discrimination and occasionally harshly enforced, the present Immigration Act is an enormous advance over the system that existed prior to 1962. It is still, however, a piece of legislation which severely restricts entry to Canada and favors certain people over others; these are the principal objections of those who would like to see Canada's gates opened much more widely to immigrants than they are at present.

The current Immigration Act in effect makes the annual level of permissible immigration to Canada a "technical" issue in that the level is tied to perceived absorptive capacity. The only possible modification is through occasional special consideration, largely improvisational, for groups of refugees, e.g., the "boat people," and certain individuals who gain ministerial support. In this way the government has almost completely taken the immigration issue out of public reach. Tied, in the government scheme of things, to the economy and general population policy, immigration is not an issue for general discussion, being considered as too technical an issue for rational debate. While there is some merit in such a view, it does result in Canadians' being excluded from involvement in one of the most important strands in the country's make-up, one, in fact, to which almost all Canadians owe their origin. It is certainly legitimate to ask whether such a profoundly Canadian issue as immigration is really best left to technocrats and bureaucrats, and whether they are in any way better qualified to judge than the population as a whole.

One undeniable result of the changes in Canada's immigration policy is that there has been a steady annual decline in total immigration; only 86,000 in 1978 for example. The admissions quota for 1979 was set at 100,000 but this was boosted by special provisions for approximately 20,000 Indo-Chinese refugees. The 1980 figure was set at 120,000 including about 30,000 such refugees. With a 75,000 annual loss through emigration it is obvious that immigration is now contributing very little to Canada's total population growth. In addition, if for every 25,000 new immigrants only 14,000 new jobs must be found, then immigration is not a great contributor to unemployment in Canada, particularly when so-called Independent immigrants must almost guarantee their continued employability in the workplace before gaining permission to enter Canada, and those who are sponsored cannot become a public charge.

By 1978, 74 per cent of all immigrants fell into the categories of Family Class and Assisted Relative Class (corresponding loosely to the previous Sponsored and Nominated categories) and only 20 per cent were Independents, that is, those allowed to immigrate entirely on their own merits and for whom the "tests" are most stringent. This first percentage has been rising steadily since 1973 when it was only 47 per cent, an indication that family reunification is the stronger force in Canada's immigration policy and that expansion of the work force through immigration is both decreasingly important and increasingly selective.

Statistics Canada no longer compiles figures on the ethnic origin of immigrants. Instead it gathers information on such matters as their citizenship, birth place, country of last permanent residence, and intended destination in Canada. These figures show that a significant proportion of immigrants—one in eight—are making at least their second move in coming to Canada, since they were not born in nor were they citizens of the country of their last permanent residence. In part, this reflects the general unsettled nature of the modern world, but it also represents an important fact about post-industrial society: the availability of a transient work force in the world owing little commitment to specific locations and seeking the best possible opportunities, Richmond's transilients. Many post-World War II immigrants to Canada actually brought with them skills and abilities proportionally well in excess of those in the existing Canadian population. Many too were thoroughly urbanized and either professionally or technically oriented toward life in a post-industrial society. It is not at all clear where the loyalties of such people lie, whether to an ethnic group, an economic or social system, a region or country, or to some other set of values. Many such immigrants move on or return home, a phenomenon amply documented during the same period. What seems quite clear is that recent immigrants do not fit easily into either of the existing modes, either Anglo-conformity or cultural pluralism, that might be said to exist in Canada.

One important result of a more selective immigration policy which favors the educated and the professional over the laborer is that many newcomers are admitted almost directly into the middle class. Whereas once immigrants were seen as a threat to manual workers only, now they are often perceived as some kind of threat to those who have achieved a certain degree of socio-economic status. The latter see themselves forced to compete with the newcomers for opportunities typically enjoyed by the "Canadian" middle class.

The middle class fear of being usurped by newcomers might be valid in some instances. It is, however, the sort of emotion that lends itself to indiscriminate xenophobia. In one case, the 1978 CTV program "Campus Giveaway" accused Chinese university students, referred to as "foreigners," of taking university places from "Canadians."[16] The protests sparked by the program pointed out that the "Campus Giveaway" students were Canadian citizens or landed immigrants. All were residents of Ontario; none was a visa or foreign student. Ultimately, the CTV president was forced to issue a public apology admitting that the network's research and facts were inaccurate and that the program itself was "racist."

While the "Campus Giveaway" episode failed to make the case that new immigrants are stealing jobs from Canadians, it succeeded in showing that the middle class and the media will respond to the threat—real or imagined—in much the same way they have traditionally gone after working class immigrants.

One reason for conflict and misunderstanding is that the composition of Canada's "ethnic" population has changed considerably over the years since Confederation but there has been reluctance to accept this change. Northern Europeans (particularly Germans, Dutch, and Scandinavians) predominated in the nineteenth century. By 1931 a Ukrainian, Polish, Jewish, and Italian presence was also strongly established in Canada. Further groups were added later, particularly after World War II, for example, Greeks and Portuguese, and very "visible" groups such as Blacks, Asians, and Chinese. This is only to mention some of the most salient characteristics of the change and is in no way meant to de-emphasize such groups as Czechoslovaks, Russians, Lithuanians, Hungarians, Koreans, etc., who have also immigrated and helped to diversify Canada's population. If one looks specifically at the period from 1951 to 1973, it is possible to see some of the effects of the changes made in the Immigration Act in 1962. In 1951 the ten leading source countries for immigrants to Canada were nine European countries (all except Yugoslavia being western European) and the United States. In 1973 only Britain and Italy remained from the 1951 European list, and Greece and Portugal had been added. The United States remained too, but the other five main source countries were Hong Kong, Jamaica, India, the Philippines, and Trinidad. A very considerable change had occurred.

This shifting pattern of immigration has also produced some interesting differences in the age and linguistic composition of the various ethnic groups themselves. In the German, Dutch, Jewish, and Ukrainian populations, the proportion of Canadian-born is much higher than it is in the Chinese, West Indian, Greek, and Portuguese populations. The former groups are also "aging" populations, gaining few new members through immigration. Likewise, the proportion of unilingual anglophones and bilingual anglophones (that is, speakers of English and an "ethnic" language) is also higher, generally considered to be a sign of greater assimilation. But again the pattern is different among the groups, depending on the experiences of the immigrants and their feelings about how they can best accommodate to the society in which they find themselves. Even though the number of replacements has been small in some groups since World War II, many, particularly newcomers from eastern Europe, have had a strong sense of ethnic or national identity and of its being thwarted. Consequently, recent immigrants of this kind have tended to find themselves among the strongest supporters of ethnic causes, of language maintenance, and of official moves to encourage multiculturalism.

It is sometimes easy to forget how different was the situation met by settlers who arrived in Canada prior to 1930 from the situation met by their successors after World War II. (There was comparatively little immigration between 1930 and 1945.) The earlier groups of settlers faced harsh conditions and considerable isolation, both rural and urban. They were forced to band together to survive and they found a social climate which was not at all sympathetic to any notions they might have entertained about social mobility. In such circumstances the maintenance of traditional cultural ways, their religions, and their languages was important for both physical and psychological survival. Poor roads, isolation, and the lack of newspapers and other media encouraged the retention of traditional patterns. After World War II, rapid industrialization, the development of the media, new provincial school systems, comprehensive social policies, changes in immigration policy, and the development of new varieties of national consciousness all produced a very different climate for both the new immigrant and the descendant of the old, a climate which may indeed have made assimilation to majority ways both easier and more likely. A modern subtle Anglo-conformity appears to have superseded the older more brutal kind.

In other ways too a greater subtlety has entered Canadian life. Old habits die hard; they can be kept alive by dressing them a little differently and not so conspicuously. For example, discrimination against minorities has always been part of Canadian life. Except in rare instances it has not been practised as openly, or as violently, as in such countries as the United States, South Africa, Uganda, or Vietnam but it has been constantly present nevertheless. The franchise has been denied or withdrawn, land ownership and use has been restricted, immigration policies have been formulated on a racial basis, and schooling and language provisions have been altered. Obstacles have risen in employment practices, payment of wages, and housing covenants. The media have been particularly intolerant and have often created ill-feeling rather than do anything to lessen tension. Even today with Human Rights Commissions and Boards coast to coast incidents of discrimination are still frequent and, as was apparent in the 1978 "Campus Giveaway" attack on the Chinese community in Toronto, extremely difficult to redress, although on this particular occasion community pressure forced the CTV network to issue a formal retraction and apology.

Against this backdrop of widespread, if muted, discrimination, it is somewhat strange that in the 1970s there was a sudden concern in Canada about an "increase in racism." Racism has always been a part of Canadian life. Slavery was condoned until the early nineteenth century. British Columbia has had a long history of opposition to Orientals and South Asians. Various groups have suffered from time to time on the Prairies: Mennonites, Hutterites, Ukrainians, and so on. In Nova Scotia the Blacks have experienced a long history of injustice. The French outside Quebec have nearly always suffered. Inside Quebec xenophobia has been a recurring theme in the life of the province. There was an anti-Semitic riot in Toronto in 1933. Indians everywhere in Canada have suffered planned discrimination and are still ignored, if less actively mistreated. There was really nothing new in the racist outbreaks of the 1970s except that the conditions for dealing with such outbreaks had changed. Today, it is regarded as unacceptable to be overtly racist, but milder forms of the disease may be found everywhere. Groups exist to expose racism when it occurs and there is a legal framework, rather weak to be sure, within which to deal with incidents. If racism in Canada is not as virulent as it is elsewhere, it is largely because Canadians have been lucky, not that they have been particularly virtuous.

Ethnic immigrant groups have always faced a certain amount of discrimination from members of the two charter groups. They have been perceived as competitors for jobs and opportunities. They have been regarded as "inferiors," culturally, educationally, and even biologically. They have been suspected of disloyalty in times of war and regarded as "undemocratic" in their political leanings. Their language loyalties have often made them especially suspect. In general, nativist Canadians have tended to fear them as being un-Canadian and to stereotype them as ignorant, uncultured, and unworthy. As features of Canadian life, prejudice and discrimination are as old as the country itself.

In retrospect, one must regard as quite unwarranted the superiority that the English and French have long felt in the presence of others in Canada. The contempt and fears expressed by politicians (such as John A. Macdonald), professors (such as Stephen Leacock), clerics (such as Bishop Lloyd of Saskatchewan), journalists, and the ordinary citizen were completely unjustified.[17] Immigrants had little time and opportunity to indulge in "high culture," were largely excluded from normal social and political activities, and had no economic weight. Survival came first; prosperity and full participation were something for future generations. But one can also ask why there was necessarily so much pride in the kinds of colonial institutions so favored by the charter groups; why was so little attention devoted to developing "Canadian" institutions and so much to perpetuating copies of English ones, or, in the case of the French, Gallic ones? In one sense this feeling of superiority led to a possible loss of opportunity to build a culturally pluralistic nation and to the continued perpetuation of apparently irreconcilable differences, that is, to the situation that exists today. But, then again, it could also be argued that the opportunity never really existed at all, in that the basic English-French flaw in Canada's history necessarily had to perpetuate differences based on ethnicity and discriminatory attitudes.

The period surrounding World War I must be seen as critical in the development of Canadian attitudes toward immigrants. The first years of the twentieth century saw a tremendous influx of new people to Canada, an influx unparalleled in the history of the country. The Prairie provinces were settled at last but not by the English or French. They could not be completely made over in the image of Ontario but that did not stop such an attempt being made. The outbreak of war in 1914 also strained the Canadian establishment. It was loyal to the Empire, indeed imperialistic, but a large part of the population was not: the French and many newly arrived immigrants. It was also Protestant; the French were not, nor were many of the new arrivals. The years of World War I were therefore trying times for everyone.

During those years the Ukrainians, for example, were regarded as disloyal and treated as "aliens" who could be disenfranchised. They were indeed torn by the European war, and, lacking any kind of sophisticated leadership, found themselves the victims of a variety of discriminatory actions initiated by both levels of government. Internment, press censorship, accusations of disloyalty, and confiscation of property were used to control and, if possible, eliminate any kind of dissent. The Ukrainian language was directly legislated against, along with all languages other than English, when Manitoba changed its school regulations to curtail bilingual instruction. The "red scare" that followed the Russian Revolution also hurt the Ukrainians. By 1920 then, the Ukrainian community in Canada had lost much of what it aspired to possess in 1914. In 1914, even though signs of oppression were there, Ukrainians could still hope to see their language taught in schools, their culture preserved, and their identity remain unthreatened. By 1920 their language rights were gone. The war had demonstrated to them how "Canadians" intended to deal with "aliens" in their midst, and a clear message had been delivered that Anglo-conformity was to be regarded as the norm expected of newcomers to Canada, even though it was conformity to principles which had shown themselves largely bankrupt in the trenches in Europe.

Racial prejudice in Canada, however, has been far more strongly displayed against people of Chinese and Japanese ancestry than against almost any other group. In particular, various governments of British Columbia, in their moves against the Chinese from the 1870s on, and the federal government itself, with the Chinese Exclusion Act of 1923 and the invocation of the War Measures Act against the Japanese of British Columbia in 1942, have actively legislated against, and colluded with each other, concerning the Chinese and Japanese. The importation of cheap Chinese labor to help build the railroad, followed by the abandonment of the Chinese once the task was done and the attempt to exclude other Chinese from coming, was a sad enough episode in Canada's history. But in 1942 it was to be far surpassed in vindictiveness and repression by the forcible removal of 21,000 people of Japanese descent, many of whom were Canadian citizens either by birth or naturalization, from the British Columbia coast, the confiscation of their property, and the abrogation of their rights. This act far exceeded in its effects the expulsion of the Acadians from Nova Scotia two centuries before. Such treatment of the Japanese showed how strongly any kind of Canadian identity was based on notions of flag (the Union Jack), color (white), and language (English). Other "alien" groups, for example the Germans in World War I and both the Germans and Italians in World War II, suffered far less, having a greater cultural similarity to the English and, of course, not being so conspicuously different in appearance. Comprising a larger population in Canada, they also found a certain safety in numbers.

One of the reasons why immigration policy may have been reduced recently to a technical issue is that a fairly open policy now would see a dramatic shift in the kind of immigrant who would be attracted to Canada: mainly people from the third world. This shift is already apparent in those who do manage to enter: West Indians, Asians, South Americans, and Mediterranean peoples. The "visible minorities" would become even more visible and Canada has not had any great success in dealing with such minorities. In this respect then the current immigration policy eliminates discussion of racism, but does so by being "racist" in the sense of attempting to stabilize the racial composition of the country in its present form. The two charter groups remain relatively unthreatened by such a policy and can even justify it to themselves and others as one determined by economic considerations alone.

Apparently familiarity breeds acceptance rather than dislike only when groups that come into contact with one another have certain differences which all are prepared to overlook. In Canada "color" appears still to be a difference not easily overlooked and generations of familiarity have not proven long enough for all barriers to break down. That is why the Blacks of Nova Scotia, the native peoples of Canada in general, and the Asians of British Columbia are still treated in ways that can only indicate residual discrimination. (The recent firebombings of East Indians' homes in British Columbia and related acts of violence against the community are reminders of how easily residual discrimination can explode into vicious assault.) It is also why West Indians and South Asians in Toronto feel threatened and unite occasionally either to protest incidents when their rights appear to have gone unprotected or to have been ignored or even brutally infringed. But if more than 200 years of familiarity between the English and French in Canada have brought about the situation one sees today, it is perhaps not so surprising that 100 years of immigration have created problems of the same kind.

In certain respects Canadian society is more tolerant today than it has ever been. Its immigration policy is "in theory" non-discriminatory, its population is heterogeneous, and each province has a law proscribing various kinds of discrimination. But still people are assaulted because they are South Asians, do not get jobs because they have this or that characteristic, cannot easily buy property because they do not reside in a particular province, cannot be educated in their mother tongue because they speak English within Quebec or French outside, or are deprived of some benefit or respect because they are from Poland or Hong Kong, or are Black or female, or lack "Canadian experience." And many think this situation is as it should be, that language, ethnicity, color, sex, and so on should still be used to apportion opportunities in Canada!

Canadians exhibit little deep commitment to any principle of equality for all. Many are still hesitant about, even resistant to, taking in any strangers at all within Canada's gates. In his 1958 book *A Nation of Immigrants* John F. Kennedy, later President of the United States, acknowledged how important immigration had been in the development of the American nation.[18] Australians too are very conscious of the importance of immigration in the development of their country and of its continued prosperity. In contrast, Canadians are much less enthusiastic, even though all except the native peoples are descendants of immigrants themselves. The reason is quite simple: Canada's founding myth focuses on the existence of two charter groups, the French and the English, and immigration is in a sense a "problem," one which threatens the delicate balance between the two groups and alters the original bilingual, bicultural nature of the "union" of these two peoples. As Freda Hawkins observes in her book *Canada and Immigration*: "The absence of firm conviction about immigration in Canada has led to great uncertainty in its management and considerable difficulty in its operation."[19]

Instead of any great national enthusiasm for immigration, both the Canadian public and its elected leaders have been somewhat wary of making changes in policies that have evolved over the years. There is a fear of the unknown. The various balances in Canada are extremely delicate: political, linguistic, ethnic, religious, economic, regional, and so on. Large-scale immigration has the potential for upsetting these even more than they are upset by disputes among the already existing population. So while there may be strong individual proponents of policy changes and while certain issues do surface to public attention from time to time, the policy that prevails is one of letting into the country sufficient numbers to keep immigration alive but never to allow immigration itself to become a conspicuous issue.

The policy has always been designed for the specific purpose of nation-building: settling new land, and finding people to chop lumber, mine ore, build railroads, subways, and sewers, heal the sick, and teach the children. It is no coincidence that the department is called Employment and Immigration. The policy has also been designed to compensate for emigration, since Canada is also a country that many have deliberately left, either to go "home" again or to inhabit "greener" areas to the south. From time to time significant numbers of refugees have come to Canada. However, they have always been admitted as "exceptions" to the prevailing policy and in relatively small numbers if any long-term view is taken. Even then Canada has tended to be quite selective in who has been admitted. Canada's immigration policy can be generally characterized as follows: During periods of strong economic growth, the nation-building philosophy tends to dominate and the doors are thrown open more widely to a broader range of immigrant workers; when the economy is weak, selectivity and discrimination tend to prevail.

While at certain times most Canadians have agreed that some, be it minimal, immigration is desirable to achieve certain national goals, at other times controversy has raged over the desirability of adding to the population in this way rather than through natural increase, the method chosen by the French in Quebec for example. Early Loyalist settlement discouraged United States acquisitiveness and removed the imbalance in the population which favored the French. Prairie settlement opened up vast tracts of land so that a nation could be established stretching from the Atlantic to the Pacific. Refugees were admitted in the twentieth century for humanitarian reasons. All these moves satisfied some kind of national policy or derived from a national consciousness which agreed that something had to be done about a specific problem. In times of economic hardship, however, attitudes towards immigration have tended to polarize. The majority apparently resist immigration at such times fearing that it will exacerbate unemployment and make economic recovery even harder while at the same time promoting social ill-will; a small minority claim that continued immigration in such times actually creates opportunities and stimulates the economy in the new demands it creates for goods and services, particularly as immigrants tend to fill jobs the unemployed native-born will not take even in the worst of times. Traditionally the first view has prevailed and is indeed reflected in the government's policy of "absorptive capacity," a policy which explicitly links the numbers admitted to unemployment figures.

This principle of "absorptive capacity" in Canada's immigration policy quite clearly demonstrates that immigration is also designed to serve the corporate interest in Canada. Employment and Immigration is but a single government department. The policy is in no way humanitarian and altruistic. While it encourages the better educated to leave developing countries, it refuses the poor, and those who suffer most must not even attempt to come to Canada. From time to time a humanitarian door is opened as "refugees" are admitted, but again this is infrequent, haphazard, and even in part self-serving.

While Anglo-conformity has provided the predominant framework for the accommodation of newcomers to most of Canada, this is not to say that the predominant culture has gone unaffected. It does show very definite signs of modification. There is no mistaking that the regional cultures of the Atlantic provinces, Ontario, the Prairie provinces, and British Columbia are different from each other, differences which must be ascribed as much to their population mixes as to any other factor. And just as the accommodating culture has been changed and is different in different places so are the accommodated groups: they are different from the grandparents or cousins in the old countries and they are often somewhat different from their fellow ethnics in other parts of Canada.

There is no doubt that Canadian society as a whole has become culturally more diverse during the twentieth century and that this increase in diversity has helped ease the burdens of adjustment for recent arrivals, who are themselves more diverse culturally than their predecessors. In the last twenty years or so Asians, South Asians, and various Blacks have contributed to the increased cultural diversity of Canada and have done so without much of the friction their predecessors aroused in more distant times; nor have they encountered as much hostility as their compatriots who chose to go to Britain.[20] But that friction has diminished only as a result of an increased tolerance for differences in Canadian society, an increased tolerance won by their predecessors in a process which sometimes exacted a heavy price on the various strangers who came to Canada's gates, particularly when they were not fair-haired, blue-eyed, preferably Protestant, English-speaking, and so on.

Certain cultural baggage was refused entry through intolerance; some is still refused entry because it seems to have no place in Canadian life as the majority wish to live that life. Immigrant groups in Canada have always found it difficult or impossible to maintain certain of their traditional practices when such practices have conflicted with those of which the majority approve. Communal land holding, pacifism, and religious and linguistic education have been notable sources of conflict and have led to legislation to restrict traditional patterns of behavior. But deliberately discriminatory legislation is not the only kind which can affect an immigrant group. Measures designed to regulate the conduct of the majority itself can run directly counter to a minority's practices. Muslims in Canada are confronted with laws which require compulsory car insurance, regulate divorce, child custody, and inheritance, protect women's rights, forbid polygamy and first cousin marriage, and require or prohibit certain kinds of dress for safety purposes. Such laws do not permit Muslims to live a "full" Muslim life in Canada and tend to reduce Muslimism from being a total way of life to being a "religion," just like other religions. Many Muslims fear that such a reduction can only be detrimental to the Muslim community in the long run since the result must inevitably be a watering down of Islamic consciousness with a loss one by one of those characteristics which make it viable, the Arabic language being one of the key ones.

There is a definite sense in Canada that some cultures are "better" than others, and that the majority can rightfully impose its will on minorities. Any policy of cultural pluralism is constrained from the beginning by this belief. No group is therefore free to do as it pleases within Canada, for all are bound by certain rules and agreements which the two charter groups have laid down for those who have followed them.

But the larger of the charter groups, the English, treads cautiously these days. It perceives itself to be threatened; Britain no longer rules the waves; the Empire is long gone; and the Commonwealth is but a pale substitute. The English no longer even comprise a majority within Canada. Secularism is on the increase so religion counts for less and Protestants are now often outnumbered by other religious groups, particularly by Roman Catholics. The French have asserted their rights to their "heritage" and the third force has been heard from. The traditional elites have been penetrated and human rights legislation forbids or restricts attempts to keep others "in their place." In brief, where the English once stood firm and acted deliberately, for example, in such matters as language legislation and education, now they tread cautiously, if they move at all. The English are a group on the defensive, rather than the offensive, with all the consequences and dangers attendant on such a mainspring of policy.

It was John Porter's thesis, expressed in a variety of publications, that there were important differences between the United States and Canada in the treatment of immigrants.[21] In the United States "the melting pot" approach quickly gave immigrants the opportunity to identify themselves with a new nation in which all, theoretically at least, were equals and no opportunities could be denied on the basis of characteristics the immigrants brought to the country with them. Ethnic identification was not lost but it was not important either. In Canada, on the other hand, the "charter groups" of the English and French treated immigrants differently, in a "mosaic" approach, depending on their country of origin. They were fitted into occupations in an already existing social system and were not encouraged to think in terms either of opportunity or mobility. The result was a "vertical mosaic" which perpetuated a certain class structure, which valued ascribed status higher than achieved status, and which created a continuing concern with ethnicity in the population so that ethnic origin has become a salient feature of Canadian social structure.

But even promoters of this concept of the vertical mosaic for Canadian society acknowledge it as having less rigid application in different places and at different times. It seems less applicable to Alberta, for example, than to Ontario, and within Ontario less applicable to the social structure which exists today than to that of the early 1950s. Perhaps part of the less rigid appearance must be ascribed to the greater subtlety with which power is used today. A rhetoric of social egalitarianism, equal rights for all, and non-discrimination makes the exercise of raw power somewhat indecent, although it does not rule it out completely. The invocation of the War Measures Act in 1970 adequately testified to that fact. The sharp cutting edges of the vertical mosaic have been replaced by blurred, less abrasive ones. The pattern is still there; it is just not easy to see and for that reason alone may actually be more insidious than it was in certain respects, being that much harder to deal with.

While Canadians often pride themselves on having adopted some version of a "mosaic" rather than a "melting pot" approach to immigrants, there may be much less difference between the United States and Canada in actual practice. Canadians certainly tried "melting" through Anglo-conformity and there is plenty of evidence that some of this approach still prevails. There was also no large Black minority group in Canada. Perhaps one major difference between the two countries is simply that modern Canada is still a nation of recent immigrants in contrast to the United States, making them more conspicuous and less assimilable in spite of very strong attempts to "Canadianize" them. It may have been sheer numbers, not a difference of intent, and the absence of the aforementioned Black minority that created any distinctions that exist between Canada and the United States in the selection of immigrants and treatment of minority groups. And, of course, Canadians have been a little less ideological about their actions because of the inherent English-French division in their country!

# 7

# THE ISSUE OF ETHNICITY

One of the greatest paradoxes of modern times is that while developments in transportation, in the mass media, and in the corporate ways of doing business have turned the world into a "global village," that village itself has become more and more fragmented as a community. The ethnic consciousness which underlies much nationalism, regionalism, and factionalism has perhaps never been stronger than it is now in a world of multinationals, global alliances, and satellite telecommunications. Uniqueness has never appeared to be more important to individuals and recognizable collections of individuals. Ethnicity tends to be a powerful divisive force in modern society, even though for individuals it may allow the achievement of very specific objectives. This "tribalism in modern dress" is a very conspicuous feature of contemporary life.

Ethnic conflict is certainly not a new phenomenon in the world: tribes have always fought one another; religious groups have persecuted or have been persecuted; and empires have fragmented under the strains of national sentiment. What we have today is a kind of extension of ethnic tensions and concerns within the boundaries of nation states in such a way as to threaten their very survival. The nation states that evolved from nineteenth century imperial structures are in turn threatened by the same force that created them, the reluctance of one or more composite groups to accept a *status quo* which appears not to be in their best interests.

Some of the ethnic consciousness that exists today undoubtedly springs from the alienating conditions of "modern life." An industrial, technological society, growing ever more materialistic and secular, with a bland universalistic culture that herds people into impersonal social systems must necessarily prove distasteful to many. A few may actually welcome the resulting anonymity and freedom, but it is likely that many will feel alienated, particularly those who have also experienced, directly or indirectly, the trauma of migration. In such circumstances ethnicity provides a sort of refuge, a "safe house" to retreat to, and a source of spiritual renewal.

Much has been written concerning the revival in recent years of ethnicity in North American life, particularly "White" and "middle class" ethnicity. Important works have even dismissed the "melting pot" philosophy of the United States as a myth and ethnicity has been discovered to be something that has always been present in American life and just more conspicuous today.[1] Whether it is conspicuous only because it has become fashionable is another matter. Before the Civil Rights movement in the United States and the later success of *Roots*[2] there was a certain "un-American" quality to ethnicity—except at election times when politicians deliberately sought out the "ethnic vote." Today, it is quite permissible to be concerned with such matters. What is different about Canada is that it has never been "un-Canadian" to the same extent as it was "un-American" to look to one's ethnic roots, the historic English-French split in Canada providing any necessary justification. Consequently, the ethnic revival in Canada may not appear to be so pronounced as the one that occurred in the United States but it has not gone uninfluenced by the latter. As is well known, Canadians often see their society in terms of what goes on to the south, whether or not there is any justifiable relationship. The resurgence of ethnicity in the United States has not gone unnoticed in Canada.

In North America in general, people's roots have become interesting to them, but one cannot be absolutely sure of the underlying reason for this interest. One view is that ethnicity is one of those basic phenomena in human existence that surface from time to time. When things are going well, it tends to stay submerged, but when dreams fail, when traditional ways are disrupted, and when existence seems threatened, ethnicity surfaces as a force which helps to strengthen and unite the disaffected. Another view is not that ethnicity resurfaces from some kind of social subconsciousness but rather that it provides a convenient lever for groups to achieve their ends in society, particularly if they face a common repression and if other kinds of leverage are not available to them. This certainly can be said to have characterized the U.S. Civil Rights movement of the 1960s which developed a modern political lexicon that has since been adapted to the needs of many other ethnic groups in the United States and Canada.[3] Perhaps both views have some validity within the Canadian context. Far from diminishing as a characteristic of modern life, ethnicity may even be on the increase. That this is true in Canada is very clear. Socially, politically, culturally and linguistically, it is perhaps the most powerful force in Canadian life in that the existence of the English-French "two solitudes" has dominated all political discussions in Canada since the nation's very beginning. Only one other factor has anything like the same significance for Canadian life, the economic structure of the country, but it goes largely ignored by the public—except at the worst of times—hidden, deliberately or by neglect, behind the linguistic and cultural differences in society.

One of the problems of dealing with ethnicity is the considerable difficulty of reaching agreement on what ethnicity itself is. There is a considerable literature on the topic but nowhere is there a definitive answer to the question: what is ethnicity? As one pair of investigators has observed:

> Ethnicity is a difficult, almost illusive, concept to define and has received the most attention in Canada's census. The history and evolution of the concept is a search for attributes by which persons can be grouped as being culturally alike. The search has focused on objective attributes even though ethnicity, in the end, is a subjective concept and depends on how individuals feel and think and how they view their cultural identity. The subjective views of individuals may not be in line with objective criteria defining ethnicity, giving rise

to a source of error in classification. The objective approach to ethnicity is, in fact, a simplifying device for a difficult classification problem, undertaken to provide a reasonable approximation to what is a state of mind for most individuals.[4]

A subjective concept is always a slippery one to deal with and the Canadian census has never fully come to grips with this issue, thus making all the data on ethnicity that have been collected in various censuses difficult to work with.

Since it is necessary to choose a definition, one offered by Wsevolod Isajiw proves to be reasonably satisfactory:

> an involuntary group of people who share the same culture, or...descendants of such people who identify themselves and/or are identified by others as belonging to the same involuntary group.[5]

From such a definition one can observe how it is that ethnic group identity is usually regarded as a two-way street. Those in an ethnic group see themselves as different from others in some way, primarily through their ancestry, and outsiders also recognize this difference as a characteristic of the group. The real difficulty lies in deciding what differences constitute *ethnic* differences: culture, language, religion, and even color or race are quite readily recognized, but age, sex, sexual preference, income or lack of it, and social classes are not. Even though "feminist" and "gay rights" groups often tend to act much like ethnic groups, they do not satisfy the "ancestral" criterion.

An ethnic group must be concerned about two aspects of its existence. One is those things which serve to unite its members: for example, a common language; a system of shared beliefs; a particular set of food, clothing, or residential preferences. The other is the maintenance of some kind of boundary between it and all other groups. A boundary which is weak will allow movement in and out and will therefore tend to weaken the group. A high rate of exogamy, that is, marriage outside the group, will obviously weaken it in contrast to almost total endogamy. Strong boundaries will also protect groups which have strong internal conflicts. Boundary maintenance is a very important factor in explaining why the French have persisted in Canada (through keeping Quebec for themselves), the Hutterites on the Prairies (through exclusiveness and very controlled colonization), and even the urban Jewish (through endogamy and a strong sense of collective responsibility, among other things).

Ethnicity is both a subjective mental construct and a highly symbolic one. It is something too which must be constantly created and recreated, but is no less real for that, as one can see from the example of such a group as the Black Muslims in the United States. Many newcomers to North America have "discovered" their ethnicity only after arrival on the continent. As Joshua Fishman has observed:

> In some instances, indeed, it was only in America that many immigrants *became aware of their "groupness,"* i.e., of their common origin and their common past, as well as of their current problems. Thus it was that only *after* immigration did language loyalty and language maintenance become aspects of consciousness for many.
>
> As their seemingly primordial ways of life crumbled —ways of life that had protected the mother tongue and had been protected by it in turn—novel institutions and organizations came to be established that had been unknown in the "old country."...While certain relics of ethnicity remained, and at times attained far greater prominence than they had originally enjoyed (various ethnic costumes, foods, celebrations), others were substantially altered while many were entirely lost. It is in this context of overriding social change, of a grasping for continuity at the same time new means and new ends were being pursued, that language loyalty and language maintenance efforts most frequently came into play.[6]

This phenomenon of recognizing one's ethnicity only after arrival in North America has been a particularly noticeable feature of Ukrainian ethnicity in Canada.

Within Canada, language has often been one of the most important keys to ethnic identification. The basic English-French polarization of the country almost guarantees that this should be so. But there has also been considerable pressure exerted on immigrant groups to give up their languages. This pressure has very obviously weakened the "ethnicity" of some Canadians, e.g., Ukrainians. Others seem not to have been so deeply affected, e.g., Jewish and Scandinavians. Some groups which have maintained a strong ethnic consciousness have always spoken English, e.g., most Scottish, Irish, and Welsh and many immigrants from various other parts of the Commonwealth. An ethnic consciousness is therefore not directly dependent on what language is spoken, but because language seems such a vital part of ethnic identity for many groups, e.g., Ukrainians, its loss is very important. A marked decline in ethnicity might see the beginning of an era in which ethnic groups would be transformed into minority social groups, groups not identified directly through race, religion, culture, language, and so on, but through differential ability to enter fully into the mainstream of Canadian life. The paradox though would be that to the extent any such group did enter the mainstream, to that extent too it would tend to disappear since the criteria used to establish its minority status would cease to be meaningful.

However, no such decline is in sight within Canada. What one observes is a society in which the bond of ethnicity provides for many the most important means for achieving certain objectives. As objectives differ so does the concept of ethnicity which applies. One important characteristic of ethnicity in such a society is that it must be periodically refashioned by every group and remain sufficiently flexible to accommodate shifts between groups and the development of new groups. A key fact about Canadian existence is that its people have always been capable of such refashioning and have always kept ethnicity a live issue in their national life.

The ethnic question asked in Canadian censuses has had a long and mixed history as the political complexion of the world has changed. In the pre-Confederation period the question was used mainly to find out what proportion of the population was of

French origin: from the very beginnings of their settlement in North America the French were concerned with knowing how their population stood in relation to others and whether they were declining or increasing as a people. A question on ethnicity has been a feature of every Canadian decennial census since 1871, with the exception of 1891 when the only question on the topic was one which asked those of French ancestry to declare themselves. In later censuses the origins of all Canadians were sought using a variety of questions.

Ethnicity was originally conceived in terms of "racial" origin with descent being defined patrilineally, that is, through inheritance on the father's side. Since race was an important issue in Canada's immigration policy, various official publications having to do with censuses in the various periods contained remarks about such information being necessary if "assimilation" (even "biological" assimilation) were to be possible. Phrases and words such as *racial or tribal origin, nationality, ancestry, descent, stock* and *extraction* are readily found in discussions of the concept of ethnicity that lay behind the census question that was asked from time to time. There is, of course, no scientific definition of *race*. Gradually, however, ethnicity became associated with culture and to some extent language but not with complete consistency. Patrilineal descent, however, remained a strong component of the definition, except when color was a factor: before 1951 a person of mixed Black and White parentage was non-White for statistical purposes even if the father was White.

Sometimes the question has been regarded as an inherently divisive one to ask Canadians. Prime Minister John Diefenbaker construed it to be so, but his attempt to remove the question on ethnicity from the 1961 census ran into strong opposition. His plea to de-emphasize "hyphenated Canadianism" was rejected, most strongly by French Canadians, who saw the question as providing data which would clearly indicate to other Canadians just how large a proportion of the population they were and therefore how justified they were in claiming some kind of equality with the English. Other groups also saw the data which the ethnic question provided as confirming their claim that

Canada was a multicultural and multilingual society. The ethnic question is, therefore, unlikely to disappear from future censuses when the data it generates can be used for such ends.

As a result of problems with the 1971 census patrilineal descent was abandoned in the 1981 census in favor of a question concerning the origin of "ancestors." Multiple responses were not encouraged but were to be accepted (and processed) if offered. This last decision resulted from the experience with the 1971 data which showed that many respondents wanted more than one label for themselves and, even more so, for their children, particularly when neither "Canadian" nor "American" was indicated as an acceptable response. The main differences between the data generated in 1981 and earlier data will be in the use of the concept of ethnicity as membership in an originating ethnic or cultural group rather than through patrilineal descent or race together with the possibility of recording a multiple response.[7] Obviously, there will be considerable difficulty in comparing the 1981 results with any and all previous results when the 1981 results become available some time in 1983, not in time though for inclusion here.

There are very obvious difficulties in using ethnic data from the various censuses. The specific question asked has varied from census to census and even a small change in the wording can produce large differences. Changes in the political composition of Europe, changes in the immigration law, and changes in census-taking methods make the historical comparability of data on Canadian ethnicity more than a little suspect. When one realizes that such attributes as race, religion, color, patrilineal descent, national origin, and language have all been used from time to time and in various mixtures, it becomes necessary to approach all census data on the topic with a degree of caution. Examples are easy to cite: if the census definition of ethnicity with its emphasis on patrilineal descent is followed meticulously, it would eliminate the Metis of Canada as an ethnic group entirely; the increase of single-parent families must surely have influenced the "ethnic" identification of children when the marriages were exogamous; and ethnicity is well-known to be a changeable thing for an individual and reclassification is quite possible within a lifetime: from German to Dutch, Polish to Ukrainian, Russian to

Jewish, and so on. Changes in administration, from the use of enumerators to self-administration, also have their effects, particularly in increasing the number of "no responses" to particular items and making literacy demands which cannot always be met. The social and political climate in which the 1981 census was taken will further confound comparisons with earlier figures.

There are certain difficulties in using data from the censuses of 1961, 1971, and 1976. The questions concering such matters as ethnicity and language were either phrased differently or asked differently. The order in which possible responses are cited can have a significant effect on the answers which are given and this order was changed. In addition, the 1971 census used self-reported data whereas the 1961 census gathered its data through officially appointed census takers. It is generally agreed that certain biases do exist in the data and attempts have been made to correct these. The data from the 1981 census will also not be directly comparable to the results of previous censuses for the same reason that changes will be made which, though small in isolation, can loom large when carried over into millions of responses.

One peculiarity of the Canadian census is that it does not recognize a "Canadian" or "American" response so far as ethnicity is concerned. It allows respondents to record such answers to the question on ethnicity but discourages them. "Canadian" and "American" have to do with citizenship so far as the census is concerned. Somewhat surprisingly, 99 per cent of the respondents to the census accede to this constraint. Few insist on writing "Canadian" or "American" or declare that they do not know anything about their ethnicity. One cannot help but wonder what conclusion one should draw: that Canadians have a poor sense of identity? that they are proud of their origins? that they willingly submit to the demands of authority? or some other conclusion?

There is also the peculiarly Canadian use of the term *ethnic* itself, one deplored by the Royal Commission on Bilingualism and Biculturalism when it commented as follows on the Canadian usage:

. . .it is common practice in Canada to restrict the term

"ethnic" to groups which are neither British nor French. Ethnicity then appears as a strange, possibly distasteful phenomenon: "ethnic" seems to be given a sense something like "foreigner."[8]

The commissioners objected to this usage even though they quite understood that it had arisen in a social context in which there are two dominant groups, the English and the French. An *ethnic* in Canada is a person who is of neither English nor French descent. The only exceptions recognized are the native peoples—and sometimes Americans!

In all discussions of Canadian ethnic groups one must keep in mind certain facts. Previous to 1981, all Canadian census data on ethnicity are based on a specific concept of ethnicity: the ethnic, cultural or linguistic group of the paternal ancestor who first immigrated to North America. The census disallows or tries to discount "American" or "Canadian" ethnicity; it allows religious, political, and linguistic designations (no matter how crosscutting these may be); it changes as the world's political climate changes (as any inspection over the years of the system of ethnic labelling shows); it requires no documentation from those sampled; and it tried to ignore, if it could, how people regarded themselves in favor of classifying by the patrilineal rule thus denying the possibility of "ethnic mobility." A disinterested observer could hardly fail to conclude that the very presence and form of the ethnic question on the census would appear to perpetuate differences which serve little useful purpose in society and downplay any feelings that citizens might have about the value of being "Canadian."

If ethnic groups are conceived of as being minority groups in society, they must find ways of relating to the majority. Sociologists make a sharp distinction between the process of "cultural assimilation" and that of "structural assimilation." In the former process, a group identifies with the dominant culture by giving up some of its special characteristics in favor of adopting those of the dominant culture. However, it may try to keep many of its traditional structures and institutions, modifying them as little as possible as circumstances change. The process of structural assimilation, on the other hand, requires that the dominant group in no way discriminate against the minority group and allow its members to have complete and equal access to all the opportunities that lie within it. They, in their turn, either do not develop or give up traditional practices, institutions, and so on. While cultural assimilation may occur without structural assimilation, resulting in a group becoming "Canadianized" but still deprived of access to power and status, it is much more difficult to achieve structural assimilation without cultural assimilation. It might happen if a genuinely multicultural society were to develop, but Canada is far from being an example of such a society. A genuine multicultural or culturally pluralistic society would be one which exhibited complete structural assimilation and resisted cultural assimilation. Canadian multiculturalism falls far short of this ideal.

Most ethnic groups that have come to Canada have tried to develop a certain measure of institutional completeness, realizing that without this they face rapid assimilation. Not all have been successful in this endeavor to preserve group viability through developing enough institutions to preserve the group's special characteristics and delay or combat assimilative tendencies. Some groups, however, have become not only viable, they have become militant. A group can become militant if its members feel they are being deprived of certain advantages which other groups appear to have and which, by uniting, they can have too. The Ukrainians of the Prairie provinces and the Italians in Toronto are viable groups, just as are the Hutterites in their way. The French of Quebec are a good example of a truly militant group, allied against English Canada, but many other groups are also militant to some extent: the native peoples, Ukrainians, West Indians, Doukhobors, just to cite a few examples. At the other extreme some immigrant groups, the Dutch and Scandinavians are good examples, have never developed the necessary full range of institutions to become viable and seem to have no prospect, even if they wished to, of becoming militant.

A strong sense of interdependence is also probably necessary for the survival of a minority group, particularly if it is small in numbers. That is, the members of the group must actively seek ways of identifying with and coming to rely on one another. Isolation from the majority is one solution. Another is to develop a society within the larger society so that almost all the needs of the group can be satisfied within it. This means the development of a group's own economic, managerial, and professional structure as well as the necessary social, cultural, and linguistic institutions. When members of a group congregate, as did the Ukrainians on the Prairies and the Italians, Greeks, and Portuguese in large cities, they make it possible for some to achieve social mobility within the group by becoming business proprietors, doctors, lawyers, teachers, and so on. However, this can be a very limited kind of mobility if the resulting clientele is entirely "ethnic." What would be interesting to know is just what kinds of shifts this minority professional class makes in its professional and social lives toward one or other of the charter groups and how their children intend to pursue their education, training, and employment; that is, what is the extent of their mobility, where will their loyalties lie, and how effectively will they pass on the advantages of social mobility to their children?

The "urban village" environments established by groups such as the Italians and Portuguese in Toronto are also a very necessary part of the transition to a new life. They allow bridges to be built between the cultures and provide a system of "cultural brokerage." They have been a feature of settlement throughout North America, as evidenced in the settlement histories of such cities as New York, Chicago, and San Francisco, as well as Canadian cities. Any group which has very different character- istics from the host group faces serious problems of adjustment to the new circumstances. It can isolate itself in colonies or underpopulated areas or it can concentrate itself in fairly dense numbers in urban areas. Both strategies protect members of the group, allow institutions to develop within some kind of shelter, reinforce bonds, and slow down changes which might otherwise prove disruptive to individuals. Continued rural isolation provides the better environment for long-term perpetuation of traditional ways and Canada's most successful "isolationist" groups are predominantly rural. In the towns and cities the second generation usually begins to bridge the gap between the dominant society and the ethnic group, the urban village environment loses much of its attraction, and mobility of various kinds starts to break up the earlier group cohesiveness. The education of the young in one of the official languages is a major component in any shift that occurs, providing as it often does the kinds of mobility to the children which the parents find unattainable.

A further factor in the enhancement of group identity is lack of acceptance. When a group feels discriminated against, its members tend to unite to protect themselves and the institutions they perceive to be under attack: for example, their language, religion, economic well-being, or culture. The Blacks of Nova Scotia, eastern Europeans on the Prairies, Hutterites in Alberta, West Indians and South Asians in Toronto, and now to some extent the English in Quebec are groups which have reacted to attacks by uniting to meet a common danger. Rarely, the opposite occurs and the group deliberately takes a kind of path of least resistance, deliberately resolving conflict through an act of assimilation. One such group was the Japanese of British Columbia, who, after the indefensible discrimination and dislocation experienced in and after World War II, reacted not through either retaliation or drawing more closely together but by attempting to disappear into the society that had so badly treated them. Only recently have the Japanese emerged to assert their ethnicity once more, which, interestingly, includes the demand for reparations for abuses suffered during the war.

The most conspicuous features of ethnicity are probably the physical characteristics of group members and their choices in such matters as dress, food, religion, and language. A group can do little about the physical appearance of its members: even a highly assimilated Black is black. Dress is an optional characteristic: one can choose to wear a kilt or not, a turban or not. The choice is a statement, possibly of course, a religious or cultural statement, but one which asserts something about the person's identity. In religion one can stay "traditional" or assimilate to various degrees, but since religion is a private matter, little notice may be taken of a person's choice by others. Language is in many respects like religion. Each is a deeply personal characteristic which can be submerged or asserted. If asserted, it becomes conspicuous and in the absence of any other very visible difference it becomes the overt mark of ethnicity, the signal that other values and beliefs than majority ones exist.

Religion and language, therefore, tend to provide strong bases for ethnic identification. They undergird cultural predispositions. When both are different from those of the majority culture, there is possibly greater strength than if one is alike. Assimilation, however, can proceed through either. In an increasingly secular world, religion is threatened almost everywhere and, in a Canada polarized by English-French language differences, all other languages face difficulties. If adopting a major Canadian religion and giving up the ethnic language did open wide the gates of social mobility in Canada, ethnic groups might be even more threatened than they are now.

Since there are many different religious groups in Canada and of necessity there is likely to be some accommodation to the new environment, religious practices tend to be modified to a greater or lesser degree to suit new circumstances: Catholics from very different backgrounds find themselves worshipping together, as do Jews and Muslims; religious leadership must be found from new sources; and social and economic conditions set limits on what can be done when state support is denied for certain religious practices. Educational practices also restrict what can be done and demand of the faithful that they themselves provide certain opportunities, particularly the opportunity to learn an ancestral language. The net result is often a "liberalization" of old religions; sometimes, as in the Mennonite community, the result is a fragmentation of an original group into sections covering the spectrum from very traditional to quite accommodative religious practices. In all cases, though, it has meant some rapprochement between the religious and the social parts of life, with each influencing the other.

The result is often a considerable weakening of traditional ethnic ties. Joshua Fishman has pointed out that the Roman Catholic Church was second only to the public school system in the United States as a de-ethnicizing force. Any preservation by arriving Roman Catholic groups of traditional parish organization and government, idiosyncratic kinds of religious services, and very specific rites threatened the hard-won respectability of the Church as a whole. It was also perceived as an obstacle to asserting control in a unified manner over all Catholics. In such circumstances the use of English was a unifying force. The situation is not without its parallel in English Canada where the French have long had difficulty in gaining what they have considered to be their fair share in influence and appointments within the Church and where Roman Catholics from non-English and non-French backgrounds have tended to drift into English congregations. Fishman was led to conclude that organized religion does not provide a dependable source of support for ethnic aspiration or language maintenance, since its ends are far less worldly and the means to those ends may be changed at will to suit the times.[9]

Churches face other problems too as ethnic institutions. As congregations age and the young become less adept in the language in which their elders worship, there is an increasing danger that they will be lost either to another church or to a non-religious way of life. Accommodation becomes necessary if the church is to survive: it becomes bilingual to serve everyone. But such bilingualism is necessarily at the expense of the old unilingual form of worship and seems almost inevitably headed to a new unilingualism in the majority language. Roman Catholics and Lutherans have gone through this process repeatedly, as have numerous other groups. Only when there are very strong beliefs about the "right" language of worship, e.g., Hebrew, Arabic, and so on, can such a process be slowed down or halted. In such circumstances too it is very important to find the "right" religious leaders and this, of course, has been a very serious concern of many different religious groups in Canada, since an indigenous source is not always available and "imports" may not always understand the special needs of the situation.

Ethnic dilution certainly takes place in Canada through actual defection from "traditional" churches and practices. The greatest gainer from defections from traditional non-Catholic religions is the United Church. This fact is not altogether surprising. The United Church is a genuine "Canadian" church, so is attractive to anyone seeking a national rather than an ethnic identity. It is middle class in its orientation, again a characteristic which would satisfy a desire to show that one has "arrived." It is also part of a mild ecumenical movement, and therefore provides a suitable compromise for those who wish to make a change but not a drastic change. And, finally, it is in no way a particularly demanding church, requiring considerably less of its adherents than most traditional faiths, being in many ways a child of the liberal and secular times in which it was born.[10]

Traditional church affiliations may even be weakened by immigration. There is usually quite a different pattern of church-going between those in an ethnic group born outside Canada and those born within. Such a difference may serve only to weaken feelings of ethnic identity and the main beneficiaries are likely to be religious groups established within Canada with which the immigrant may have little or no contact, e.g., the United Church, Anglicans, and Baptists. Or there may be a switch from one kind of Catholicism to another. For example, while over 81 per cent of the Ukrainians in Canada who were born in the present-day Soviet Union or Poland are either Ukrainian Catholic or Greek Orthodox, only 46 per cent of those born within Canada have those affiliations. In contrast, over 48 per cent of the Canadian-born are affiliated with either the United Church, Roman Catholicism, or the Anglican Church but only 10 per cent of those born in the Soviet Union or Poland have these affiliations. There is one very marked exception to this general pattern: the French in Canada are more devoutly and uniformly Roman Catholic than immigrants from France.[11]

There is plenty of evidence of the weakening of religious ties in Canada as a whole. Insofar as religious commitment buttresses ethnic identity and the use of a language other than English or French, any weakening from any cause is likely to lead to some loss of that language. Interdenominational marriages, for example, have increased significantly in number in the last twenty years. The 1971 census figures showed that while the Jewish and Roman Catholic groups still overwhelmingly chose marriage partners within the groups (better than 80 per cent of the time), even that percentage had fallen from 1961. This decline was apparent in almost all denominations, and on the whole more than one-third of the marrying populations crossed a denominational boundary to marry. And, as such boundaries continue to weaken, they become that much easier to cross.[12]

Data available on interethnic marriages in the 1961 and 1971 censuses show that the native Indian and Inuit, Jewish, French, and English groups in Canada tend to select marriage partners from within their own ethnic groups: in the 1960s fewer than one male in five from these groups went outside the group to choose a marriage partner. Among other groups interethnic marriage was much more frequent. Indeed, for Canadian-born members of other ethnic groups, if Asiatics are excluded, a male would more likely be living with a wife chosen from outside his ethnic group than from within: 80 per cent of Scandinavians; 70 per cent of Italians; and over 50 per cent of Ukrainians. A greater rate of interethnic marriage is also found among those who move away from original areas of settlement than among those who stay.[13]

Ethnic groups may have very different views on assimilation, interethnic marriage, and shifts in religious affiliation. Some may see assimilation as very desirable. Disappearance into the larger society may be welcomed, particularly if it is accompanied by recognition and success. Individuals may find this route easier to take than do groups; they may very deliberately remove any "ethnic" characteristics from their identities such as distinctive names, religious affiliations, manners of dress, and so on, so as to blend in with the majority. On the other hand, certain other groups would regard any attempt to hasten assimilation as a coercive move. The very legitimacy of the society in which they find themselves would depend on its tolerance of their differences and of their ethnicity. Often this is because the homeland is no longer available to them and maintenance of a separate ethnic identity has become a kind of spiritual trust.

But the host society can seek to weaken ethnic identification in various ways too. If it is fairly open, it may be possible for an "ethnic" to enter it quite easily, particularly if there are no overt differences such as color to overcome. In this sense English Canadian society has been more open than French Canadian society, and both have been more open than Japanese society, for example. Ethnicity may also be reduced as a personal identifier as other kinds of identifiers assume greater importance for the individual in an open society. Religion is a good example: one can convert or shift to worship in another tongue, as when French Roman Catholics in Toronto join English parishes. Another kind of shift is when one becomes more attached to a job, profession, vocation, marriage partner, organization, or some such thing than to anything else, so substituting this new connection for an older interest in roots or ethnic origin. Perhaps the strongest (though statistically rare) form this shift takes is getting involved in a system of class identification rather than one of ethnic identification so that personal mobility is seen to depend on climbing a social class ladder, where ethnicity is irrelevant, rather than being stuck with one's ethnic group in a particular bit of the overall mosaic. Mobility of any kind, social, occupational, or even residential, tends to go along with a reduced sense of ethnic identification and a greater sense of "Canadian" identification. It is also likely to be accompanied by much less frequent use of formal and informal ethnic associations. In this way ethnic identity yields to class identity.

Ethnicity may not work at all to the advantage of the individual. Those who identify closely with their ethnic group are necessarily constrained in their behavior by that association. The stronger the identification the greater the constraint. If individual mobility is to be prized, then the individual must feel free to act without irrelevant constraints as circumstances require. Restraints are generally imposed by the host society but they can be imposed by the ethnic group itself. Ethnicity may indeed be self-fulfilling in the sense that it can cause an individual deliberately to constrain his or her own opportunities, blame society for the perceived resulting "injustice," and then consider the only remedy to be the development of an even greater ethnic consciousness both as an individual and as a group. Ethnicity may confine rather than liberate individuals without at the same time guaranteeing that the group be any better advantaged in society.

However, within Canada it seems almost impossible to free oneself entirely from the constraints of ethnicity. Although educational level, previous occupational background, and individual motivation (which tends somewhat to reflect group motivation) are important in determining how individuals become mobile in society, there is still, unfortunately, a large ethnic component which influences how great that mobility is. There is still considerable ethnic stratification and individuals are subtly (and sometimes not so subtly) constrained to occupy only certain positions in the larger society.

John Porter's well-known observation should be noted: "Ethnic and religious affiliation in Canadian society have always had an effect on the life chances of the individual."[14] The individual is always faced with the choice of giving up something to gain something else if mobility is the goal. As Vallee and Shulman have observed:

> The more a minority group turns in upon itself and concentrates on making its position strong, the more it costs its members in terms of their chances to make their way as individuals in the larger system....Among ethnic minority groups which strive to maintain language and other distinctions, motivation to aspire to high-ranking social and economic positions in the larger system will be weak, unless, of course, it is a characteristic of the ethnic groups to put a special stress on educational and vocational achievement.[15]

Ethnicity reduces the individual's life chances in this view. John Porter was himself one of the strongest exponents of that view, regarding emphasis on ethnicity as a kind of racism in a new form and a type of regressive behavior.[16] Insofar as ethnicity is concerned with the past and not the future, it tends to absorb effort which might be better expended dealing with issues which will really decide what the future of all will be like.[17]

In Porter's view, it has proved rather difficult for groups to move away from their "entrance status" to Canada. Only one group has had any conspicuous success, the Jewish. Others have tended to maintain their original status to a large degree: for example, Ukrainians have tended to maintain their mid-to-low place in the ethnic hierarchy. Even when ethnic groups do move a little in status it is usually a movement within the total collectivity of ethnic groups and therefore one which does not threaten the dominant English group in Canada as a whole or the dominant French group within Quebec. These groups still control the elites in which they are involved and "ethnics" find themselves in such elites in nominal quantities only: a lieutenant-governor here, a bank director there, and a deputy minister somewhere else.

One possible way of looking at the status of all groups in Canada, charter and ethnic alike, is to regard the amount of status available to them within a kind of zero-sum game. As one group moves up in status, adjustments have to be made somewhere else in the system to accommodate that movement; consequently, some other group or groups must be diminished in status, because status is above everything else a relative matter. There is plenty of evidence that such a view is not inappropriate. Ethnic groups must compete for limited resources: economic, social, cultural, and so on. Many English Canadians feel diminished because the French in Canada appear to be getting more than they seem to deserve. It matters not at all that everybody gets something and gets more than predecessors. All that matters is that any improvement seems to be greater in another group or groups so "more" there must mean "less" here.

Of course, an ethnic group may attempt to opt out of the system entirely, perhaps through deliberate isolation. But an ethnic group which attempts to preserve its traditional ways in all or most respects will fossilize its culture, e.g., the Hutterites. Perpetual social isolation will be the result and mobility within the larger society will not be a possibility. What many ethnic groups fear is that by making changes that will keep the door to mobility open they may reach a point (in fact they will reach a point) where change becomes a headlong rush into assimilation. Essentially, therefore, a policy of cultural pluralism seems almost certain to be dysfunctional in one of either two ways: a full traditional life can be maintained only if a separate existence with all its drawbacks, including lack of mobility, is acceptable; or full participation in the wider society can be achieved only if the group is prepared to surrender some of its most precious defining characteristics.

The paradoxes and contradictions relating to ethnicity are many. For example, studies which outline how various ethnic groups measure up to Canadian norms in such areas as education, economic success, rural-urban distribution, political affiliation, and so on leave one uncertain as to the appropriate conclusion to draw. On the one hand, such studies typically show the particular ethnic group under discussion falls behind the norms in many respects. Other groups, particularly the English, invariably do better, and some invariably do worse. But the impression one gains is that somehow all groups should match the norms in a society where social justice actually prevails. But for the group to match the norms is in a real sense for it to be just like any other group, particularly the majority group. What appears to be the point of many of these studies is a desire to document a situation, one never found, in which the group matches or exceeds certain norms which will give it "power" while at the same time being far different from the norms in such areas as language use, religious affiliation, and certain cultural patterns so that the group's distinctiveness can be affirmed. Just how far it is possible "to have one's cake and eat it," to be at the same time both distinctive and to be the same (or even better), is a fundamental problem which is rarely addressed. It appears to be more of a utopian dream than a possible social reality.

In spite of all the problems in dealing rationally with ethnicity, there is plenty of evidence that members of Canada's non-charter groups do see value in retaining a connection with an ethnic group. They may not know the language spoken by their ancestors, nor may they participate in ethnic activities and associations, but the identity itself is only rarely rejected. It can even be a powerful discovery for some, particularly those who relish their success in the wider society "in spite of" being ethnics. A remarkable characteristic of the Canadian population as a whole then is the willingness of individuals to give themselves ethnic labels. As one might expect there are mixed views about the consequences of this for social cohesion and the development of a "Canadian" identity. Some regard it as a large obstacle in that the effort spent on maintaining separate identities is a divisive force within the country and, moreover, one which locks in vast numbers of people to inferior positions in the social mosaic. An opposite view holds that ethnicity as a force actually provides a unifying strand in society: it cuts across social and regional boundaries and provides some mitigation of the sterile homogeneity that would otherwise exist.[18]

Both of these views are compatible with a third view. On the one hand, ethnicity is divisive in the sense that it keeps groups who should have common interests from uniting and, on the other, it is unifying in that it preserves the *status quo*, in effect at the expense of the same groups. As for the latter view, all ethnic groups seem to have bought the twin myths of the universal Canadian middle class and the legitimacy of the present two-party system of government. A class-based political system might have more appeal to groups that are largely excluded from power in Canada, but continued ethnic divisiveness together with a belief in the myth of mobility prevents even the left wing New Democratic Party from making great inroads into the ethnic vote. The beneficiaries are the two major parties who do nothing to dispel either myth; they quite willingly split the ethnic vote between them in various ways and then safely proceed to ignore it.

If all this were done in the interest of furthering a truly open society, it might be laudatory. A truly open society based on merit—although merit might be hard to define—would have no place for groups based on considerations of ethnicity, wealth, social class, religion, race, language, or family connections. As each of these currently reduces the openness in society and puts constraints on mobility society is less open by that much. Since all of them are effective constraints in Canadian life, to the extent they do restrict opportunity Canada is not an open society. However, it is quite clear that it was never intended to be such a society nor is it intended to be one by those who presently control the country. Statements to the contrary must be dismissed as exercises in rhetoric, exercises which are unfortunately all too frequent in Canadian political life.

Above all, it is the failure of the English and French to reconcile their differences that guarantees a continuing concern for ethnicity in Canada. Since the English and French cannot agree on what it means to be "Canadian," there can be no strong feeling about a national identity, no unifying symbols on which to focus attention, and no crises to bring solidarity. The normal situation is one of ethnic conflict. All ethnic groups find it to their advantage to make special claims, since they face only the alternative of assimilating to another group, there being no "national" identity instead which provides some kind of norm. In fact, this is exactly what has happened: groups strongly resist certain moves which will make them more like certain other reference groups in society.

It is even difficult to assess what effect the presence of large numbers of "ethnics" in Canada has on English-French differences. Their presence certainly increases the heterogeneity of English Canada and, in doing so, tends to make English Canadians more tolerant of differences, particularly of language and cultural differences. One effect could be to increase the sympathy for the French minority within English Canada. But still another possibility exists. If that heterogeneity is seen to contain within it several small but influential minorities who feel themselves much like the French in being neglected and who at the same time grant no privileged position to the French, then the French minority may regard themselves as even more threatened. This second possibility seems to offer a better description of what has actually happened. The French in Canada outside Quebec do not regard themselves as just another minority ethnic group in Canada and resent this implied "second class" status. They do not thank the English for this result.

The ethnic groups in Canada, excluding the native peoples, who do not easily fit into any scheme of things, sometimes regard themselves, taken together, as a kind of potential "third force" in Canadian political, social, cultural, and linguistic life. Just what this third force is perceived to be able to do is hard to say. It has insignificant political power because of its geographical distribution and the way in which it is split every which way, sometimes one suspects deliberately so. It is homogeneous only in that it is almost entirely anglophone. Rather powerless as a force, it is nevertheless a highly visible entity, particularly in Canada's larger cities. But in the conflicts between the English and French and between Ottawa and the regions any third force seems at best to have only a very minor role in deciding Canada's future.

# 8

# GROUP SURVIVAL
# AND LANGUAGE MAINTENANCE

It is all but impossible to draw any general conclusions about the various ethnic groups in Canada. It is not even possible to say with certainty how many different ethnic groups there are in Canada since definitions of "ethnicity" constantly vary as do the purposes for which ethnic identifications are used. Certainly there are more than 50 and possibly fewer than 100 ethnic groups in Canada, with each group having its own history of immigration and adjustment both to the "charter" groups and other groups. Every census has shown Canada's population mix to be different from the previous census and over many censuses the mix has changed dramatically: the English have declined and the "ethnics" and native peoples have increased. Few things have remained constant, except perhaps the durability of the French in Quebec. But just how profound has been the influence of the non-charter groups on Canada's social development remains an unanswered question. What the future holds for such groups is also equally problematic.

The ethnic distribution of Canada's population varies considerably across the country. Minority ethnic groups are virtually unrepresented to the east of Quebec, except in Nova Scotia where they represented just over 12 per cent of the population in the 1971 census. The Atlantic provinces, with their overwhelming English presence (except in New Brunswick), have not proven attractive to settlement by such groups. Recognizing this fact, newcomers have preferred the opportunities they have perceived to exist elsewhere, particularly, in recent decades, in the major urban centres. Therefore, they have gone to Ontario and the provinces west of Ontario. The 1971 census showed that minority ethnic groups comprised about a third of the populations in each of Ontario and British Columbia and approximately one-half in each of Manitoba, Saskatchewan, and Alberta. The groups in Ontario and British Columbia are much more diverse in their composition than those of the other three provinces; moreover, they are "newer" and more urban in orientation. The consequences of such an overall distribution is that whereas the populations of such provinces as Newfoundland and Quebec are fairly homogeneous, those of many other provinces are not, and, within these more heterogeneous provinces, Ontario is different from Alberta in the "newness" of many of its ethnic groups.

Immigration, interprovincial migration, and heavy post-war urbanization have all resulted in Canadian cities assuming very different population characteristics since World War II. Vancouver's population mix with its leavening of Italians, Chinese, and Scandinavians is very different from that of the Prairie cities of Edmonton, Calgary, and Winnipeg. Toronto is unique in that very many different factors have contributed to its growth so that it has become an extremely cosmopolitan city but within an essentially English framework. The flavor of Montreal is different again because immigration and urbanization have occurred there within the current English-French conflict and within a social and economic system that tends to be more polarizing than elsewhere.

While some ethnic groups have concentrated in certain areas of Canadian cities to produce the "urban villages" which act as bridges between the old ways and the new, these concentrations are not as dense as they sometimes appear to be. Although many Italians are concentrated in certain areas of Toronto and Montreal, many Chinese in a specific part of Vancouver, and many Germans, Ukrainians, and Poles in certain parts of Winnipeg, they still settle in these areas with people of other backgrounds. In each case the majority of the ethnic group in the city actually resides outside the most concentrated area of settlement. There is also fairly constant movement from the area of greatest concentration to other areas and replacement by new arrivals, who may be from an entirely different ethnic group. Such movement often results from a desire to be in some ways more like members of the host society. It need not necessarily signify any willingness to change one's cultural characteristics, but it may well lead members of the next generation to do so. Some evidence exists that within Canada's major metropolitan areas patterns of residential segregation are actually decreasing, not necessarily a happy omen for the ethnic groups involved.[1]

It is very easy for outsiders to regard the various ethnic groups as homogeneous in composition, that is, to resort quickly to stereotypes. This is a very serious mistake and one likely to lead to injustices of one kind or another. Perhaps the worst error of all would be to group all Blacks together or all South Asians. These two groups are possibly the most heterogeneous of all groups in Canada. The members of each came to Canada at various times from various parts of the world, and all kinds of social, educational, cultural, and religious differences can be found in the groups. They are at quite the other end of a continuum from a very homogeneous group like the Hutterites. Unfortunately, too often the members of such groups are treated as though they belong to some undifferentiated and undifferentiable mass of "inferiors," an attitude which is characterizable only as racist.

In another important respect too, ethnic groups are often not homogeneous. As different waves of immigrants have come to Canada to join a group already established here, different segments of the "old" society may be represented among the newcomers. Recent Ukrainians, for example, have tended to be intellectuals rather than farmers, like their predecessors. Recent Chinese arrivals have tended to be better educated than the average Canadian and are quite different in most respects from the laborers who helped to build the railroads. Many recent South Asian and West Indian immigrants are professional or semi-professional in their background. In contrast, the majority of Greeks, Italians, and Portuguese have brought few such skills with them and have had to generate their professional elites within Canada. One effect of the changes in immigration policy in the 1960s was a tendency actually to increase the differences among immigrants who arrived under the new regulations:

independent immigrants, those who came under their own devices, had to demonstrate their ability to survive and prosper through their qualifications, whereas nominated or sponsored immigrants needed little more than an assurance of help from close relatives already in Canada.

Many recent immigrants are much better educated than their predecessors, often in the language, culture, and history of the region of their origin. It is not unusual to find them possessing strong political, national, linguistic, and religious views: these may well have "pushed" them to leave. Such immigrants can provide a sort of leavening for the ethnic groups they join on arrival. But that is not always the case. They may instead find their concerns to be somewhat at odds with those of the "older" ethnics whose view of the "old country" must necessarily be different and whose view of the "new" cannot be the same. The older ethnics will also have made certain compromises with other cultural groups in Canada, compromises which might appear to be "betrayals" to newcomers. The level of the cultural and intellectual functioning of the newcomers may also be quite different; they may be more idealistic and put much more emphasis on symbolic issues than on the practical matters of daily living.

Newcomers to an ethnic group also provide replenishments for those who have been lost by assimilation. The group may have to refashion itself constantly to accommodate them as they arrive but it is in the nature of ethnic groups in a new land constantly to reshape themselves anyway. Without such replenishments it may be difficult for ethnic groups to survive indefinitely in Canada, confronted as they are with the dominant charter groups.[2] Current Canadian restrictions on immigration do not offer much hope though. In the absence of replenishments through immigration ethnic groups will undoubtedly continue to exist for a considerable period as social collectivities in Canada, but they are unlikely to function in quite the same way as before.

Two major inescapable facts about the ethnic groups in Canada are their sheer diversity and the threat they face from the charter groups. If only by uniting as a third force can they survive and maintain their identities, then that battle is being lost constantly. They seem incapable of finding any enduring ground on which to unite. Physically, they are spread through a vast land in small numbers, especially when they live outside major centres such as Toronto, Montreal, and Vancouver. The groups also tend to have very different needs and aspirations: one has only to compare Scandinavians with Hutterites, Jewish with Portuguese, and Jamaicans with Vietnamese. Furthermore, it may be only in the large cities, such as the three just mentioned, and perhaps in a few other areas, e.g., parts of the Prairie provinces, that individual ethnic groups can maintain themselves as viable entities for a further generation or two largely in the manner of their present arrangement. But beyond that point in time their future begins to look very bleak indeed.

The Ukrainians are one of the most politically active ethnic groups in Canada. They have had much to say on a variety of topics, particularly federal policies concerning bilingualism and multiculturalism. But, even this well organized group faces severe problems of continuity in Canada. It is an "old" group, it lacks replacements, it shows strong assimilative trends, and it is faced with a social and political situation within Canada which does nothing, or very little, to slow down the rush to even greater assimilation.

Ukrainians comprised just 2.7 per cent of Canada's population in the 1976 census with well over 80 per cent of those of Ukrainian origin being Canadian-born. They are located mainly in central Canada and in the Prairie provinces, but, unlike the French for example, do not control a specific tract of land, nor have they congregated so compactly as either a rural group such as the Hutterites or an urban one such as the Jewish. If ethnic survival depends on controlling a territory over which the group exercises considerable political and economic control and within which it develops a set of social institutions, then Ukrainian survival in Canada is severely endangered. As a small minority spread somewhat thin and wide, both in rural and urban areas, and with no solid grasp of any part of the national economy, Ukrainians have little direct political power. Being fairly well integrated into Canadian society, and with almost no hope of growth through immigration, assimilation is a very distinct possibility. Ukrainians therefore must make a conscious effort to maintain their language since few can ever hope to use it as the language of work, and Ukrainian culture must struggle to survive in the great ocean of "North American culture." What is truly remarkable is that Ukrainians have survived so well in spite of all these obstacles. They have done so because they have found ways to keep their religion, culture, and language alive; indeed in this respect they may be the best organized of all ethnic minorities in Canada.

Ukrainians in Canada have been held together both by their similarities and their differences. Their religion has been important and so has been their language. But that religious life itself has centred around a conflict between two churches, the Orthodox and the Catholic, each with its own rites and loyalties and each uniquely Ukrainian in its development as an entity within Canada. Political disagreements have united the community even as they have divided it; pro-communist and anti-communist Ukrainians differ strongly about the political future of Ukraine, but such differences serve to keep alive both the idea of Ukraine and the language of the debate itself, Ukrainian.

Ukrainians are subjected to many of the same influences as all other residents of Canada. Urbanization is one, and it has brought about some interesting consequences for the Ukrainian community. The 1971 census showed that 59 per cent of all Ukrainians lived in one of the 22 Canadian Census Metropolitan Areas included in that census. Over half the metropolitan Ukrainian population lived in three such areas—Winnipeg, Edmonton, and Toronto. Each area had over 60,000 people of Ukrainian descent, with Edmonton the fastest growing in its Ukrainian population. The other areas had from 14,000 to 31,000 Ukrainians—in descending order: Vancouver, Montreal, Calgary, Hamilton, and Saskatoon—all large enough to support "ethnic" institutions. Edmonton and Winnipeg, with approximately 12 per cent of their population Ukrainian and with their continuing ability to attract Ukrainians from settlements elsewhere on the prairies, are the most characteristically Ukrainian cities. In 1971 the Prairie provinces still contained 80 per cent of all rural Ukrainians. In comparison, Ukrainians in Toronto comprise just over 2 per cent of the metropolitan population and several other ethnic groups are more numerous; consequently, Ukrainians are much less distinctively part of Toronto's multicultural mix than certain other groups and much more threatened by assimilative tendencies in spite of their real numbers there. In such circumstances it is very necessary for the Ukrainian urban community to build and maintain strong institutions if it wishes to preserve its identity.

One can see how successful the Ukrainians were in preserving their ethnicity when they first moved into Winnipeg. Like many newcomers to the city, they settled first in the Northend and tended to isolate themselves. They were not as successful as the French and Jewish in developing a strong ethnic consciousness, but were more successful than groups such as the Poles and Germans. However, by establishing church groups, newspapers, and social institutions the Ukrainians achieved a considerable "community" feeling as well as a perception that they were different from other groups, a very necessary component of "ethnic" identification. In other words, they managed to achieve "ethnic urban village" status for themselves. Today there appears to be some weakening of this community spirit in Winnipeg. Economic success has led many Ukrainians out of the Northend to suburbs which are much more heterogeneous in their ethnic composition. Religious and political divisions have shown few signs of abatement and have caused some of the younger generation to opt out of the Ukrainian community rather than to involve themselves in the conflicts of their ancestors. The young are also less secure in their ability to use the Ukrainian language and more doubtful of their Ukrainian identity then the previous generation. They are also ambitious and more willing than their parents to pursue the "North American dream"; ethnicity tends to get in the way of realizing certain kinds of ambitions. On the whole, then, Ukrainians in Winnipeg now rank behind the Jewish and the French in those characteristics that would tend to keep a minority group strong, and assimilation is the ever-present threat.[3]

Assimilative trends are very clear in Ukrainian life in Canada. There is a movement toward the city and away from the traditional Canadian roots of Ukrainian community life in the more marginal farming areas. In addition, traditional religious affiliations are weakening as more and more Ukrainians adopt one of the pan-Canadian religions rather than continue traditional forms of worship. Exogamous marriage is also on the increase. All these trends result in what is to many Ukrainians the most threatening trend of all, the marked decrease in the use of the Ukrainian language, especially in the younger generation. Each successive census shows that the population which describes itself as Ukrainian looks more and more like the overall Canadian population in its demographic characteristics.

The trend among Ukrainians to adopt non-traditional religions is shown in the census figures measuring religious affiliation to the two traditional Ukrainian churches, the Ukrainian Catholic and Greek Orthodox. Whereas in 1831, 82.6 per cent of Ukrainians were affiliated to one of these churches, in 1971 only 52.2 per cent were and even fewer (49.7 per cent) among urbanized Ukrainians. Church membership is often regarded as one of the strongest forces in maintaining ethnic identity. It offers opportunities to use the mother tongue, provides a community of shared objectives, and helps bridge the gap between the old life and the new by attempting to offer a complete intermediate existence. Consequently, any lessening of membership in traditional churches usually indicates a serious weakening of ethnic identification and any transfer to non-traditional pan-Canadian churches can be taken as a sign of transfer to another set of values and expectations.

Not only has there been a shift in church membership within the Ukrainian community away from Ukrainian Catholic and Greek Orthodox affiliation toward membership in Roman Catholic, United Church, Anglican, and other churches, but the characteristics of the traditional church population have changed. The Ukrainian Catholic and Greek Orthodox churches tend to attract first- and second-generation Ukrainians so that about 70 per cent of their membership is drawn from those groups. On the other hand, more than half of the Ukrainians who are affiliated with other religions are third-generation Ukrainians. These figures from the 1971 census seem to indicate that to this generation of Ukrainians "being Canadian" is more attractive than "being Ukrainian." This conclusion is confirmed by the fact that those third-generation Ukrainians who have left the traditional churches have less than a 10 per cent Ukrainian mother-tongue facility while those who have remained have about a 45 per cent rate of retention.[4] This last figure shows how necessary it is for even the traditional churches to minister to Ukrainians in the dominant language of the society in which the vast majority of Ukrainian Canadians are located, that is, in English. So now activities, including even religious services themselves, may be conducted in English, and Ukrainian language classes may be offered as an inducement to those who wish to reaffirm or even rediscover their "roots."

Another indicator of a weakening of traditional religious ties is provided by the incidence of exogamous, or outgroup, marriage. Ukrainians are tending more and more to marry outside their traditional religions and even outside the Ukrainian community itself. In 1931 the proportion of exogamous marriages in the Ukrainian community in Canada was a mere 18.5 per cent. By 1971 this proportion had increased to 61.3 per cent. Of course, some Ukrainians who marry outside the traditional religions may still marry fellow Ukrainians, those who have adopted for example the Anglican or the United Church denominations without at the same time abandoning entirely their Ukrainian identity. But the tendency toward assimilation increases as members of the community give up one by one such things as traditional religion, endogamous marriage, and Ukrainian as the language of the home and then as mother tongue, and as they slowly adapt to the norms of Canadian society as a whole.

Ukrainians, just like the vast majority of French Canadians, have always assumed that to lose their language is to lose their identity as a people. Yet this assumption is hardly one that has been confirmed in other groups. For example, Glazer and Moynihan's work in the United States showed fairly conclusively that ethnic identity is not necessarily sacrificed if the ancestral language is lost.[5] However, if the language has a profound symbolic value to the group, loss may be followed by complete assimilation. The group seems to give up when its most precious asset is gone.

In the 1921 census nearly 92 per cent of those of Ukrainian

origin in Canada said that Ukrainian was their mother tongue. By 1971, only 48.9 per cent said so, with an even larger decline (to 45.9 per cent) among those who were urbanized. In the same year only 22.8 per cent said that Ukrainian was the most frequent language of the home. These figures show a startling decline in the use of the Ukrainian language in Canada. The pull toward the use of English is considerable, particularly if one remembers that ever since the 1941 census well over 90 per cent of Ukrainians have also claimed to be able to use English, this proportion actually being 97.8 per cent in 1971.[6]

Of course, one can speak a language with varying degrees of fluency. In the Ukrainian community there are marked differences in fluency in Ukrainian. Fluency decreases significantly with generation. Most first-generation Ukrainians are completely fluent; most third-generation Ukrainians either do not speak Ukrainian or speak it with considerable difficulty. Those who are fluent are also more likely to be less well educated than those who are not (if recent immigrants are excluded, particularly those to Montreal and Toronto). Endogamous marriage also tends to be associated with fluency. So, too, to some extent is where one lives: rural family-oriented communities offer better support than does a large metropolitan area like Toronto. Winnipeg and Edmonton, with their larger proportions of Ukrainian population than Toronto, offer opportunities to use Ukrainian which Toronto does not, and even those less fluent in the language are tempted to use it in daily living both inside and outside the home. In Edmonton or Winnipeg it is simply easier to be Ukrainian than it is in Toronto.

Language loss is apparent in both rural and urban areas, but less so in the former. Regardless of circumstances, however, third-generation Ukrainians show a great decline in their knowledge and use of Ukrainian when contrasted with their parents and grandparents. In the metropolitan areas Ukrainian is most commonly used by first-generation immigrants, and Canadian-born Ukrainians are more likely than not to use English as the language of the home. Many may not speak Ukrainian at all. With immigration virtually at a standstill and the Ukrainian community continuing to urbanize, the Ukrainian language is

severely threatened in metropolitan areas, and so, therefore, is
Ukrainian identity. In spite of its numerically considerable
Ukrainian population, Toronto offers a most precarious situation
for the continuation of the Ukrainian language, but even
Ukrainian communities in Edmonton and Winnipeg may well be
threatened unless they can find ways to preserve their identities
while still actively participating in Canadian life.

An interesting relationship is discovered if ethnic self-identification is related to opinions about the necessity for language
retention. One study showed that of those who identified
themselves as "Ukrainian Canadians," 84 per cent expressed
strong support for the retention of the Ukrainian language. But of
those Ukrainians who identified themselves simply as "Canadians," only 64 per cent expressed such support and 28 per cent
were actually indifferent to the matter. The split was also
independent of generation, being apparent in both first- and
second-generation Ukrainians. Evidently in the Ukrainian
community those who have the strongest ethnic self-identification
also have the strongest views concerning language retention.[7]

There is also evidence that younger Ukrainians, for example
university students, do not regard language loss as the greatest
danger to their ethnic self-identification. A more highly rated
threat than erosion of the Ukrainian language at home was
continued exogamy. Traditional church membership and attendance at ethnic schools were judged as important in preserving
ethnic identity. The same study confirmed what other studies
have revealed: Ukrainian self-identification is less strong than
either Jewish or French self-identification but stronger than either
English or Scandinavian self-identification.[8] That the latter two
groups rank low in this regard is to be expected. The
Scandinavians have rather deliberately assimilated to the English
pattern in most respects and the English need have no anxieties
concerning who they are in Canada, being very securely in the
majority.

As the Ukrainian population in Canada ages, with a growing
proportion being Canadian-born, religious support is still strong
even if actual church-going might have decreased. But
involvement in the politics of the "old country" is less attractive to

the young than to the old and less to the native-born than to the new arrivals. Finally, even if exogamy is increasing and use of the Ukrainian language is decreasing, most Ukrainians in English Canada regard their case for public support for the teaching of Ukrainian to be every bit as meritorious as public support for the teaching of French. They are the leading exponents of the position that the ethnic groups outside Quebec should be on a par with the French outside Quebec so far as language is concerned.

The federal government does not support this position, having opted instead for a policy of both multiculturalism and English-French bilingualism, but in reality it does little at all to slow down the assimilation of minority ethnic groups. Not everyone regards this governmental failure to act as necessarily harmful, particularly as individuals are affected:

> The Ukrainian who becomes less ethnic is more likely to reach higher income levels than his same generation counterpart who remains totally ethnic. It would seem that the implications of a national policy designed to encourage the retention of ethnic behavior under present conditions in Canadian society are not totally positive.[9]

The implications may not be positive for individuals, but for group survival the policy itself may well be essential. This, however, is just another instance of how paradoxical is much of Canada's social and political existence.

The situation of Ukrainians in Canada can be further illustrated by making brief comparisons with certain other ethnic groups. Undoubtedly the most successful ethnic group in Canada has been the Jewish people no matter how one defines success. Endogamy, residential patterns, attempts to create institutional completeness, a strong sense of the past and of its horrors, a ritualization of Jewish history, and a feeling that strength, even survival, lies in unity are among the factors that keep the Canadian Jewish people together. Language is not an important factor: whereas the traditional Hebrew is maintained as a unifying language of religious importance, English is perfectly acceptable as the language of secular affairs. Economic success, though not complete since the highest positions in the elites have not been opened up to Jews, has also been attained, and, in this respect at least, Porter's thesis concerning immigrant groups to Canada being doomed to remain in their entrance status is apparently refuted. A strong sense of identity, a commitment to certain fundamental values, particularly self-sufficiency and education, and a willingness to participate fully in society would seem to assure the group's continued survival.

There is quite adequate evidence to show how the Jewish people of Toronto for example changed to accommodate to the wider Canadian society after World War II. Ethnicity became a positive rather than a negative factor, something to be asserted rather than merely protected. This change was largely due to the experiences of World War II, continued, but possibly more subtle, discrimination, the impetus given by the founding of Israel, and the continued need for solidarity in the face of such events as the "Six-Day War" of 1967. Although the Jewish people took to their synagogues as symbols of ethnic identity, in actual religious practice they tend to favor Conservative Judaism over either the Orthodox or Reform varieties. Conservative Judaism allows Jews both to maintain their ethnic traditions and to participate in the wider Canadian society; on the other hand, Orthodox Judaism tends to isolate its followers from society and Reform Judaism increases assimilative pressures.[10]

The Jewish population of Montreal is more tightly knit than its Toronto counterpart. A contributing reason has been the recurrent waves of anti-Semitism in Quebec. While Jews have always experienced discrimination outside Quebec, overt anti-Semitism has long been more apparent within the province than without. The fact that the Jewish population of Montreal saw their opportunities within that part of Quebec life dominated by the English rather than the French and that the educational system pushed them toward the English merely widened the gap between the Jews and the French. It also did nothing to alleviate feelings of distrust. The controversies over Bill 22 and Bill 101 served merely to reinforce a belief that many Jews had long felt, that they were not particularly welcome in Quebec. But the language legislation also tended to split anglophone Jews from francophone Jews (about 15,000, mainly from Morocco). The latter have generally felt quite happy with legislation that allowed them a kind of mild revenge against the more well-entrenched and successful anglophone Jewry. So this is still another variation in the kinds of skirmishes that take place within the language wars that are a continuing part of Canada's history.

In contrast to both Ukrainians and Jews, the Germans, Dutch, and Scandinavians have become almost "invisible" ethnic groups in Canada in spite of their large size relative to all other groups, even the Italians. Being Northern European, they "blend" quickly into the predominant English majority. They have also exhibited a strong desire to learn English, to succeed in the adopted society, and to establish a variety of contacts with "Canadians." Consequently, they have expended very little effort on developing "ethnic" institutions. For example, if they are religious, as, say, the Dutch, they have tended quickly to adapt to worship in English within their denominations or to shift to a "Canadian" church, particularly the United or Anglican. Two wars have also contributed to the Germans' keeping the lowest possible profile for lengthy periods. From time to time members of the groups emerge to show something of the various bits of culture they have retained, but usually in a very subdued fashion. The fact that these groups show some of the lowest degrees of language maintenance of all groups in Canada is not unexpected in such circumstances.

The Japanese in Canada are another group with a very low profile. The Issei, or first-generation Japanese, brought with them traditional Japanese values: a sense of community, obligation, and gratitude, perseverance, self-effacement, and devotion to family. They met discrimination and isolation and brought up their children, the Nisei, to conform to the demands society seemed to place upon them. Consequently, the Nisei have tended not to use the Japanese language and to adopt the values of the culture in which they were born. Nor did the injustice of the treatment they received in World War II, when they were forcibly compelled to leave the west coast, dissuade them from this course of action; if anything it did the opposite, convincing many that they had not actually gone far enough to be like the majority. Many of the Nisei became successful again when the war ended. Now some of the Sansei, the third generation, find themselves concerned about their identity, though their search is conducted along modern-day lines. While many intermarry with non-Japanese, do not know their ancestral language, and seek to be "Canadian" rather than "Japanese" or "Japanese Canadian," a significant minority look back for their cultural roots, believing that part of being "Canadian" is being "Japanese" since it can never be being "English." They have also discovered that it is possible to be Japanese without either speaking Japanese or following many of the traditional ways and that ethnicity can be refashioned out of an interest in one's heritage rather than in attempting to recreate the past.[11]

In contrast to these ethnic groups whose members nearly always spoke a language other than English on arrival in Canada, there are ethnic groups in Canada who arrived speaking English. Canada's Black population is almost entirely anglophone, a major exception being recent arrivals to Quebec from Haiti. Most Blacks in Canada originated from other parts of North America or the Caribbean. Loyalists moved with their slaves to Nova Scotia, free Blacks also moved there and to Ontario, and some Blacks settled in the Prairie provinces during the nineteenth century. Not all stayed, for the United States drew many back after the Civil War as Canada proved not to be quite the attraction it had first appeared to be. Blacks found themselves given less than they had been promised, they faced discrimination in education, employment, housing, and the use of public facilities, and, in general, were treated as inferior human beings. Recent Black arrivals come mainly from the West Indies, although again there is a small representation from other countries now that race is no longer an overt selection criterion in Canadian immigration policy. Since most speak English on arrival, one must assume that any differential treatment they receive is related to color rather than any other factor. Canada has never had a "color problem" of the magnitude of either the United States or South Africa, mainly because until recently Canadian immigration policies have kept out the non-White. Canadian racism, therefore, has tended to be of a different kind from American racism, more like the variety found in Japan, exclusionary rather than discriminatory. But for those who got around the exclusions, racism has always been present when seeking schooling, a job, housing—even when trying to serve the country in wartime.

One important factor that militates against Blacks' taking a more assertive role in society is that they are not at all a unified group. Nova Scotia Blacks and West Indians have little in common with each other, and neither feel very close to American Blacks, either to those who have become militant in the United States or those who have for one reason or another come to live in Canada. In a way ethnicity divides the Blacks. Whereas Whites are inclined to see all Blacks as alike—a dangerous racial "stereotyping"—Blacks see each other as Jamaicans, Americans, Nova Scotia Blacks, and so on, with each group having its own particular agenda in Canadian life. Blacks, therefore, do not comprise a single ethnic group in Canada, even though for some purposes they are often treated as a single group, possibly by analogy with the racial situation in the United States.

Language tends to be an issue with most ethnic groups, and it is even so with many West Indians, who may resent the attempts certain educators make to eradicate the variety of English they bring with them in favor of some kind of Canadian standard. In general, speakers of English fail to appreciate how emotional an issue language is to speakers of certain other languages and dialects. They do not readily comprehend what it is to have "pride" in one's language. English is so widespread in the world, in a sense so commonplace, that it just simply exists for its speakers. They take no particular pride in its great artists nor have they ever found a need to entrust its "preservation" to anyone. In contrast, the French have their academy, the Germans revere Goethe and the Italians Dante, and speakers of many other languages take a pride in either particular writers or a certain linguistic tradition. Admittedly, this pride in language exists mainly at a cultural level ("culture" in the sense of the "best" in literature, art, and music) and not at the functional level (language use in the home). It is at this cultural level that much concern about language maintenance exists: one seeks to preserve a language not merely to be able to talk to one's grandparents but also to remain in touch with the best (or the essential) in the culture of those who speak the language.

To many the really important issue is whether you can still be Italian, Ukrainian, Chinese, or Vietnamese without speaking Italian, Ukrainian, Chinese, or Vietnamese. Most ethnic groups deny such a possibility. But others find it possible to be Scots, Jewish, Dutch, or Jamaican without having any language other than English. The English language itself is neutral so far as ethnicity is concerned: it is a tool of communication. But the use of English has a highly symbolic value too. Its adoption is often a sign of a shift in cultural values or identity.

A national or ethnic consciousness obviously can be continued and maintained even when the language is threatened or almost extinct. The Irish in Ireland are no less Irish for the fact that only a very small minority speak Irish, in spite of its being the first official language of the country. Welsh national feeling has not depended on everyone in Wales speaking Welsh and the Scots have had even less reliance on Gaelic as a unifying force. Language is therefore not necessarily a mark of ethnicity: a group may assimilate to the language of another group without losing the desire to maintain an "ethnic" distinctiveness. However, this fact should not minimize the importance of language as a strong symbolic force in maintaining ethnic identity: it remains so even for the Irish, Welsh, and Scots.

The languages of many immigrant groups to Canada are not yet in such desperate straits as either Irish or Gaelic. Nor do these groups want their languages to exist in such desperate circumstances. They know well that it is almost impossible to revive a "dead" language; it is difficult enough to maintain a "dying" one. The revival of Irish has not been a success in Ireland. The one notable exception to what appears to be an almost general principle has been the revival of Hebrew in Israel. Modern Israel was faced with the task of finding a national language. Many competitors existed among the immigrant population to Israel but no language could clearly usurp the first position. Hebrew provided at the same time a unifying force and a means of avoiding a new Tower of Babel. It was also solely the language of Israel, a clear mark of national identity, and a signal to the rest of the world that finally a distinctive Jewish state existed. But the situation that existed in post-World War II Israel was obviously unique.

Within Canadian ethnic communities there exists a measure of disagreement concerning the necessity of language retention if a genuinely multicultural Canada is to exist. While nearly all agree that language maintenance is a "good thing," not all regard it as essential to preserving ethnic identity. Some indeed argue that ethnic identity can continue to exist in a multicultural society in the absence of non-official languages. They either see as inevitable the loss of those languages or ascribe to other characteristics of the group a greater importance than language in maintaining the identity of the group. If language is made the key to survival of the group, then its loss will mean the death of the group: language should not be the key symbol of the group's identity. The language issue is therefore critical in determining what a multicultural society should be like, but it is not one about which all parties to the discussion may be expected to agree.

In Canada, the host society, whether English or French, has traditionally been rather unsympathetic to the maintenance of minority languages. For example, in the 1950s and 1960s school authorities in English Canada responded to the large influx of children who could not speak English by devising programs to change these children as quickly as possible into "New Canadians." The key was language training through teaching English as a second language. The quite deliberate goal was assimilation. The immigrant languages were regarded as obstacles to be overcome. In retrospect, one can see that the programs adopted were not very successful. Much of the teaching was inadequate and the deliberately assimilative goal often produced conflict, particularly when cultural assimilation did not lead to structural assimilation and actually brought into the open some of the inequities of social organization in Canada. The move toward multiculturalism in the 1970s may be construed as one designed to repair the deficiencies of earlier policies.

However, as Vandra Masemann has shown, attempts to develop multicultural programs in the schools of Toronto roused considerable controversy in the mid-1970s.[12] While there was little disagreement that instruction in English for immigrant children should and could be improved, there was much more disagreement on what the goal of that instruction should be: assimilation, or bilingualism and the deliberate retention of the home language. Controversy also focused on whether or not some attempt should be made to have provincial laws changed to allow a language other than English or French to be used for instructional purposes. In the end those favoring a kind of modified *status quo* prevailed. The schools were to concentrate on improving English instruction and developing better understanding among cultural groups of the contribution each has made to society. The policy of Anglo-conformity was continued, even though in a somewhat attenuated form, a few concessions being made to reduce immediate pressures. In reality, no essential shift in policy occurred since such token efforts as the Heritage Languages Program were to be allowed rather than encouraged. The current situation is largely unchanged, and this in a city which has been more attractive to immigrants than any other place in Canada.

There has been one comprehensive study of non-official language use in Canada, O'Bryan, Reitz, and Kuplowska's 1976 publication *Non-Official Languages: A Study in Canadian Multiculturalism*.[13] The study itself has severe limitations, being confined to five metropolitan areas (Montreal, Toronto, Winnipeg, Edmonton, and Vancouver) and covering only the ten largest non-official language groups (Chinese, Dutch, German, Greek, Hungarian, Italian, Polish, Portuguese, Scandinavian, and Ukrainian). Nevertheless, it contains a wealth of data about conditions within these groups and cities, conditions which do not augur well for language maintenance. Their work led the authors to conclude that, while quite extensive knowledge of non-official languages continues to exist in Canada, this immense cultural resource is almost lost in a single generation. In some groups, even among immigrants, fluency in the language may be lost quite quickly. They note that although the various groups differ in their rate of loss these differences are minor, and that the loss occurs in a straight-line fashion:

As matters now stand, the generational transition is a powerful force in language loss, even among those groups possessing high retention rates. We have provided clear evidence that by the third generation the question is not one of retention but of reacquisition and primary acquisition.[14]

They also found that language loss was greatest in Winnipeg and Edmonton, but that although this fact could be accounted for by the more recent immigration to the other three cities, it nevertheless indicated that the issue of language maintenance was more critical on the Prairies than elsewhere.

Their investigation of the use made of the non-official languages showed that there was quite heavy daily usage in the first generation but that usage fell off in the second and third generations. The home, family, friends, and the church proved to be the most significant areas in which the non-official language was used. However, the groups differed in the actual amount of use in such circumstances, with Greeks, Poles, Portuguese, and Chinese showing quite heavy use and Scandinavians, Dutch, and German appearing at the opposite extreme.

This study, like almost all Canadian studies of language maintenance among groups who do not have one of the official languages as the mother tongue, shows that length of time in Canada is directly related to language loss. The longer a group stays in Canada the greater the loss with, of course, some individual variations in the actual rate of loss. Consequently, the Portuguese, Greeks, and Chinese have the highest retention rates, being large groups of recent arrival. They are closely followed by the Italians. A "middle" group comprises such peoples as the Hungarians, Czechs and Slovaks, Ukrainians, Yugoslavs, and Polish. In this middle group, the Ukrainians in particular are "higher" in language retention than might be expected, but eastern European immigrants in general tend to exhibit better than average retention, partly because of religious and political factors in their original immigration and ancestral homelands. The Germans, Jewish, Dutch, and Scandinavians are clearly very fast to assimilate, and being among the earliest immigrant groups in

Canada, they show very low rates of language retention.

If one looks at some of the factors in the low retention rate of German as a language in Canada, it is possible to appreciate how varied can be the influences which lead to language loss. The immigrant German-speaking population brought with it to Canada a wide range of German dialects varying all the way from the German of Austria to very Low German. Some of these dialects also contained certain mixtures of other languages, particularly Russian. In addition, the German community itself has a special High German as the language of education. The immigrant community was split into various religious and political factions: Hutterites, Roman Catholics, Lutherans, Mennonites, Austrians, Prussians, and so on. Two world wars disfavored the use of German and even "being German," and provincial educational regulations restricted or eliminated the teaching of German in schools. Institutions failed to develop or were nipped in the bud although Germans were the largest ethnic group in Canada after the English and French, comprising 6.1 per cent of the Canadian population in the 1971 census. That so little German is spoken, particularly outside certain well-known linguistic pockets such as the Kitchener-Waterloo area in Ontario, shows how strong assimilative tendencies can be.

Jeffrey Reitz shows in his follow-up study to the non-official languages investigation that among the various urban ethnic groups he studied there is almost a straight line (and sharp) decrease between the first and second and second and third generations in ethnic identification, endogamy, ethnic language retention, ethnic neighborhood residence, and ethnic church affiliation. However the decrease is not quite as sharp after the second generation as it is between the first and second. The sharpest decline of all is in language retention.[15] One can hardly fail to conclude that all languages other than English and French in Canada are seriously endangered species.

One of Canada's greatest natural resources has long been the language capabilities of its various peoples. However, from the very beginning these capabilities have been perceived to be more of a threat to the country's existence than a blessing. Canada's history is in part a history of the suppression of both native and immigrant languages, either deliberately or by calculated neglect. With immigration now slowed almost to a trickle, Canada may be at a critical moment in its history, one at which Canadians must decide whether it is worthwhile trying to arrest the decline in the language capability of its population in languages other than English or French, or whether that capability must be finally sacrificed so that the major English-French conflict can continue uninterrupted by other voices.

# 9

# A MULTICULTURAL SOCIETY:
# MYTHS AND REALITIES

Canada exhibits an extremely diverse pattern of languages and cultures.[1] The Atlantic provinces are strongly English in their orientation, both in language and culture. The exception is New Brunswick, which is the most thoroughly bilingual, bicultural part of Canada and perhaps the only province in which the federal government's bilingual policy could work as it was apparently intended to. Quebec is strongly French in orientation and increasingly so every day. But there is an important English language pocket and multicultural enclave in the city of Montreal. Ontario, except where it borders on Quebec, is English in language but a province of many cultures with English predominant. It is also only recently multicultural, the result of its attraction, particularly Toronto's attraction, to newcomers to Canada after World War II. To the west of Ontario, all the provinces are English so far as language is concerned but all may lay claim to be multicultural to some extent. The north of Canada, and the north may be defined to include the northern parts of the western provinces and Ontario, is a land of many languages and many cultures with English tending to dominate in both areas if only because of the federal government's massive presence. And everywhere within Canada, heavily populated areas are more heterogeneous in language and culture than the areas which surround them.

When the Canadian government established the Royal Commission on Bilingualism and Biculturalism, it soon realized that the term *bicultural* was every bit as contentious as the term *bilingual*. As early as 1968, the government was stepping around the issue by referring to "bilingualism" so far as language was concerned but "pluralism" when cultural matters were under discussion. The Commission itself was somewhat ambivalent on the issue, concluding that immigrants should choose to integrate with one of the two dominant cultures in Canada. Integration was not, in the Commission's view, assimilation. However, the commissioners knew that many people did not accept such a solution: they quite understood that although many of the non-English, non-French groups in Canada would accept bilingualism, they would categorically reject biculturalism. Such people perhaps regarded Canada as a country with two official languages but argued that it was fundamentally multicultural rather than bicultural. This was also a strongly stated minority view of the Commission itself.[2]

When the time came to implement parts of the Commission's Report, the government decided to reject any view of Canada as a bicultural nation, indeed any view of Canada that would give support to the idea that there was a "Canadian" culture which was worthy of "official" support. The government's policy was announced on October 8, 1971, as one of "multiculturalism within a bilingual framework." As outlined in a statement tabled with the government's response to the fourth volume of the Report of the Royal Commission on Bilingualism and Biculturalism, the Government of Canada said it intended to do four things. It would support all those cultural groups, resources permitting, "which have demonstrated a desire and effort to continue to develop, a capacity to grow and contribute to Canada." Second, it would "assist members of all cultural groups to overcome cultural barriers to full participation in Canadian society." Third, it "would promote creative encounters and interchange among all Canadian cultural groups in the interest of national unity." And, finally, it would "assist immigrants to acquire at least one of Canada's official languages." All the federal parties concurred in this policy.

The 1978 government document *Multiculturalism and the Government of Canada* was a further attempt to explain the federal government's involvement in multiculturalism.³ Like equivalent documents for the policy on bilingualism, it seems to be an attempt to counter both ineffective previous explanations and public antipathy. According to this document, the objective of the Multiculturalism Directorate is

> ...to encourage and assist, within the framework of Canada's Official Languages Policy and in the spirit of existing human rights codes, the full realization of the multicultural nature of Canadian society through programs which promote the preservation and sharing of cultural heritages and which facilitate mutual appreciation and understanding among all Canadians.⁴

To this end the Directorate supports such activities as seminars, conferences, exhibitions, artistic and cultural activities, and so on. There is also "provision of support for teaching of ancestral languages in classroom settings but outside the formally organized school systems," support which includes money for teaching aids, teacher training, and operating costs.⁵

It is apparent from reading this 1978 document, as it is from reading an earlier 1973 background document prepared for the First Canadian Conference on Multiculturalism, that the government included almost everything it could to show how responsive it is to the needs of Canadians who are neither English nor French. Even Fitness and Amateur Sport gets its mention!⁶ What is apparent from reading the document is how thin the effort is spread: a film here, some radio programs there, a document available in several languages somewhere else, and a reminder in still another place that certain rights are available to all. The document also shows that perhaps the widest contact the government has with ethnic groups is through the advertising it takes out in the ethnic press: the government's interest in and support of the ethnic press is very apparent. How political rather than altruistic that interest is may be a subject of some concern to many!

Governments other than the federal government have found it either convenient or expedient to adopt a policy of multiculturalism. For example, the three cornerstones of Ontario's policy are equality, participation, and appreciation.[7] The first involves a commitment to combat discrimination against individuals in employment, education, justice, recreation, and all aspects of life in the province. The second aims to bring together the various ethnic groups in a community in order to understand and share their cultural diversities. The third has the intention of helping the various groups retain and share their cultures, including their languages. The major emphasis appears to be on anti-discrimination to ensure that individual rights are not jeopardized; a lesser emphasis is on the provision of public monies to conduct significant group programs.

The major effort of the program appears to go into such areas as the provision of "reception" and "orientation" facilities for recently arrived immigrants, the development of information services, and the sponsorship of a variety of programs designed to teach English to the newly arrived. Anti-discrimination policies and a concern for harmonious race relationships are also prominent. The Heritage Languages Program permits schools to offer extra instruction in languages other than English or French, and a concern is shown for a whole spectrum of cultural activities.

It is interesting to see that under its multiculturalism policy the Government of Ontario includes programs designed to reach both the French and the native peoples of the province. It lists its French language services and the support it gives to bilingualism in the province alongside what it does for other groups. In like manner the government's effort to do something for the large native population through schools and social services is subsumed under multiculturalism. Neither group, the French nor the native peoples, finds this inclusion to be anything but a hindrance to its objectives. Each group believes itself to be "special" in some specific respect and fears the loss of that uniqueness if it is treated like all other non-English groups in the province.

In practice the multicultural policies initiated by the various governments in Canada provide a limited amount of assistance and financial support to ethnic groups. This support seems designed to allow such groups to maintain some of their organizations and certain aspects of their cultures. To that extent ethnicity is to be encouraged as a desirable "Canadian" characteristic, a view which regards the Canadian nation as a "mosaic" of peoples. The policies are quite clearly not designed to enable groups to establish organizations and institutions which would compete in any serious way with those of the English and French charter groups, for example, separate publicly funded educational facilities. Such a move would delay the "Canadianization" of the ethnic groups, for an essential part of the multicultural policies is that the ethnic groups must "participate" in the life and culture of the whole community. The key word is *participate*. But to members of the ethnic communities themselves, participation, as defined in the various policies, appears to imply the surrender of certain key attributes and an eventual submersion and loss of distinctiveness for those communities.

Critical in any debate on multiculturalism is the issue of language: how to curb the erosion of the ethnic languages. Closely related is the issue of the French language outside Quebec and the special status French has under the Official Languages Act and now under the Constitution Act. For many ethnic groups, particularly the Ukrainians, the granting of any special status to French outside Quebec is something to be resisted as discriminatory. While they are quite willing to grant the English language a privileged status in Canada, many Ukrainians are unwilling to accord either the French language or the French who have settled outside Quebec an equivalent "charter" status. The French are just the same as they are in this view and therefore deserve no better—and, of course, no worse—treatment. This view is particularly prevalent on the Prairies and even to some extent in Ontario. To give any privileged status to French would be to acknowledge that one's own position is reduced to the status of being an "ethnic." It would also place all ethnics in a permanently institutionalized second-class position behind both the English and French. This consequence is particularly unacceptable on the Prairies where the French appear to be no less recently arrived than any other group and no more successful. Somehow the Official Languages Act has promoted the French ahead of equally worthy candidates and the result is resentment: if any privileges are to come the way of the French, they must also be granted to any other minority group that wishes to enjoy them. In this view multiculturalism implies multilingualism not bilingualism. Languages such as Ukrainian deserve all the privileges presently reserved exclusively for French.

When one looks at attempts, however, to preserve Canada as a multilingual country, one cannot be sanguine about the results. The report on the *Non-Official Languages* provides no hope for optimism.[8] Whereas nearly everyone agrees that language retention is very important in maintaining group identity, among those who do not speak one of the two official languages on arrival in Canada language loss begins immediately. Most immigrants do learn some English or French, often just enough to get by in very restricted circumstances. But typically their Canadian-born children become bilingual and tend to use their mother tongue only to a limited extent. And their children's children are even more limited in their use of the ancestral language, with 60 per cent or more having no knowledge of it whatsoever and 80 per cent rarely or never using it. Some groups are much more concerned about this phenomenon than others, e.g., the Chinese, Ukrainians, Italians, and Greeks. On the other hand, the Portuguese are as yet apparently little concerned, probably because of their recent arrival and unfamiliarity with the phenomenon. Some long-settled groups, such as the Scandinavians and Dutch, having lost much of their original language capability, would now like to see a revival. Most groups regard language retention as a kind of cornerstone in maintaining their cultural distinctiveness in Canada; hence the attempts some have made to allow or require schools to teach languages other than English or French and even to have these languages approved for basic instructional purposes.

But almost universally in Canada the language of instruction in the public schools, colleges, and universities is either English or French. Of necessity, there exist many programs designed to teach one of these languages to newcomers. Instruction in English or French as a second language is designed to raise the students' level of proficiency in the language to enable them as quickly as possible to function as equals in the classroom. Some provinces, such as Ontario with its Heritage Languages Program, Quebec with its Programme d'Enseignement des Langues d'Origine, and Alberta with its permissive policy toward a variety of languages, do allow languages other than English or French to be taught for enrichment purposes. The intent is that children will learn to appreciate both languages and cultures rather than being required to sacrifice the old for the new. However, these are by no means bilingual programs; the languages are not used equally. They are at the most maintenance programs in which English or French is the primary language through which educational and social mobility will be achieved and the other language and culture is regarded as something valuable to be preserved rather than to be used, almost a kind of museum artifact.

The alternative for many groups is to provide their own ethnic schools outside the normal school day. But such schools, though widespread, are not very successful. Parents realize this fact and, while also recognizing that the home is extremely important in language maintenance, look to the institutional support which could be offered by a public system committed to language retention. As the authors of the *Non-Official Languages* study observed:

> There is very strong and clear support among many members of Canada's ethnic minority groups for inclusion of the non-official languages in the courses of instruction and as vehicles of instruction in the public schools—especially in the elementary schools.[9]

But one must also be realistic and ask whether even such a curriculum would produce the desired results. There is a substantial body of evidence that schools specially designed to protect minority group interests may not be especially successful. It is extremely doubtful whether such schools (whether language schools, religious schools, or social-class oriented schools) can carry most of the burden of perpetuating those very qualities that brought them into existence, particularly if they lack strong prior and concurrent support from the home and community. For example, there seems little reason to believe that children who leave the separate school systems of Canada are any more moral, religious, God-fearing (or God-loving) than those who leave the public school systems. Even when there is strong home and community support for the specific activities for which a minority-group school is established, the school itself may produce little more than marginal support for these activities. One study of Jewish education in Toronto concluded by endorsing the observation of the Task Force Report on the Future of the Jewish Community in America that "there is evidence...that formal school experience is not the best vehicle for identity formation by comparison with programs of family education, communal service, or planned Jewish experience."[10] This observation concerns the group in Canada which has been *most* successful in maintaining its ethnic identity while succeeding in the wider society. Other groups with less determination are not likely to be more successful than the Jewish; in fact, it would be reasonable to expect them to be much less so.

The pessimism that the authors of the *Non-Official Languages* study felt concerning the future of those languages is quite clear:

> We investigated a number of other organizations and activities which might encourage the retention of the non-official languages. These included the question of more visits to the old country, the establishment of summer camps for children, the establishment of group cultural centres and the provision of more books in the ancestral language. ...Generally, these organizations do not currently play a very substantial role in language retention, but they may well be developed to do so. Currently, they receive most support from those who already have some knowledge of the ancestral tongue and least from those whose linguistic retention is very small or has vanished.[11]

Not only are there external problems arising from inadequate public recognition and support, but internally the communities themselves do not know how they can best achieve their objectives. The authors also acknowledge the importance of continued immigration for maintaining many of the resources and agencies necessary to perpetuate language skills: "Our data clearly indicate that some of these agencies would undergo substantial difficulties if immigration should be markedly curtailed."[12] Since immigration has been markedly curtailed, it is reasonable to expect that without massive external aid the immigrant languages will become increasingly moribund.

The maintenance of multilingualism through programs which support many different pairs of bilingualisms would be a costly proposition if it were feasible. That feasibility itself is another concern. There are many examples throughout the world of countries which have struggled, or are struggling, with bilingual and multilingual populations, most without success. For example, India is a vast pluralistic multilingual society where it has been necessary to have the languages classified for different purposes so as not to create unnecessary frictions: home language, link language, regional language, national language, official language, library language, literacy language, and world language. For the average Indian multilingualism is more likely than not a norm. Bilingualism is regarded as an attempt at nation building or elite building when it involves Hindi or English or some other highly standardized language. Sheer size, numbers, and diversity continue to prevent the development of a language common to all and keep alive the tolerance which multilingualism seems to promote. So multilingualism is at the same time both an obstacle to some kind of national efficiency and a guarantee against that efficiency becoming a kind of tyranny.

Bilingual education is officially entrenched in the Soviet Union, a country of well over 100 indigenous languages. In the Soviet Union, however, the goal is quite explicit: to spread Russian as a universal language while maintaining local languages, the policy of Russification. This is not an acceptable goal to many of the language minorities. For example, the Ukrainians see Russian linguistic imperialism marching hand in hand with Russian cultural imperialism, with both threatening Ukrainian language and culture. Nevertheless, the 1970 Soviet census showed that 36.3 per cent of Ukrainians gave Russian as their second language.

In a country like Wales bilingual education refers to a somewhat desperate attempt to keep alive the Welsh language.

English is the predominant language of Wales and Welsh very much a runner-up. In a society which is becoming ever more English in orientation and industrialized in its economic life, bilingual education may, at best, arrest the decline of Welsh. However, revival seems highly improbable.

In the United States bilingual education has focused on providing instruction in both the home language and English for children who do not have English as their first language. In 1968 the United States Congress passed the Bilingual Education Act, an extension of the 1965 Elementary and Secondary Education Act. Partly as a result of the Supreme Court decision in the case of *Lau v. Nichols* in 1975 and partly from other pressure Congress also passed the Equal Educational Opportunity Act of 1974, which extended bilingual education in certain circumstances. Bilingual education in the United States is generally interpreted to mean the provision of instruction in the native language concurrent with the teaching of English, with the aim of assimilating children into the English-speaking mainstream. It is a form of "compensatory" education. The 1974 Act requires local and state educational agencies to provide "children of limited English-speaking ability instruction designed to enable them, while using their native language, to achieve competence in the English language."

Sometimes biculturalism is promoted alongside bilingualism and sometimes literary skills in the native language are also developed. But on the whole bilingual education in the United States is a transitional compensatory measure aimed at a "disadvantaged" segment of the school population; genuine language maintenance programs are virtually unheard of. United States law ensures the rights of all children to equal educational opportunity but that opportunity is essentially one within an anglophone society; the only requirement imposed on school authorities is that they must, if necessary, use another language to provide a bridge into that world of opportunity. The goal of American education is that of making children full participants in the American way of life, which means providing them with a knowledge of English if necessary and an understanding of the culture in which they are expected to use that knowledge for personal advancement. Canadian "heritage language" programs may in reality have some of the same characteristics, mollifying as they do the feelings of ethnic communities and hence lowering resistance to what the hierarchy of educators perceive their real task to be: making newcomers into good law-abiding citizens who can be fitted into their proper slots in Canadian society.

One very obvious contrast between the situation in the United States and the one in Canada is that whereas the Government of the United States has poured billions of dollars into its language programs the Government of Canada has been much less generous, particularly in its support of multiculturalism. A remark such as the following from a 1978 Ministry of Supply and Services pamphlet entitled "Notes on Multiculturalism" is either quite ingenuous or deliberately misleading:

> There are those who might question the wisdom of spending large sums of money to further the cultures of a multitude of minorities. A history of Polish immigrants, a film on a Ukrainian family in Winnipeg—these may seem like unnecessary frills at a time when the national purse is not exactly bulging.

"Large sums of money" are certainly not what the Canadian government has spent. In fact, the federal government has consistently budgeted little money for its multiculturalism program and failed to spend even that. In 1980 the federal government's budget to support its policy of multiculturalism came to $10.8 million, that is, less than one cent per person per week throughout Canada. One can contrast this "generosity" with various responses to the corporate world in times of "difficulty," for example, to farm implement and automobile manufacturers and to oil companies. "Corporate welfare bums" get tens and hundreds of millions to stay alive in order to safeguard the profit motive, but a language is worth only nickels and dimes!

Little manpower has been assigned to implement policies and strong ministerial support has been lacking. Initially this situation might have been anticipated if for no other reason than that there was a minority government which could not afford to alienate its French supporters. It also had its hands full with implementing the policy on bilingualism, and the buoyant spending mood of the 1960s was gone forever. Grants were given out, but they were small and tended to divide ethnic groups, both internally and one from another. A divisive tokenism has resulted which effectively seems to stunt any growth of a "third force" in Canada despite the official pronouncements of policy makers. In the absence of any coherent policy and real commitment "multiculturalism" has remained a slogan rather than a reality. The inability of ethnic groups to unite in common cause or to make any concerted effort to gain influence through the ballot box has resulted in the major political parties being largely able to ignore, in reality if not in their rhetoric, all linguistic and cultural groups other than the English and French.[13]

Jeffrey Reitz, an informed observer in this area, has stated that much more money and an entirely different principle are called for. He concludes his own study, *The Survival of Ethnic Groups*, by pointing out that the federal government's multicultural program supports such matters as language instruction. However, his own research led him to the conclusion that it is the economic rather than the cultural organizations of ethnic groups that need support, for without viable economic organizations ethnic groups may not be able to maintain themselves in Canada. However, Reitz is not at all optimistic that support for ethnic businesses, for example, will work in the current economic system. It may already be too late for that solution.[14]

Not all groups concern themselves with the obvious inadequacies, even contradictions, of federal and provincial policies concerning multiculturalism. Such groups as the Greeks, Portuguese, Italians, and Chinese tend to be less involved and apparently less concerned with multiculturalism than groups such as the Ukrainians. The concerns of the former groups are more immediate: fitting into the economy, surviving, overcoming discrimination, and putting down roots in a new country. They either have not developed an adequate middle class group or have one which is still not readily accepted in the wider society. Unlike the Ukrainians they currently lack the leadership that can draw both public attention and the attention of the group itself to those factors which will influence long-term group survival. However, social inequality, discrimination, and lack of government support may actually provide them with the incentives they need to ensure group survival.[15]

Multiculturalism seems to have only very limited appeal to a significant proportion of newly arrived immigrants. Such people often want to find jobs and learn English above everything else. They want to have some kind of assurance that they are being accorded the same rights and privileges as others and that they are fully protected by law from exploitation. Association with an ethnic group and immersion in its concerns may be too restrictive and inhibiting, and may confine rather than liberate. The availability of training in English, help in using the existing social services, and the absence of discrimination may be far more important to many newly arrived immigrants than the opportunities provided by a strong ethnic organization to cling to the past rather than come to an accommodation with the present.

Both commitment and money seem to be lacking almost everywhere so far as successful implementation of multiculturalism is concerned. The Canadian public too seems largely unaware of existing programs and of what is possible, or, if aware, is not necessarily sympathetic. The only people who consistently push for fuller and better implementation of multiculturalism are ethnic group leaders. These are often the same people who have been active over the years in keeping ethnic consciousness and ethnic language alive in private after-hours schools and other institutions.

The general public lack of concern in Canada for multiculturalism is well attested. What support there is is not very strong. Multiculturalism might be a good idea, but not good enough to spend significant amounts of money on. So long as multiculturalism is unlikely to affect either the way society works or the way public monies are spent, it merits support; to the extent it might change life in Canada it produces an unsympathetic reaction. French Canadians are, if anything, less sympathetic than other Canadians, regarding any promotion of non-official language groups as a demotion for themselves. They do not regard "ethnics" as potential allies in a struggle against the English but as competitors in a situation where the rewards are fixed and each party must get what it can at the expense of as many others as possible.

A 1977 survey of Canadian feelings about, and perceptions of, the government's policy on multiculturalism led the investigators to conclude that public knowledge of that policy was not widespread, with only one in five knowing about it.[16] Most people perceived the government's policy to favor a "permissive" attitude toward the survival of minority groups rather than a "supportive" one. On the whole, however, multicultural attitudes were generally positive, respondents being slightly in favor of cultural diversity within Canada. So far as particular programs were concerned, there was evidence of greater acceptance for some, such as "community centres" and "folk festivals," than for others, such as "radio and television shows in languages other than English or French" and the "teaching, in regular school programmes, of the languages of the major cultural groups who have settled in Canada." Respondents actually tended to reject the last two programs. The authors concluded that it "may well be that Canadians think that the idea of multiculturalism is good, that some of the programmes are enjoyable, but they do not want to get involved."[17]

In looking at multiculturalism in Canada, as it is endorsed by various governments, one cannot really escape the feeling that what is being seen is gesture without substance. Perhaps the only reason why a multiculturalism policy has been in any way acceptable to English Canada is this realization, that it has actually changed nothing. Subtle Anglo-conformity still prevails. As one observer has trenchantly written:

> Canada, within very narrowly circumscribed limits, has multicultural characteristics. At least it is an heterogeneous society with two clearly dominant cultures. Canadian multiculturalism operates within the limit of a broadly Christian context; it operates as well within the limit of a western European—either French or English—pattern of family and political organization and within the more universal pattern of international capitalism as far as the economy is concerned. In what might more cynically be viewed as the

> realm of the innocuous, the extraneous, and, most often, the quaint, true multiculturalism is tolerated and encouraged. This realm of cultural alternatives includes cuisine, folk dance, costume, song, literature, and the like. It also includes religion, narrowly defined as worship, which in modern society has been demoted from the earlier place among the cultural universals. In the final analysis Canadian multiculturalism is political ideology, even possibly a subtle device to melt the variant immigrants down into homogeneous stew.[18]

This point of view has been echoed by others. The ethnic studies curricula currently found in Ontario, Alberta, and other Canadian provinces have been criticized. They do not appear to be genuine and spontaneous responses to an emerging understanding of cultural pluralism, but instead seem to indicate only some mild tempering of old Anglo-conformity.[19] Admittedly, such programs have changed from being *for* minority group children to being *about* minority groups in Canada, a change for the better, but Palmer and Troper declare that more is needed:

> To evolve as a viable field of study in the schools, it is essential that studies must be encouraged without entanglements in filial-pietous generalities—wise men, heroes, great events, and an unending series of contributions. The controversies, tensions, and frictions that have characterized the history of ethnicity and pluralism in Canada must be recognized and honestly approached. It must not be hidden under layers of brotherhood rhetoric and folk music. To do so would not only sugar-coat the truth, it would also misrepresent the ethnic experience of students, which remains the key to wider understanding.[20]

However, that is just the kind of reality the schools generally seek to avoid: it is "too difficult" to deal with, "too contentious," and too likely to arouse sleeping dogs.

Multiculturalism as an official state policy has not been a success. Very few indeed have spoken out strongly for the policy as it is currently administered. Much more numerous and outspoken have been its critics. French critics, for example, see it as a means of promoting the English language at the expense of the French since they recognize the assimilationist reality of English Canada. Multiculturalism buys the English the time needed for assimilation to work and in its denial of French culture increases the threat not only to French culture but also to the French language. The policy also represents to them a denial of what they consider to be the basic fact of Canadian life: the country's fundamental biculturalism. Multiculturalism reduces the French language and culture to a status a little ahead of Ukrainian language and culture but far behind that of English language and culture. Accepting the policy is equivalent to acknowledging that Canada is predominantly English in culture, since the French firmly reject Prime Minister Trudeau's repeated claim that there is no "official" Canadian culture. To them it is quite clear that "official" has nothing to do with reality, a reality in which English language and culture dominate.

Some critics argue that multiculturalism perpetuates the Canadian vertical mosaic in that it effectively locks in all the ethnic groups to the positions they now hold in society with, of course, the English firmly positioned at the very top of the Canadian social structure. The policy simply affirms the *status quo*. Not everyone accepts such a pessimistic view. Some ethnic group leaders are firmly of a view that a genuinely multicultural society is necessary to accomplish certain goals which they regard as desirable. Only a multicultural society will allow people to retain the invaluable "psychic" connection they need with their roots. To surrender such a connection for very doubtful personal mobility in society may be a poor trade. There is absolutely no guarantee that assimilation will bring equality with the "charter groups" in Canada in any reasonable length of time since the current social structure of Canada is so rigid.[21] Multiculturalism is the only alternative.

If ethnic groups are allowed to melt into the larger society the surest beneficiary will be the English. The French will gain nothing from such assimilation. In fact, they will be even more jeopardized than they are at present as their proportion decreases in Canada. It can be argued therefore that it would be in the best interest of the Quebecois to promote multiculturalism in English Canada; denying it in French Canada through restrictive legislation will also be counter-productive.

Sometimes in practice the federal government's policy appears almost to be a cynical one of "divide and rule," one deliberately designed to promote factionalism and deprive ethnic groups of any real power. A problem with multicultural programs and grants is that people in government decide who gets what, not the ethnic groups themselves. The grant awarders have their own ideas about what should and should not be supported. In this way all ethnic groups are put into a position not unlike the one long experienced by native peoples: they must depend on others to decide what is worthwhile and must constantly face the danger of being "co-opted" to serve the ends of others. As policies are turned into programs, one sees the consequences: the resulting endeavors tend to provide ethnic groups with a few symbolic accommodations while doing nothing to meet substantive needs. A folk festival here, a radio program there, a glowing reference in a speech somewhere else, and an advertisement placed in an ethnic paper may placate those who want some kind of recognition but who do not really understand how ineffective, indeed how irrelevant, all of those things are in changing their lot in life. There are those like Phillippe LeBlanc, the Director of the Multicultural Development Branch of Ontario's Department of Culture and Recreation, who actually resign (as LeBlanc did in April, 1979) because they believe that multiculturalism is being promoted for narrow political objectives rather than out of any real social concern, a charge denied of course by the responsible minister. Again there is a paradox in all this: "divide and rule," neglect, and interethnic conflict may benefit those who wish to see ethnicity continue as a factor in Canadian life. If ethnic consciousness depends to a considerable extent on inter-group conflict and jockeying for position in society, then a well-articulated and adequately funded policy of multiculturalism could very well lead to a reduction of conflict and a very considerable lowering of ethnic consciousness. Certain groups in Canada have flourished in persecution, real or imagined, and discrimination. Such treatment has helped to maintain group cohesiveness or at least slow down the rate at which the group loses what special characteristics it has. Groups which have not undergone this kind of experience have tended to assimilate quickly. The paradox is that these characteristics maintain group identity in that they create conflict, but when society refuses any longer to regard them as matters of conflict, they lose their potency and may quickly be lost. Consequently, acceptance tends to weaken ethnicity. The failure of multicultural policies might actually be a better guarantee of the continued existence of ethnic groups than success.

One difficulty in judging multiculturalism as a policy is defining what "success" is. Some critics argue strongly that multiculturalism is essentially a very conservative, even atavistic, social philosophy. It encourages people to look back rather than forward and to try to reorder the present according to systems that existed at some other time and in some other place. In this respect it must be doomed to inevitable failure since it is quite impossible to recreate either the past or conditions which exist elsewhere. Hence multiculturalism is a romantic impossibility and not at all a realistic option. This fixation on the past is a frequent criticism. Hughes and Kallen have commented on various existing multicultural programs:

> Their emphasis is on the preservation of *traditional* arts and crafts, and *traditional* ways of viewing and doing things ("folk" or "museum" culture) rather than upon the growth and development of *living, Canadian* cultures....Current multicultural programmes may serve, for some Canadians, to revive or strengthen *ethnic* identity and commitment, but they do not encourage large-scale, direct inter-ethnic exchange or the redistribution of resources necessary for greater minority penetration of majority institutions. In effect, they emphasize diversity and short-change national unity.[22]

They further observe that the government's multicultural policy of integrating minority ethnic groups into society is, in effect, a modified version of the old, dominant Anglo-conformity model, but it now officially allows for the persistence of the ancestral culture of ethnic minorities while unofficially ensuring that these are maintained in a subordinate position within that society.[23]

These various views of multiculturalism are not necessarily as contradictory as they appear. The official policy has that kind of "all things to all people" look about it, when indeed it has any appearance at all. It has been badly articulated, poorly publicized, inadequately supported, and thoroughly underfunded. A policy of great promise to some, it is anathema to others, and, for the vast majority, it hardly exists at all.

Perhaps the flaws in what passes for multiculturalism in Canada are unavoidable and the policy is doomed to failure. The inadequacies and contradictions in it appear almost insurmountable. First of all, by divorcing bilingualism from biculturalism and then denying biculturalism in favor of multiculturalism, the federal government seems to have destroyed the basic connection that exists between language and culture, a connection of tremendous social and psychological importance. It has also downgraded the place of culture in a society in which cultural differences are an inherent part of the country's make-up, and has reversed a century of traditional belief that Canada is a bicultural country. Once the Royal Commission on Bilingualism and Biculturalism reported, bilingualism became a pragmatic issue: providing services to taxpayers in the official language which they preferred. The government did continue to recognize that the new policy also retained a symbolic element, deriving from a recognition of the historic duality of the country, but, in denying the bicultural basis of Canadian society, it proclaimed a kind of bilingualism lacking the deep emotional commitment required for success.

A policy which tries to give equal emphasis to bilingualism and multiculturalism must be inherently flawed. If Canada is to be bilingual in English and French, it is only because it is biculturally so. Multiculturalism cannot co-exist with bilingualism so long as the French believe that bilingualism must entail biculturalism. Such a belief is not likely to change. But biculturalism fails because of massive under-representation of the French in the economic life of not only the country as a whole but even of Quebec in particular. The geographic distributions of the two languages and cultures is also a formidable obstacle. Moreover, biculturalism is rejected by the federal government and found unacceptable by much of English Canada and many ethnic group leaders.

If Canada is multicultural, it must be either multilingual, bilingual, or unilingual; only the first seems to mirror reality. It is quite obviously not bilingual, except regionally. However, regional bilingualism distributes French almost entirely within Quebec and English everywhere else. Personal bilingualism is actually multilingualism, a situation in which individuals speak two or more different languages in all kinds of combinations. Canada is certainly not unilingual although it is increasingly becoming a country of two unilingualisms as French and English become increasingly segregated regionally and both groups continue to pursue their assimilationist goals.

One of multiculturalism's particularly damaging flaws is its selective emphasis. The policy is designed to preserve the "best" in the cultures that different groups bring with them to Canada. However, newcomers sometimes bring baggage which might better have been left behind. Racism and discrimination, for example, are sometimes part of that baggage. While there can be no doubt that the English and French in Canada have discriminated against peoples of other origins—and still assure themselves certain preferences today—there can also be no doubt that numerous other groups have brought with them attitudes and beliefs which are also either racist or discriminatory. At times these hostilities flare up between factions of the same group. "Old world" loyalties and hatreds abound and these seem to do little or nothing to help the development of some kind of "Canadian" consciousness. A genuine multicultural society would have to be a pluralistic one so far as values and beliefs were concerned. It is difficult to imagine what such a society would be like in which widely different, even contradictory, values and beliefs prevailed. Certainly present-day Canadian society is not pluralistic in this sense. It is unlikely too that this kind of pluralism is really what many ethnic groups want—they are unlikely to be any more tolerant of values and beliefs that they do not hold than is Canadian society currently tolerant of polygamy, widespread drug abuse, and so on. It is not at all clear how a multicultural policy can effectively encourage some characteristics of a culture and discourage others and still remain "neutral." One would surmise that it is actually impossible to do so, for it is impossible to tinker with cultures in this way. Moreover, those who dominate society have little desire to tinker anyway; they intend to continue to dominate.

The cynicism that can arise when the federal government (and other governments too) proclaims the virtues of its multicultural policies is a perfectly reasonable response. Not a few groups regard multiculturalism as a temporary sop, one inadequately funded and of a nature designed to ease the ethnic communities into oblivion. Even the Ukrainians, the principal advocates of multiculturalism, are showing signs of disillusionment with its policies. Whereas bilingualism was a federal commitment, multiculturalism still has all the appearance of being a piece of empty rhetoric.

# 10

# Unheard Voices

Any discussion of just where the native peoples of Canada fit within the various schemes of things confronts one immediate and overriding problem: the native peoples simply do not fit. Attempts to make them fit have failed constantly but still they continue. An indisputable fact of Canadian life is that about one citizen in twenty has almost no place in that life. What is even more tragic is that the native peoples are the direct descendants of those who settled the land ages before the "ethnic" groups and even the two "charter" groups arrived. They are at the same time Canada's original people and her national shame, one that has not gone unnoticed in the court of world opinion.

It has been estimated that when Europeans first encountered the native peoples of North America in the region today known as Canada perhaps a quarter of a million such people existed spread throughout the area. They spoke a wide variety of languages and had developed very distinctive cultural patterns in their different areas of settlement. During the early years of contact the native peoples themselves were forced to move from place to place either because of pressures from European settlers or voluntarily as they migrated into one another's territories. Now their descendants live mainly in areas those settlers did not want to occupy. But even that situation has changed. Today, many of those areas seem to offer the promise of a great wealth of natural resources, so once again pressures have been placed on the native peoples either to move or to forego what "rights" were left to them, even to abandon entirely every vestige of their ways of life, languages and cultures included. Usually nothing is offered in return, and, when something is, it is offered grudgingly and niggardly.

Today, Canada's native peoples comprise approximately 5 per cent of the country's total population, well over one million. It is also a young population with a high birth rate, and even though mortality is extremely high, it is a growing population in contrast to many other groups which see their numbers and proportions in decline. It is therefore an increasingly conspicuous population. The native peoples are also better educated than they have ever been, more urbanized, and more militant about their concerns. Not fitting within any scheme of things, they are a "problem," one that governments and the general public alike can neither legislate nor wish away. The country seems to lack both the mechanisms and the collective will to resolve the future of the native peoples, and debates on such issues as English-French and federal-provincial differences direct attention elsewhere—without in any way resolving those issues either.

The native population is very small in numbers in eastern Canada in relation to the non-native population.[1] Only in Ontario does it exceed 2 per cent of the provincial population and the proportion drops as low as 0.6 per cent in Newfoundland. To the west and north the proportions are considerably higher. Manitoba and Saskatchewan respectively have native populations of 16.7 per cent and 19.0 per cent while the figures for Alberta and British Columbia are 7.5 per cent and 8.8 per cent according to the 1971 census. Major concentrations are in the Yukon with 45.7 per cent and the Northwest Territories with 80 per cent, which, it should be noted, is almost exactly the same percentage as the French population of Quebec. While no one seriously questions the right of the French to control Quebec, any proposal to allow the native population to control the Northwest Territories evokes strong opposition, particularly from the non-native minority there. Numerically, the largest number of native peoples is actually to be found in Ontario with 223,000 and British Columbia with 217,000, but several other provinces are also well represented: Saskatchewan with 175,000; Manitoba with 170,000; Alberta with 138,000; and Quebec with 114,000. Significant numbers or proportions of Indians exist throughout Canada, distributed mainly in the northern areas of the provinces, but, like other Canadians, the native peoples are moving more and more into towns and cities, particularly in the Prairie provinces. In contrast, one small group of fewer than 20,000, the Inuit, live in almost complete isolation in the far north.

One basic fact that must not be ignored in discussing the native peoples of Canada is that they are not one people but many. The Inuit are quite different from the Dene, the Crees from the Kwakiutl, and the Siouan from the Micmac, both in culture and in language. The native peoples are in almost every way as diverse in their overall composition as the people who make up the rest of Canada's population. Within the native population, however, no groups dominate as do the English and French in Canada as a whole. This cultural and linguistic diversity is the reason behind the claim that the native population of Canada is a "group of nations" quite distinct from the rest of Canada's people. Moreover, it is a group of nations not only because of cultural and linguistic differences but also because of its unique historical relationship to those who came later.

The native population of Canada, with the exception of the Inuit, were taken into the country's political structure through a succession of treaties signed between the Government of Canada and Indian bands. Then, under the Indian Act of 1876 and successive Indian Acts, the Canadian government proceeded to spell out just who was an official "status Indian," that is, an Indian eligible for the protection and benefits provided under the Indian Act. After the initial registration period, an Indian for purposes of registration under the Indian Act was someone born of an Indian father.

However, status could be lost in certain ways, the most common of which occurred when a status Indian women married a non-status Indian man, a move which removed her and their descendants from registration. However, a non-status Indian woman marrying a status Indian man could achieve status for herself and their descendants. The Indian Act therefore makes patrilineal descent its cornerstone even though patrilinearity has never been any more important than matrilinearity to Indians themselves.

The 300,000 or so status Indians in Canada, that is, those natives who are registered under the Indian Act, are organized for administrative purposes into more than five hundred bands on approximately 2,200 reserves. The 70 per cent who live on the reserves have certain government services provided for them, particularly health, education, and welfare services. They may also have rights to certain lands adjacent to the reserves. The federal government has traditionally adopted a paternalistic role in its treatment of the status Indians, tending to see them as a small minority of the total Canadian population, one which should be encouraged to assimilate and disappear into the majority as quietly, quickly, and conveniently as possible. However, the century-long existence of this policy eloquently testifies to its conspicuous failure.

Those Indians who are not eligible for registration or who have lost their status through that Orwellian concept "enfranchisement" sometimes call themselves Metis, half-breeds, or just "Indians." They number at least 800,000 and this number has grown considerably at each new count. With minor exceptions they have no commonly held land nor do they have the protection and benefits of the Indian Act. They are considered to be citizens of the province or territory in which they reside and not wards of the federal government. In their life styles, beliefs, and language use, they may be no less "Indian" (indeed may be more so) than many status Indians who are their neighbors, but the laws of Canada say they are not Indians. Legal "Indianness" in Canada is the arbitrary creation of the White settlers of Canada; it is an entirely divisive creation so far as the native peoples themselves are concerned.

Of the various non-status Indian groups, the Metis, the descendants of the marriages of French or Scots men with Indian women, have much the same feeling about "nationhood" as some of the status Indian bands. They did try to asset their right to nation status in 1870 and again in 1885, and their leader, Louis Riel, paid with his life for the failure of the second attempt.

Although the Canadian government classifies the native peoples into certain categories, to the majority of Canadians somebody who looks "Indian" is an Indian, that is, Indians are an undifferentiated mass within the larger society. Moreover, as native people follow the general Canadian trend toward urbanization, they are becoming more and more conspicuous, but usually in the context of "skid row," welfare, and poverty. Not everything about the resulting situation is entirely bad. At one time the native peoples identified closely and solely with particular tribes or languages. As a result of schooling in English, urbanization, and loss of status this kind of narrow identification has diminished over the generations. Now "Indianness" itself has become the identifier. The advantage to the native peoples of this broader definition of self is that it gives larger groups more power: a claim to "nationhood," as with the Dene; or a claim to speak for all status Indians, as does the National Indian Brotherhood; or a claim to speak for all Metis and non-status Indians, as does the Native Council of Canada. Unfortunately, it also tends to encourage a loss of those very things that are most distinctive about the component parts of the various groups: the different languages and traditional cultural patterns.

In general, the native population of Canada has fared somewhat better under the French than under the English. For example, the French have always been more prepared to marry Indians than have the English, if conditions necessitated. The large Metis population of the north attests to this fact. Indians in Quebec are generally more affluent, more used to good relations with local authorities, and, until recently at least, less militant than Indians elsewhere in Canada. They have found that learning French has made them acceptable in Quebec society even though it has not advanced them to any high level there. In contrast, outside of Quebec, Indians have experienced considerable discrimination in English Canada, particularly in the Prairie provinces and British Columbia. Forced to learn English, they have found that such learning undermined the traditional cultures without allowing access to a new one.

The Inuit of Canada are a small and very special group of native peoples. They do not fall within the jurisdiction of the Indian Act but, because of provisions in Section 91 of the British North America Act charging the federal government with responsibility for "Indians, and lands reserved for Indians," they are a federal responsibility. Moreover, since they have signed no treaties with the Government of Canada their differences from either status or non-status Indians are further increased. They have no special land set aside for them and have retained good claims to their traditional lands, never having surrendered these by treaty. The federal government recognizes these claims as it also does its responsibility for providing for health, social, and educational needs. Isolated from one another and virtually cut off from the rest of Canada's population, the Inuit tend to be more concerned with Inuit problems than with either the issue of where Indians in general fit into Canada's structure or how the Inuit in particular relate to other native peoples. They have tended to take an independent position, for example, in the James Bay settlement; and only an attempt by the Quebec government to substitute French for English as the language of instruction for the Inuit of Quebec brought them into contact with the wider language politics of Canada.

The native peoples of Canada were not always as disadvantaged as they are today. In the period of first contact with Europeans the native peoples were sought out as either allies against the Americans, trading partners, or religious converts. They were regarded as "noble savages." The strategies used in dealing with them were nearly always accommodative, perhaps exploitative, but they were neither assimilative nor expropriative. The native peoples were treated with a fair degree of dignity. The major goal of the settlers and traders was to make as much profit as possible from the new lands that were being opened. They had no grander motives. Moreover, there was considerably less fighting than in the settlement of much of the rest of the American continent. The Indians of Canada were not regarded as enemies to be overcome by conquest and the treaties that were signed were made between equals, or such was the Indian view of those treaties. The Hudson's Bay Company and the North West Company were noteworthy employers of this strategy of dealing with the native peoples in the lands given to them in their charters. The presence of so many Metis today largely attests to its success. Only with Confederation did the situation change, and it changed drastically to the detriment of the native peoples.

After Confederation the Government of Canada deliberately went about opening up the west to build a nation that would stretch from coast to coast. To do so, it had to establish the Canadian-United States boundary, deal formally with the Indians and build a transcontinental railroad. The treaties with the Indians and the various Indian Acts from 1876 ensured that the Indians settled mainly where the government wanted them to settle, thereby enabling the west to be opened up to farming and to be shielded from United States' expansionism. An era of paternalism toward the Indian population began. The Indian Act even proceeded to define who an "Indian" was. The decline of the Indian also began. Status Indians were treated as inferior beings, pagan and uncivilized, who were to be brought gently along to final "absorption" in the major society through a variety of manipulative and bureaucratic means. Over the years this attitude has meliorated but it has not at all disappeared. Non-status Indians became the responsibility of the provincial governments, a responsibility these governments have been generally quite unwilling to assume. What one sees today is the consequence of this treatment of the native peoples: a population living largely apart from other Canadians in a kind of caste system, with high unemployment and poor education, housing, and health. The many hundreds of millions of dollars spent on status Indians each year changes little. And outside the federally controlled system there is the still larger system of misery in which the non-status Indians exist. To be an Indian in Canada is to be at the very bottom of the Canadian social hierarchy; it is to be last in everything. This then is the plight of Canada's *first* people!

The consequences of this strategy of dealing with the native peoples have been disastrous to them. In the federal schools, for example, only English was to be used, even in those schools which were in Quebec. Use of the native language was forbidden. Indian culture and behavior were to be replaced by White culture and behavior. The Indians were even divided up among the competing churches to become Catholics or Protestants according to who had the "rights" for particular bands. At the same time these deliberately assimilative policies were carried out in almost complete isolation from the White community in highly segregated facilities and in social circumstances which virtually prohibited any mixture of Indian and non-Indian populations except at the very lowest level of society. The inevitable result was widespread destruction of those very characteristics that gave the Indians their distinctiveness—their languages, their cultures, and their beliefs—with a sprinkling of government handouts the only compensation, and even these never freely given and often much resented by the general public.

The Indian Act, the legal instrument behind much of the native peoples' misery, is a piece of legislation that must arouse quite ambivalent feelings in any thinking person. On the one hand, it is most obviously a piece of severely discriminatory legislation. It marks out status Indians for special treatment, providing them with certain lands and services, but controlling them too as though they were children, in a kind of guardian-ward relationship. Being the only group in Canada treated this way, the Indians are therefore in a special relationship with the federal government, but one which has never done them much good. On the other hand, without the Indian Act, status Indians might be even worse off than they are now, with absolutely no protection for certain aspects of their life, cultures, and languages. They would be at the very bottom of the social ladder in Canada, as indeed they are, but with no one to turn to and no protection at all. Indians protected by the Indian Act realize how much more fortunate they are in this respect than their fellow Metis and non-status Indians, who lack this protection. The federal government is constitutionally obligated to do certain things for them, and it does these things through the Indian Act; the provincial governments have no such constitutional requirement laid on them to provide any kind of special treatment for the Metis and non-status Indians in their jurisdictions. Therefore, many status Indians tend to believe that the Indian Act offers them assurances of protection and makes them "citizens plus" by singling them out for special consideration, the only group in Canada so treated. In contrast, Metis and non-status Indians tend to see the Indian Act as a sign of oppression and the treaties which the Indians signed with the Whites as instruments of colonization.

They point to continued discrimination as the clearest indication of their mistreatment and tend to look elsewhere than the rewriting of the Indian Act and the renegotiation or reinterpretation of the treaties for relief.

One of the consequences of the Indian Act was to confine many Indians to life on reserves, tracts of land set apart for them, often very unsuitable land for their ways of life and much too little of it. But now the reserve system has become part of the Indian way of life. The reserves are the only "homes" the nations have. While the reserve system was instituted to protect Indians from exploitation and give them the opportunity to "develop," that is, to become more and more like the Whites, the Indians themselves accepted neither purpose. They did not want protection so much as preservation of their ways of life, and they certainly did not want to assimilate to the Whites, constantly rejecting much of what they saw in the new society that had been brought to Canada.

Today, just like other Canadians, the native peoples are developing a preference for life in towns and cities rather than on rural reserves. Status Indians are moving off the reserves; in some parts of Canada the proportion of status Indians living off the reserves is well over one-third. The urbanization of the native peoples has become an issue in the Prairie provinces. Since urbanized Indians are very likely to be unemployed, in poor health, and the victims or perpetrators of petty crime, they require social services which provincial governments claim are a burden on their treasuries. This is particularly the case in Manitoba, a province lacking the recently acquired wealth of Saskatchewan and Alberta. Adding to provincial "frustration" is the inability of the same governments to exploit lands controlled by native peoples for taxation purposes. The Indians cannot help therefore but feel that they are treated as social parasites no matter what they do—stay on the reserves or move into town.

Within the towns and cities Indians generally find themselves living in the poorest areas and the worst conditions. Although urban Indians try to maintain contact with the reserves from which they come, such contact inevitably diminishes over time and consequently fewer and fewer opportunities exist for the young to participate in Indian cultural activities and to use their native languages. Intermarriage with Whites, or common-law arrangements (often necessary for an Indian woman to preserve her Indian status), also weakens traditional bonds and characteristics without at the same time doing very much to lessen the discrimination that is experienced. The trend is therefore toward the establishment of a class of uprooted urbanized native peoples trapped in a culture of poverty and apparently doomed to remain at the very bottom of every social and economic scale in Canada.

Given this fact, one can see why nearly all status Indians cling to the reserve system. It is all they have. Even as the native peoples urbanize, the reserves retain their importance to them. The reserves offer a refuge to the urban Indian who can go "home" again if things do not work out in town, or who can go back to water roots there. The reserve system therefore acts as a kind of necessary safety valve in Indian life today. Without it the urbanizing Indian would be completely uprooted, doomed for the foreseeable future to a life of poverty and discrimination, and unprotected and uncared for in a society which continues to refuse to native people almost any chance of achieving economic independence and self-respect.

The reserve system and the Indian Act have become very emotional issues to many Indians, harmful as both have been and continue to be. The devils they have come to know are still better than the devils they fear will be unleashed on them if the Act and the reserves were to disappear. One can even argue that the preservation of the reserves and the system of status under the Indian Act benefit all native peoples, not just status Indians. Without the protection these afford a minority of native peoples, all would be dispossessed beyond even the levels which exist today. The native peoples would become no more than the lowest class of poor Canadians. Only the Indian Act continues to focus some kind of national consciousness and conscience on their continued plight. Only the Indian Act stands between the native peoples and complete assimilation into "Canadian" life, an assimilation which would be the final act of cultural genocide for over a million people.

In retrospect it is easy to see how this assimilationist policy has been pursued by the federal government. Until after World War II the policy was one of segregation for the Indians in the hope that they would be "civilized" in the exclusion and isolation of the reserves. That policy failed, and after World War II it proved impossible to maintain this kind of separateness and distance from society. Consequently, a new tactic was tried:

> After 1948, the government decided to pursue the same main aim, assimilation of Native people into the majority society, by treating them together with and in exactly the same way as other citizens. This policy was, in fact, a way of killing two birds with one stone for the federal government. Not only could it justly be considered to be working hard at the job of assimilating Native people, but it was also able to divest itself of the job of administering a good many of the services to Native people that are not normally federally administered services.
>
> It received considerable co-operation from the provinces. . . . the fact that the province gained control of some federal funds in return for its services was probably an important factor. And the provinces have the advantage of not being bound by the federal government's legal description of an "Indian."[2]

This new policy peaked in 1969 with the Liberal government's publication of its White Paper on Indian Policy, a document written by various bureaucrats who, though they had consulted with Indians concerning a revision of the Indian Act, actually proposed in the White Paper its repeal. In effect the 1969 White Paper blamed the Indians for their plight. It proclaimed that it was their special status in Canada that harmed them and prevented their integration into the larger society. It was time to terminate the old policy (much as the United States government had done in the 1950s with disastrous consequences). Consequently, the government proposed to repeal the Indian Act, to have provincial governments assume responsibility for Indians, to provide temporary financial help for economic development, and to appoint a commissioner to look into the various land claims. This "de-Indianization" program would take only a few years according to the formulators of the policy. Indians however were virtually unanimous in their opposition, which they expressed in such statements as the British Columbia Indians' *Brown Paper*, the Alberta Indians' *Red Paper* and the Manitoba Indians' *Wahbung*. Reform of the system to give native peoples control of their lands and their own destiny was what they wanted, not abolition of the only piece of legislation that gave them any protection at all from cultural genocide. They did not care at all for this version of Prime Minister Trudeau's "Just Society."

The Indians of Canada saw themselves about to be abandoned to a fate they had long feared: the complete loss of their identity as a people. If the 1969 proposals were implemented, Indians would be Canadian citizens just like anyone else and they would have to make their way in Canadian society as best they could. All Indian groups saw how hopeless that task would be, given their position as the absolute bottom of Canadian society. They saw the proposed new policy as a betrayal of their treaties and as an abrogation of their rights. Opposition from them and from other Canadian groups sympathetic to their plight compelled the government to withdraw the proposals, and the overt attempt to change the *status quo* failed. But how far did the overt policies of the 1969 White Paper become the covert policies of the 1970s? Certainly much that happened in the 1970s to the native peoples would have followed from the implementation of the 1969 policy. Withdrawing the paper actually seemed to change little, except possibly the rate at which the changes were to be made. And where there was no change there was a continuation of the policy of benign neglect. Perhaps this neglect was no more clearly apparent than in the federal government's categorical refusal to allow any kind of native peoples' representation in the constitutional discussions, particularly those of 1980-81. In those negotiations too the federal government showed its willingness to drop guarantees of treaty and aboriginal rights, rights ambiguously restored in the final draft of the new constitution only after considerable lobbying and protest.

But then it is generally easy to ignore the native peoples. Isolated as they are in many small groups throughout Canada and cut off from one another by linguistic and cultural differences, the native peoples find it difficult to speak with one voice. In their general powerlessness, disunity, and inferior social position they can hardly be said to be a strong interest group. Several smaller "ethnic" groups have been able to speak cohesively and more persuasively than the native peoples. As well, native lobbying efforts do not easily arouse the sympathy of the vast majority of the other 95 per cent of Canadians who prefer to place their own problems, whatever they are—cultural, ethnic, linguistic, economic—well ahead of any the Indian population might have.

Indeed, the general public is apt to resent the "wastefulness" of the government's Indian policy. It sees the federal government spend hundreds of millions of dollars each year to little effect. It reads of waste in the bureaucratic structure and lack of rational planning and it fails to understand why things are as they are.[3] But it blames the victims, the Indians, rather than the oppressor, the system in which the native peoples find themselves, because that of course would be to acknowledge responsibility of some kind.

The main system has been one of tying Indians down to specific bits of land, the reserves, in an attempt to turn them into "farmers" while concurrently "civilizing" them. But Indians have resisted such attempts, wishing to preserve their own views of their relationship to the land, finding themselves anyway unable to farm the poor lands they were given, and regarding the education offered them as uncongenial and even alien. As a result the government has increasingly found itself in a patron-client relationship with the Indians under its jurisdiction, a relationship satisfactory to neither party but one hard to change. The total effect is to maintain the Indians in an inferior social position, the recipients of handouts (as their benefits are considered by most non-Indians), and to disregard their aspirations as a collection of "peoples" in favor of treating them as a disadvantaged social group.

In a nation which is itself in many ways still a colony, if not two or even more, there is within it another colony—the native peoples. If a colonized people are a group which is constantly exploited, patronized, and kept in political, social and economic dependency and inferiority, then the native peoples are a colonized group.[4] Moreover, there seems to be no escape from that status. A century of attempts to assimilate them has ended in failure. The last great attempt was the policy enunciated in the White Paper of 1969. The native peoples and the "native problem," continue to exist, an embarrassment to Canada in the United Nations, and a dilemma which neither governments nor the majority population seem to be able to handle.

Only the Inuit among them have managed to survive the various traps that all other native peoples have fallen into. Their "Indianness" derives from the British North America Act not the Indian Act, and their isolation has been a second blessing. They have been the most successful of the native peoples in preserving their identity. Never having had the doubtful benefits of the Indian Act and cut off and isolated in land which until recently has had little worth in the eyes of others, they have managed to preserve much of their traditional culture and language while adopting some of the material possessions of their southern neighbors. It is partly for these reasons that the Inuit Tapirisat of Canada has never been able to work closely with other native peoples' organizations: the problems of the Dene, the concerns of the Metis and non-status Indians, the proposed changes in the Indian Act, the slow urbanization of other native peoples, all of these are matters remote to the continuation of the Inuit way of life in the north.

At the present time, the most charitable interpretation one can give to federal-provincial treatment of native peoples is that it is attempting to integrate them into the Canadian "mosaic" within the federal government's policy of bilingualism and multiculturalism. As this policy is practised, they will ultimately become francophone if they live in Quebec and anglophone elsewhere, meanwhile qualifying for certain types of funds to maintain some of their distinctive cultural attributes so that others can remark on their charms, talents, and handicrafts. They will have little or no special status, due to continued attenuation of the Indian Act, but in theory all doors to advancement will be thrown open. The success of such policies demands almost an overnight change in the hearts of everyone who is not an Indian to accept Indians as equal and worthy citizens. Many millions of miracles seem called for! The price the native peoples will be forced to pay is considerable. It will inevitably include an abandonment of their languages, cultures, territories, and history, that is, the price will be cultural genocide. It should be no surprise to anyone that they regard such a price as far too high for still another set of promises to be broken at the convenience of others.

In one respect the native peoples are like amost every other group in Canada: they associate their continuity and identification with the preservation of language and culture. This is an abiding Canadian social phenomenon. But just like other residents of Canada who have neither English nor French as their mother tongue, the native peoples of Canada are gradually shifting toward the use of English, and this until recently has been the case even in Quebec. The 1971 census revealed that of the 313,000 status Indians and Inuit only 57 per cent declared that they had a native language as the mother tongue. This percentage was even lower for those who were urbanized: 33 per cent compared with 69 per cent in rural areas. However, even fewer used a native language in the home: of all those who had a native language as the mother tongue, only 77 per cent used a native language in the home; the corresponding urban proportion was 53 per cent and the rural proportion 81 per cent. Consequently, only 18 out of every 100 urbanized native people used their native language in the home. And even though 56 out of every 100 rural dwellers did, the overall figure for Canada was 44 out of every 100, well under half of this population. An analysis by age groups also showed quite clearly that the native languages were in decline since they were used less and less in each successively younger age group in the population. The only sub-group which showed itself to be an exception to the trends was the Inuit, among whom more than 85 per cent still retained their language both as mother tongue and home language. The Inuit's continued isolation was apparently the most important factor in their language retention. In view of the fact that the schools long attended by the Indian population of Canada have used English as the language of instruction considerable language loss is to be expected. Perhaps what is really surprising is the actual persistence of the native languages: they have survived in the most unfavorable circumstances, undoubtedly because of the almost complete ineffectiveness and irrelevance of much of the schooling that was provided.

Native language loss has another important dimension: it is directly related to distance from the White population of Canada. Barbara Burnaby's analysis of the linguistic situation of the Indian population of Ontario led to the not surprising conclusion that urbanization brought about decreased use of the native languages. This decreased use was also related to proximity to major White settlement: native language maintenance was greater in the north, less in the mid-north, and least of all in the south. Finally, those Indians who had more schooling and higher incomes than the average for all Indians also showed the greatest language loss.[5] In Canada in general a definite pattern of language loss prevails: the more southerly and the more urban the greater the loss. Urbanized native peoples in the south show the least incidence of language retention. However, there are a few exceptions. The northern native peoples of British Columbia and the Yukon show fairly low native language retention both as mother tongue and language of the home, whereas the Blackfoot of Alberta and Micmac of New Brunswick have managed to preserve their languages quite well, with over 90 per cent retention of mother tongue in both cases.

The rate of language loss has also apparently increased since World War II as the federal government adopted policies designed to help the native peoples "catch up" in the segregated confines of their reserves. And the effects of urbanization are hard to resist. W.T. Stanbury's 1971 study of 1,095 Indians living off the reserve in British Columbia revealed a sharp increase between 1954 and 1971 in the proportion of those who spoke only English, an increase from about 5 per cent to over 30 per cent.[6] Moreover, the better educated the off-reserve Indian the less likely was that person to use a native language or even to know one. However, many off-reserve Indians did try to maintain their languages and cultures: a quarter of them tried to use an Indian language at home and even more had tried to teach it to their children; Indian stories and legends were passed on; and most Indians visited the reserve at least once a year. A significant effort was being made to hold onto the Indian language and culture but the pressures toward assimilation were considerable. Recently, a growing "Indian" consciousness has helped to stop the decline and even reverse it in some cases. Fortunately, too, much of the "White" education has not taken and still does not take, as evidenced by the high drop-out rates in schools. This rejection of schooling has helped in its way to keep Indian languages and ways of life alive. In many respects White education for Indians is like attempts to make "Christians" out of them: successful for a while superficially but with little or no deep and lasting effect.

Canada's native peoples realize how important the preservation of their languages is to the preservation of their ways of life. They have managed to preserve much of their linguistic heritage in spite of attempts to eradicate native languages in the schools established on the reserves. In recent years the move to integrate Indian students in provincial schools is seen by them to be just as much of a threat to their languages and cultures as was the establishment of schools on reserves. Such integration in the guise of equality means assimilation to the culture of others. Indians realize that their children cannot be given a firm basis in their native languages if they are faced with learning another too soon and with using it as the language of instruction within a curriculum which almost totally neglects their Indian heritage.

To a limited extent the federal government has acknowledged this desire on the part of the native peoples to assume responsibility for the education of their own children. In 1972 it opted for a policy of native control over native education. This policy involved hiring Indian and Inuit teachers and para-professionals, giving native peoples representation on local school and education committees, and attempting to modify the curriculum to make it more suitable to the needs of native children. By the mid-1970s the Indian Affairs Branch of the Department of Indian and Northern Affairs could claim that in the 1,974 federal and 34 provincial schools offering instruction to children of native peoples there were programs in 23 of the 54 different Indian languages and dialects spoken in Canada. The situation is sometimes not as rosy as the official description would have us believe. Too often when native peoples are encouraged to run their own schools, they find the Department of Indian and Northern Affairs exerting control in subtle and not so subtle ways: Indians can run their own schools without interference only if they run them the way the Department would run them were it still in control since that way is "best" for the Indians. Neo-colonialism is still very much in fashion.

One of the points that Justice Thomas R. Berger made in his *Report of the Mackenzie Valley Pipeline Inquiry* was that even in 1977 native peoples still had little effective control over their children's education in spite of official pronouncements to the contrary.[7] He was led to comment as follows:

> The new policy provides for instruction to native children in their mother tongue during the first three years of school. This has not come about: the language of instruction is still English, and the Alberta curriculum is still the basis of northern education.[8]

Nor has the attempt to train native peoples as bilingual teachers been very successful. As Berger said, the real issue is not good faith or sincerity but the fact that "one people cannot run another people's schools."[9] He added:

> There are many elements and factors to be considered in the implementation of a program to ensure the survival and development of the native languages, but it is quite clear that the school system is at the core of it.[10]

Once again we see the schoolground becoming Canada's favorite battleground in the linguistic wars which are the country's real national sport.

Many Indians, particularly those younger ones who seek leadership roles, insist that the decline in native language ability must cease and be reversed if possible. They regard language preservation as the key to cultural preservation. Indian cultural ways have been subverted one by one by Whites: the Indian's religion, language, social bonds, and economic viability.

Competition and a search for social status have been promoted to replace co-operation and sharing as virtues. A revival of the Indian languages will create a barrier that will preserve traditional ways and stop the headlong fall into the oblivion of assimilation into the lowest stratum of White society. Other Indians want the best of both worlds; they seek to retain their Indianness but at the same time want to succeed in a society which they regard as very different from the one they would have preferred but nevertheless one they cannot avoid. In this respect they are like many of the "ethnic" groups in Canada.

Howard Adams, a Metis spokesman, argues in his book *Prison of Grass* that instruction in English should be delayed in schools for Metis and Indian children. They should first of all be taught about their history and culture in their native language. English is the language of colonization. If introduced too early, it will undermine the ability of native children to learn anything at all. To those who share Adams' views, it is only to be expected that colonizers have always attempted to teach English to native children right from the first years of education and that at one time even the use of native languages in the schools was forbidden.[11]

An observer like Barbara Burnaby is not at all optimistic about the future of native language education. So far as Ontario is concerned, she sees such education beset with many difficulties since no clear consensus exists on what should be done. Very large amounts of money are needed if even the existing level of native skills is to be maintained, and much more money if it is possibly to be increased. According to Burnaby, the focus of attention should be on those children who already speak a native Indian language when they come to school; these children should become bilingual and be given opportunities to increase their language capability in both languages. However, she considers that it is already probably too late to do anything for those native children who come to school with English only. Resurrecting a native language for them is hardly a viable proposition. Unfortunately, in many areas of the province these are the majority of native children.[12]

One of the basic problems the native peoples face in Canada is speaking with a voice that gets listened to. They do not find it easy to organize, they do not always trust the leadership that surfaces, and they are well aware that even though Indian voices are sometimes heard they are rarely listened to. Unfortunately, there are few signs that this situation is likely to change for the better.

The three major groups of native peoples have organized themselves, with federal government financial help, into three organizations: status Indians into the National Indian Brotherhood; non-status Indians and Metis into the Native Council of Canada; and the Inuit into the Inuit Tapirisat of Canada. But there is considerable rivalry among the groups. Status Indians do not want their rights jeopardized by any kind of legislation which would recognize the non-status Indians and Metis at the expense of the protection afforded by the Indian Act. The resolution of aboriginal land rights is also a divisive issue, with the major disagreement being between the two Indian associations. The Inuit tend to go their own way, seeing a greater affinity in their problems among the Inuit of Alaska and Greenland.

If the results of uniting in associations have not been impressive, they have at least drawn the attention of many Canadians to the problems the native peoples face. The associations themselves must necessarily do their work in a *lingua franca*, in this case English, a fact which can hardly do anything but weaken the native languages themselves. Disagreement appears more usual than agreement; for example, the Dene of the Northwest Territories want a separate nation and are willing to work independently for that goal or with the Metis, but the latter do not accept Dene leadership. Such an objective actually cuts across the organizational structure. This is merely a single instance of lack of agreement and of inability to work together. Native organizations in Canada are no less balkanized that many other Canadian institutions. There is some reason too to believe that the federal government is not at all opposed to this balkanization. Divide and rule is one of the oldest philosophies of administration just as is the co-option of dissidents through providing government positions for the various leaders who emerge in the local, provincial, or national native organizations:

if you can't beat them, buy them.

It is difficult to judge to what extent the leaders of such organizations as the National Indian Brotherhood and the Native Council of Canada really do speak for the people they claim to represent. (But then how true is it that the federal government "speaks" for the people of Canada and the Premier of Ontario "speaks" for the people of Ontario?) Some of the native peoples see the federal government somewhat cynically co-opting Indians to do the job the government itself once did. By distributing funds, by not being very strict in accounting for how these monies are spent, and by allowing a well-paid "leadership" to develop, the government is able to claim that it is recognizing "responsible" Indian options. But, in reality, the government may be getting only the opinions it wants. Moreover, the new native elites now work alongside the old White bureaucrats in a modified colonial structure possibly far more threatening than the old because it now has all the trappings of legitimacy.

Whatever the "responsible" leadership says, one can be sure that the native peoples disagree considerably among themselves on how best to guarantee their future in Canada. Even on such a specific issue as the Indian Act there is great diversity of opinion. Some native peoples would like to revert to the position they held at the time the treaties were signed, that is, to go back to traditional ways of life and attempt to undo as much as possible of the harm the Whites brought to that life. Members of the American Indian Movement want almost to reinvent the past, to have virtually nothing to do with the Whites, and they have shown themselves willing to accept few compromises. Others feel that their only hope is to play the Whites' game: retain what one can of Indian life but compete in the larger society and integrate as fully as possible into its institutions. Assimilation into wider Canadian society is the goal of still others although one should observe that in recent years not a few Canadians have found it somewhat advantageous to rediscover their "Indian" ancestry, which is, of course, the opposite of assimilation. For many, the major problems are actually those of getting a job, having a better house, and providing better for the family. Whether that goal can better be achieved assimilated, integrated, or separated is a purely practical, non-ideological matter. For others, language, culture, and all that goes with these are important.

Any pan-Indian movement must also overcome traditional tribal attachments which, of course, the reserve system continues to foster. Its success may well depend on native peoples' willingness to sacrifice their concern for differences among themselves in favor of uniting against all those who are not Indians, in much the same way as Blacks in the United States united in the 1960s. Indians may therefore find unity in deciding who they are not, rather than who they are, a well-attested phenomenon in ethnic group formation. But the success of such a move may also depend on a willingness to engage in open conflict with those they perceive to be their natural opposition.

Conflict is often an important ingredient in ethnic consciousness. It can provide the incentive to organize. As the native peoples of Canada have more and more found themselves in conflict with other Canadians they have realized how badly they have been treated. Consequently, they have developed their own networks of communication, associations, newspapers, and so on, but unfortunately often with the "help" of their natural opposition. Confrontation tactics over such matters as schools and land claims have been employed occasionally but to no great success. Given the somewhat rigid social structure within which Indians find themselves at the bottom, confrontation may even have been somewhat counter-productive. Success depends on winning recognition of some kind of equality between the two parties—as in English-French confrontation in Canada and Black-White confrontation in the United States. Canadians have never acknowledged such equality in dealing with the native peoples. The result is a growing frustration at not being taken seriously and a desire on the part of some native peoples to try other means to succeed; for example, the doctrinaire policies of the American Indian Movement or direct requests to the Queen in 1982 to have the Canadian government honor old agreements and disallow new legislation.

And there are those who, like Howard Adams, believe there can be no solution to the problems the native peoples of Canada face without a complete reordering of society, and not just

Canadian society. Adams regards the native population as colonized peoples within a country which is itself a colony. Moreover, the real oppressor is capitalism as an economic system. Only a complete social and economic reordering can bring about the changes that are needed to make any substantial differences in their way of life. This revolutionary Marxist approach has, as yet, found few sympathizers among native peoples, just as it has found few among Canadians in general. But so long as other solutions are tried and fail it remains a possibility, one that cannot just be made to go away as being quite unthinkable.

The native peoples are being pressured on all sides and they find few supporters. The federal government would like them to be citizens like everyone else regardless of the social cost to them. The provincial governments covet the lands they occupy. Exploration companies want unhampered access to the north. Just about everyone wants to end the spiralling costs of the present wasteful system. The native peoples are everybody's victims. Two of the greatest current threats come from the provinces with their desire to exercise more control over everything and everyone within provincial boundaries, and the failure—if it can be called such, since failure implies some genuine attempt to meet an objective—of the federal government to settle the land claims of the native peoples.

In some ways land claims have become the focal issue of the "Indian problem" in Canada. It is around such claims that both levels of government meet with the native peoples. If the claims made by native peoples are successful, much of the Yukon and Northwest Territories and large tracts of the Prairie provinces will belong to them to do with as they please. To put it mildly, that outcome is feared by the governments of those areas. They want to exploit the very same lands for their natural resources; to them the Indians are an obstacle to "development." The federal government's role in the whole affair is ambiguous, to say the least. The Liberal government has long wanted to exercise some control over those same resources but at the same time it has spent millions of dollars to fund research into the land claims of the native peoples. Neither its desire to control natural resource development nor its funding of such research has endeared the federal government to the provincial governments. There has indeed been bitter rivalry on the first issue. But either caught in the middle or disregarded, depending on the specific point that is being discussed, are the native peoples themselves.

One spurious claim the native peoples have long dismissed is one still heard quite often: it is that the corporate development of natural resources in the disputed lands would benefit them greatly if they would just let others get on with exploration and extraction. Indians well realize that northern Canadian developments offer only temporary unskilled work to them and tend to disrupt their lives irreparably. Neither permanently useful skills nor permanent jobs result. Even when a real attempt is made to build some kind of community in which the native peoples are integrated, after the resources are depleted the native peoples are left with facilities that can no longer be used and expectations that can no longer be met. They are left the victims of development, not its beneficiaries.

The justification for the land claims of native peoples in Canada can be found in the Royal Proclamation of 1763 which provided that Indian lands would be protected from settlement and exploitation until the Indians formally surrendered their rights to the Crown. A long succession of treaties resulted. Current claims, which involve nearly half of Canada's total land mass, arise from a variety of circumstances: some lands were never covered by a treaty, for example lands occupied by the Inuit; many treaties have been "broken" or certain provisions have been unfulfilled; and still others require renegotiation because, according to the native peoples, the treaties did not properly record the original understanding between the native population and the government's negotiators. In particular, Indians maintain that any belief that the native peoples surrendered their land to the Canadian government must be false since land cannot be surrendered, only shared. Likewise, any rhetoric from the federal government that renegotiation must lead to the "extinguishment" of land rights cannot seriously be entertained since such a concept is unthinkable.

The most contentious treaties have been Treaty 8 of 1899 and Treaty 11 of 1921. The Dene regard these documents as treaties between sovereign peoples guaranteeing peace and friendship. They are not treaties which cede lands. The treaties were made hurriedly so that in the first case the Klondike gold rush could go ahead without difficulty and in the second case so that oil discoveries in the north could be exploited. The Dene claim that the treaties have been violated repeatedly and that what they want now is not a proper extinguishing of their land rights but a legal understanding with the people of Canada concerning how they can continue to live on their own lands.[13] As Justice Thomas R. Berger wrote in his *Report of the Mackenzie Valley Pipeline Inquiry*:

> The Dene had signed Treaties 8 and 11 on the understanding that they would be free to hunt and fish over their traditional territory, and that the government would protect them from the competition and intrusion of white trappers. Yet, contrary to treaty promises, an influx of white trappers and traders into the country was permitted to exploit the game resources almost at will, and soon strict game laws were necessary to save certain animal populations from extinction. The enforcement of these game laws caused hardship to the native people who depended on the animals for survival.[14]

Father Rene Fumoleau's detailed account of the events leading up to the signing of the treaties in his book *As Long As This Land Shall Last* clearly documents the understanding that the people of the Athabasca-Mackenzie District had of the agreements: they were being asked to share their land not surrender it, an alien incomprehensible concept, and in return they were to be protected from encroachment by outsiders. He also recounts what happened after the treaties were signed: the broken promises; the imposition of restrictions on hunting and fishing; and the slow destruction of traditional ways of life. While the Indians believed that in return for sharing their land their ways of life would be protected "as long as this land shall last," they found themselves rapidly pushed to one side as people from the south moved freely northwards and extended entirely alien social and economic systems into Canada's last frontier.[15]

Although there are numerous and various land claims in Canada, little progress has been made in settling them, the federal government apparently believing that delay is to its advantage: it puts further pressure on the native peoples; it tends to divide them; and it seems to have decreased the public's sympathy with the whole issue of land claims. There has only been one major land claim settlement in Canada, that between some of the native peoples of Quebec and the federal and Quebec governments, brought on by the desire of the government of Quebec to build the great James Bay hydroelectric dam.

The James Bay and Northern Quebec Native Claims Settlement Act of 1977 can hardly be called a model for other agreements to be negotiated with the native peoples. The Quebec government deliberately went ahead with its giant hydroelectric project without recognizing native rights in the area or obtaining a formal surrender of land, as was required by the legislation which extended Quebec's boundaries in 1912, the Quebec Boundaries Extension Act. Native appeals to the courts to prohibit construction until a settlement was reached ultimately failed, so in 1974 the native peoples were faced with a *fait accompli* and they had to settle for what they could get. The Grand Council of the Crees and the Northern Quebec Inuit Association were forced to bargain with the Government of Canada, the Government of Quebec, the James Bay Energy Corporation, the James Bay Development Corporation, and Hydro Quebec to gain a settlement. They gave up their rights to 410,000 square miles of land in Quebec for $225,000,000, to be paid over twenty years, plus certain other rights to hunt, fish, and trap. Although the sum appears to be a large one, it really amounts to approximately $1,125 for each native person per year, hardly a generous settlement for all the wealth contained in the land that was surrendered, and not enough to bring many families out of poverty.

The James Bay Agreement is not unlike the earlier treaties, in which the native peoples were faced with a *fait accompli*: the courts allowed the project to begin before agreement was reached and all that the native peoples could do was to strive for the best possible settlement in the circumstances. This is hardly an honest way of negotiating differences but it has been the customary one in dealing with the native peoples. Just what the ultimate results will be is not at all clear: assimilation by 1997? Further disappointment as the monetary gains prove to be worthless and the others less adequate than believed? Or some kind of social and economic integration but not at the expense of native culture and language? Only the native groups who signed the agreement seem to be happy with it; other Indian groups believe that much too much was lost for quite paltry and extremely doubtful benefits.

One important consequence of the James Bay Agreement was that the Government of Quebec undertook to assume control over the education of the native peoples of the province. Traditionally, the language of instruction for status Indians and Inuit had been English, even in Quebec, because they were the responsibility of the federal government and its bias was toward English. Bill 101 commanded a change to French, a change the Inuit resisted to the extent that intervention by the Quebec Provincial Police was necessary to keep the peace in some Inuit settlements. The federal government has been reluctant to intervene in what it now considers an internal provincial dispute, and the Inuit and more recently certain Indian groups have attempted to resolve their differences through negotiations with the Government of Quebec. It is hardly possible to imagine anything more disruptive to school children than to have the language of instruction arbitrarily shifted in such a manner against the wishes of parents and students alike, all done to serve some remote political end.

The Dene of the Northwest Territories have no wish to settle their claims on either the model of the James Bay Agreement or that made by the native people of Alaska, which, though it provides a billion dollars in compensation, also eliminates their special status by 1991. The Dene feel particularly threatened and vulnerable since their claims stand in the way of the exploitation of oil and gas resources in the north, resources which many Canadians, for a variety of reasons, feel should be exploited soon. The Dene are not necessarily opposed to such exploitation. But if others are to use their land, they want to be properly compensated *beforehand* and they do not want part of that compensation to be promises of jobs, for such promises have traditionally been broken.

They have observed how the native peoples of Canada have always been pushed aside, Indians everywhere and the Metis on the Prairies, to allow lands to be "developed" without adequate compensation. They now fully recognize that their relationship to the land is of fundamental importance to their survival, as important in its way as is French to the cultural survival of the Quebecois.

Consequently, the Dene have laid claim to 450,000 square miles of territory and demanded that their rights to this land be recognized rather than extinguished. In this territory they want to organize themselves as a nation in order to develop their traditional ways of life, endeavors not dependent on exploiting non-renewable resources, accepting government handouts, and experiencing broken promises. To accede to this request the Canadian government would have to reverse its traditional policy of exploiting natural resources such as furs, fish, lumber, wheat, minerals, oil and gas, mainly for use by non-Canadians. This is not a change it contemplates lightly. The northlands are the only Canadian territories left for such exploitation but since the removal of natural resources has nearly always disrupted the ways of life of Canada's native peoples and now there is *nowhere else for them to go* if they are denied control of the lands they now inhabit, the issue is a critical one for their future. And they must surely have a voice in that future through a just resolution of their differences with the Government of Canada.

Justice Thomas R. Berger found himself extremely sympathetic to the views expressed by native peoples such as the Dene. His 1977 Report advocated a ten-year delay in the construction of the Mackenzie Valley Pipeline. The delay was thought necessary to establish a new system for dealing with the native peoples of the north. He wanted to avoid the usual mistakes of the past—a few written agreements quickly worked out, or imposed, and then abrogated. Berger foresaw quite clearly the social disruption that building a pipeline would cause if proper preliminary work was neglected. Consequently, he advocated an equitable settlement of land claims, one which would recognize the way the native peoples held and used land.[16]

The Dene claims have been flatly rejected by the Canadian

government. It refuses to negotiate any issue which might involve recognizing some kind of "sovereignty" for a part of Canada, much the same position it took to the proposals made by the Government of Quebec. The pressures still exist to "open up" the north. Whites there have such a desire and, though they are a very small minority, yet they manage to speak as the "legitimate" territorial voice on such matters. The majority goes unheard.

When such a situation has existed elsewhere, for example in the former Rhodesia and in the present South Africa, Canadian politicians usually adopt a very moralistic tone and lecture others on their errant ways. They might well heed the old biblical injunction about motes and beams. The plight of the native peoples in the north shows once again how disordered is Canada's linguistic and ethnic house, how unwilling Canadians are in general to tidy up the mess, indeed, how that very mess is really what identifies us to others as Canadians.

# 11

## TOWARD A LANGUAGE OF AGREEMENT

Issues concerning language and ethnicity continue to dominate much of the political discussion in Canada. Central to them is the problem of English-French conflict, a conflict from which the country was born and in which it may yet perish. The years have certainly not stilled the disagreements between the English and the French; if anything, hostilities have sharpened in recent years as the French have become more assertive and the English more defensive. The distrust each feels for the other is in no way reduced by the growing linguistic separation of the two peoples, as the French more and more solidify their position within Quebec and the English show great reluctance to change their assimilative ways without. The historic "two solitudes" grow more noticeable as each day passes.

To some extent this situation appears to be meliorated by the growing ethnic diversity of Canada, particularly English Canada. But that appearance is deceptive. "Ethnicity" and the "mosaic" are regarded as "good things" in Canada, as contributing to a distinctively—distinctive from the United States, that is—Canadian way of treating newcomers. But much of that diversity is a kind of statistical artifact, the product of censuses which maintain the myth of diversity. The reality is that ethnic groups have always been pressured to assimilate, and nearly all have found those pressures irresistible. Ethnicity has survived largely because of fairly continuous heavy immigration and to some extent the basic divisiveness which the English-French conflict produces. As immigration is allowed virtually to dry up, not even the English-French conflict will guarantee survival for other groups. The English and French have both shown themselves quite eager in recent years to campaign to win over the hearts and minds (and languages) of immigrants and ethnics. Montreal has been a major battleground but not even the Inuit have been left unaffected.

Ethnic diversity is a fact of current life in Canada, but for how long remains to be seen. What it actually contributes to the political and social well being of the country is quite unknown, nor is the possible harm it does. Arguments and reasons are advanced on both sides. It seems at times that the whole point is not to find answers but to keep the issues alive, which is also a well-attested mode of Canadian political behavior. But whatever view one holds of ethnic diversity, or of any other matter, one particular group of people stand out as exceptions, the native peoples. They are still Canada's forgotten people.

Concurrent with all such difficulties are the cold facts of late twentieth-century economic life. Economic problems largely beyond the country's control affect the lives of its people. Canada's "colonial" status—and the colonial mentality of much of its leadership—does little to help in a post-industrialized economic world. Political leaders who a few years ago portrayed the country as rich in resources now warn of severe resource shortages. Lectures on the recession alternate with encouraging speeches on recovery, and issues campaigned against are implemented upon election to office. It is as if economic matters are both beyond their control and almost beyond their interest. Certainly, these leaders do little or nothing to educate the public in matters such as the continued selling off of natural resources and the increasing monopolistic nature of Canadian business. Instead, they prefer to "educate" the public in matters that are now traditional, and to do so through the politics of confrontation.

So Canadian political life is directed toward the old issues of language and race. These cannot be allowed to die or fall into desuetude. Moreover, they are to be dealt with through confrontation: Ottawa versus Quebec; Ontario versus Quebec; English versus French; Liberals versus everyone else; Canada versus the United Kingdom or France; Trudeau versus all comers;

and so on. Even the federal government's disputes with the provincial governments fit into this pattern. It encourages divisiveness, grandstanding, power plays, elections called at the whims of various chiefs, and a continuous warring tribalism in which people are continually being asked to unite against something—to stop this or undo that—rather than to imagine the general good and adopt an altruistic stance.

Language and ethnicity are never far then from the surface of political existence in Canada because they run so deep in the nation's political life. And even though other currents are at least as deep, certain economic ones, for example, they are not allowed to have the same attention. But being unattended, they succeed, paradoxically, in changing Canadian life while those issues that preoccupy the nation's attention do little or nothing to change anything, least of all Canadians' linguistic and ethnic prejudices toward one another. Two good examples of ineffective measures which scratch at the surface of issues but do nothing to resolve them are, of course, the Liberal government's policies on bilingualism and multiculturalism. The first has been badly articulated, constantly misunderstood, deliberately misrepresented, and made overly confrontational. It was almost certainly the wrong solution—too little, too late, and too grudgingly given. By the time it was implemented Quebec found it irrelevant and the rest of Canada found it unrealistic. Whatever the "right" decision would have been, the Official Languages Act was not it. However, as Prime Minister Trudeau's child it was launched with a "damn the consequences" air about it, and the consequences have done nothing to satisfy anyone, except, for a while, some of the French outside Quebec. The multicultural policy is little more than an empty gesture. Underfunded, unsupported, and muddled, it fails to address itself to the basic issue of what it would mean for Canada to be a truly multicultural society.

Canada's only hope for a peaceful future seems to lie in exchanging confrontation for accommodation, and desires of ethnic ascendancy for those of cultural pluralism. But many factors work against any such change. The English establishment in Canada seems reluctant to loosen its reins of control, economically and politically. It does not pull those reins as tight as it once did, but it pulls them nevertheless: in the economic life of Quebec and the rest of Canada; in the federal bureaucracy and political parties; and in a rural Ontario which continues to keep a conservative provincial government in office, thus effectively dampening social change in Canada's most populous province.

The basic stubbornness of the English and French in Canada is another obstacle to progress. It is a characteristic which has infuriated Prime Minister Trudeau from time to time, but one which he unfortunately has seemed incapable of recognizing as a defect in his own character. The endemic obstinacy leads to an insistence on keeping to an unchanged agenda in political life and it almost guarantees failure before any negotiations begin. It may even be the original cause of that other obstacle in Canadian life, the abrasive, confrontational leadership style that so characterizes most of the Canadian political leadership: "always is heard a discouraging word" about someone else's views on a particular issue. Eleven players may make an effective soccer team, but they have been almost a disaster when playing Canada's national game of linguistic and ethnic confrontation.

A final obstacle is the nature of the society requiring transformation into a pluralistic one. It is something of a mosaic already to be sure, but, if one is to believe John Porter and others, it is a vertical mosaic in which opportunities are unequal. There seems little reason to doubt that as a broad conception the vertical mosaic is a valid statement of the realities of ethnic life in Canada. The English are at the top, the native people are at the bottom, and all groups must fit in between as best they can. Moreover, once fitted in, it is very difficult to move up—or even down. And all the while very definite pressure is exerted from the top down for everyone below the "charter" English and French groups to forego certain aspects of their distinctiveness, language being the crucial one. That this pressure is effective, there can be no doubt; every survey of ethnic languages in Canada shows their continuous sharp decline.

Only by creating a pluralistic Canada in which linguistic and ethnic divisions and tensions are reduced will Canadians be able to see how diverted they have been, deliberately or otherwise, from the serious business of considering who owns Canada and for what purposes. Any reduction of the confrontational style, any toning down of disputes, any willingness to accommodate others, any development of a consensual system for dealing with issues will inevitably change the whole agenda of Canadian political life. Such a change will not be easy, if for no other reason than that the adversarial system is also part and parcel of the system of British law and government that Canada has adopted. But it may allow Canadians to see what things they can do for themselves. Instead of being against so many things (the United States, Ontario, Alberta, immigrants, the English, the French, Indians, westerners, easterners, and so on—Canadians feel free to choose as circumstances dictate!) a more consensual style would allow Canadians to be *for* something, to be not just survivors but builders.

The twentieth century was once supposed to be Canada's century. It still may witness Canada's demise. What Canadians need to show is less concern with and insistence on the rightness of their personal views of language and ethnicity. Only a new political mechanism which will encourage greater tolerance of diversity will guarantee a future for all Canadians. Only when perennial issues are put aside or resolved within an entirely different strategy from the one preferred at present will Canadians be able to deal effectively with their collective destiny. If Canadians missed their chance in the twentieth century, perhaps they may be lucky enough to regain it in the 21st!

# NOTES

Chapter 1: Northern Solitudes
1. Henri Bourassa's words, quoted in Edward McWhinney, *Quebec and the Constitution 1960-1978* (Toronto: University of Toronto Press, 1979), p. 21.
2. Ramsay Cook, *The Maple Leaf Forever: Essays on Nationalism and Politics in Canada* (Toronto: Macmillan of Canada, 1977), p. 16.
3. Pierre Elliott Trudeau, *Federalism and the French Canadians* (Toronto: Macmillan of Canada, 1968), p. 202.
4. *Ibid.*, pp. 178-179.
5. Quoted in Sheila McLeod Arnopolous and Dominique Clift, *The English Fact in Quebec* (Montreal: McGill-Queen's University Press, 1980), p. 40.
6. Donald Smiley, "Reflections on Cultural Nationhood and Political Community in Canada," in R. Kenneth Carty and W. Peter Ward, editors, *Entering the Eighties: Canada in Crisis* (Toronto: Oxford University Press, 1980), p. 36.
7. Crawford Young, *The Politics of Cultural Pluralism* (Madison: The University of Wisconsin Press, 1976).
8. *Ibid.*, p. 7.
9. John Porter, "Conservatism: The Deep Bond in an Embattled Marriage." Quoted in Donald V. Smiley, *Canada in Question: Federalism in the Eighties*, Third Edition (Toronto: McGraw-Hill Ryerson Limited, 1980), p. 294.
10. Task Force on Canadian Unity, *A Future Together: Observations and Recommendations* (Ottawa: Supply and Services Canada, 1979), p. 38.
11. Cook, pp. 186-187.
12. Young, pp. 527-528.
13. John Porter, *The Vertical Mosaic: An Analysis of Social Class and Power in Canada* (Toronto: University of Toronto Press, 1965); Wallace Clement, *The Canadian Corporate Elite: An Analysis of Economic Power* (Toronto: McClelland and Stewart Limited, 1975); Peter C. Newman, *The Canadian Establishment* (Toronto: McClelland and Stewart Limited, 1975); Dennis Olsen, *The State Elite* (Toronto: McClelland and Stewart Limited, 1980).
14. Clement, p. 237.

15. *Ibid.*, p. xi.
16. *Ibid.*, p. 350 ff.
17. *Ibid.*, p. 356.
18. *Ibid.*, pp. 364-365.
19. Olsen, p. 23.
20. *Ibid.*, p. 30.
21. *Ibid.*, p. 41.
22. See Merrijoy Kelner, "Ethnic Penetration into Toronto's Elite Structure," *The Canadian Review of Anthropology and Sociology* 7:2 (1970), pp. 128-137.

Chapter 2: Official Bilingualism

1. *Book I, Report of the Royal Commission on Bilingualism and Biculturalism* (Ottawa: Queen's Printer, 1967), p. 173.
2. *A Preliminary Report of the Royal Commission on Bilingualism and Biculturalism* (Ottawa: Queen's Printer, 1965), p. 13.
3. *Book I*, p. xvii.
4. Howard Palmer, editor, *Immigration and the Rise of Multiculturalism* (Toronto: Copp Clark Publishing, 1975), p. 115.
5. *Book I*, p. xxiii.
6. *Ibid.*, p. xxvi.
7. *Ibid.*, p. xxvii.
8. *Ibid.*, p. xxviii.
9. *Ibid.*, p. xlvii.
10. *Ibid.*, p. 39.
11. *Ibid.*, p. 52.
12. *Ibid.*, p. 55.
13. *Ibid.*, p. 69.
14. Claude-Armand Sheppard, *The Law of Languages in Canada*, Studies of the Royal Commission on Bilingualism and Biculturalism, Number 10 (Ottawa: Information Canada, 1971).
15. *Ibid.*, p. 313.
16. *Book I*, p. 85.
17. *Ibid.*, p. 86.
18. *Ibid.*, p. 94.
19. Commissioner of Official Languages, *Annual Report 1973-1974* (Ottawa: Information Canada, 1975), pp. 4-5.
20. Commissioner of Official Languages, *Annual Report 1971-1972* (Ottawa: Information Canada, 1973) p. xii.
21. Commissioner of Official Languages, *Annual Report 1979* (Ottawa: Supply and Services Canada, 1980), p. 152.
22. *Ibid.*, p. 153.
23. *Ibid.*, p. 57.
24. Christopher Beattie, *Minority Men in a Majority Setting: Middle-level Francophones in the Canadian Public Service* (Toronto: McClelland and Stewart Limited, 1975).
25. Raymond Breton, "The Functions of Languages in Canada," in W.H. Coons, Donald M. Taylor, and Marc-Adelard Tremblay, editors, *The Individual, Language and Society in Canada* (Ottawa: The Canada Council, 1977), p. 92.
26. Commissioner of Official Languages, *Annual Report 1977* (Ottawa: Supply and Services Canada, 1978), p. 15.

27. *Annual Report 1973-1974*, p. 10.
28. *Annual Report 1979*, p. 28.
29. *Annual Report 1981*, p. 191.
30. J.T. Thorson, *Wanted: A Single Canada* (Toronto: McClelland and Stewart Limited, 1973).
31. J.V. Andrew, *Bilingual Today, French Tomorrow* (Richmond Hill, Ontario: BMG Publishing, 1977).
32. *A National Understanding: The Official Languages of Canada* (Ottawa: Supply and Services Canada, 1977).
33. *Ibid.*, pp. 41-42.
34. *Ibid.*, p. 78.

Chapter 3: Fortress Quebec
1. Rejean Lachapelle, "Evolution of Ethnic and Linguistic Composition," in in Raymond Breton, Jeffrey G. Reitz, and Victor F. Valentine, editors, *Cultural Boundaries and the Cohesion of Canada* (Montreal: The Institute for Research on Public Policy, 1980), p. 24.
2. Jacques Henripin, *Immigration and Language Imbalance* (Ottawa: Information Canada, 1974).
3. Richard Ares, *Les Positions—Ethniques, Linguistiques et Religieuses—des Canadiens Francais a la Suite du Recensement de 1971* (Montreal: Les Editions Bellarmin, 1975), p. 206.
4. Richard J. Joy, *Languages in Conflict: The Canadian Experience* (Toronto: McClelland and Stewart Limited, 1972). First published privately, 1967.
5. Richard J. Joy, *Canada's Official-Language Minorities* (Montreal: C.D. Howe Institute, 1978).
6. *Ibid.*, p. 5.
7. Stanley Lieberson, *Language and Ethnic Relations in Canada* (New York: John Wiley & Sons, 1970).
8. *Ibid.*, p. 4.
9. Sheila McLeod Arnopolous and Dominique Clift, *The English Fact in Quebec* (McGill-Queen's University Press, 1980), p. 89.
10. Madeline A. Richard and Douglas F. Campbell, "The Differential Effects of Religion and the Cultural Setting on Ethnic Intermarriage in Toronto and Montreal," 1971. Cited in Raymond Breton and Daiva Stasiulis, "Linguistic Boundaries and the Cohesion of Canada," in Raymond Breton, Jeffrey G. Reitz, and Victor F. Valentine, editors, *Cultural Boundaries and the Cohesion of Canada* (Montreal: The Institute for Research on Public Policy, 1980), p. 271.
11. Paul Lamy, editor, *Language Maintenance and Language Shift in Canada: New Dimensions in the Use of Census Language Data* (Ottawa: University of Ottawa Press, 1977), p. 44.
12. Charles Castonguay, "Opportunities for the Study of Language Transfer in the 1971 Census," in Lamy, 1977.
13. Joy, 1978, pp. 34-39.
14. A. Raynauld, G. Marion, and R. Beland, "La Repartition des Revenus selon les Groupes Ethniques au Canada." Unpublished study.
15. Jac-Andre Boulet, "Evolution dans la Distribution des Revenus de Travail des Groupes Ethniques et Linguistiques sur le Marche Montrealais de 1961 a 1971." Cited in Breton and Stasiulis, 1980, p. 149.
16. Claude Morin, *Quebec Versus Ottawa: The Struggle for Self-*

*Government 1960-72* (Toronto: University of Toronto Press, 1976), Chapter 11.

17. Ramsay Cook, "The Paradox of Quebec," in R. Kenneth Carty and W. Peter Ward, editors, *Entering the Eighties: Canada in Crisis* (Toronto: Oxford University Press, 1980), pp. 56-57.

Chapter 4: The Charter of the French Language

1. Richard J. Joy, *Languages in Conflict: The Canadian Experience* (Toronto: McClelland and Stewart Limited, 1972), p. 95.
2. Hubert Guindon, "The Modernization of Quebec and the Legitimacy of the Canadian State," in Daniel Glenday, Hubert Guindon, and Allan Turowetz, editors, *Modernization and the Canadian State* (Toronto: Macmillan of Canada, 1978), pp. 241-242.
3. Jeremy Boissevain, *The Italians of Montreal: Social Adjustment in a Plural Society*, Studies of the Royal Commission on Bilingualism and Biculturalism, Number 7 (Ottawa: Information Canada, 1970) p. 60.
4. John R. Mallea, editor, *Quebec's Language Policies: Background and Response* (Quebec: Les Presses de l'Universite Laval, 1977), p. 97.
5. *Ibid.*, p. 142.
6. *Ibid.*, pp. 207-208.
7. Camille Laurin, *Quebec's Policy on the French Language* (Quebec: L'Editeur Officiel du Quebec, 1977), p. 51.
8. Quoted in Peter Leslie, "Ethnic Hierarchies and Minority Consciousness in Quebec," in Richard Simeon, editor, *Must Canada Fail?* (Montreal and London: McGill-Queen's University Press, 1977), p. 112.
9. Laurin, pp. 52-54.
10. *Ibid.*, p. 60.
11. *Ibid.*, p. 72.
12. *Ibid.*, p. 73.
13. *Ibid.*, p. 76.
14. Richard J. Joy, *Canada's Official-Language Minorities* (Montreal: C.D. Howe Research Institute, 1978), p. 31.
15. Serge Carlos, *L'Utilisation du Francais dans le Monde du Travail*, 1973. Cited in Raymond Breton and Daiva Stasiulis, "Linguistic Boundaries and the Cohesion of Canada," in Raymond Breton, Jeffrey G. Reitz, and Victor F. Valentine, editors, *Cultural Boundaries and the Cohesion of Canada* (Montreal: The Institute for Research on Public Policy, 1980), p. 163.
16. Pierre Fournier, *The Quebec Establishment: The Ruling Class and the State* (Montreal: Black Rose Books, 1976).
17. David C. Gordon, *The French Language and National Identity (1930-1975)* (The Hague: Mouton Publishers, 1978), p. 139.
18. Joy, 1978, p. 28.

Chapter 5: The French Outside Quebec

1. Task Force on Canadian Unity, *A Future Together: Observations and Recommendations* (Ottawa: Supply and Services Canada, 1979), p. 51.
2. *Les Heritiers de Lord Durham* (Ottawa: Federation des Francophones hors Quebec, 1977).
3. Keith Spicer, "Banquet Address," in Manoly R. Lupul, editor, *Ukrainian Canadians, Multiculturalism, and Separatism: An Assessment* (Edmonton: The Canadian Institute of Ukrainian Studies, 1978), p. 132.

4. Richard J. Joy, *Canada's Official-Language Minorities* (Montreal: C.D. Howe Research Institute, 1978), p. 16.
5. *Ibid.*, pp. 21-23.
6. *Ibid.*, pp. 18-20.
7. Thomas R. Maxwell, *The Invisible French: The French in Metropolitan Toronto* (Waterloo: Wilfrid Laurier University Press, 1977).
8. *Ibid.*, chapters XI-XII.
9. John D. Jackson, *Community and Conflict* (Toronto: Holt, Rinehart and Winston of Canada, 1975), p. 140. Robert Choquette, *Language and Religion: A History of English-French Conflict in Ontario* (Ottawa: University of Ottawa Press, 1975), p. 249.
10. *Book II, Report of the Royal Commission on Bilingualism and Biculturalism* (Ottawa: Queen's Printer, 1969), p. 75.
11. *How to Live French in Ontario* (Toronto: The Ontario Educational Communications Authority, 1978), p. 24.
12. There is not always agreement as to which schools should be counted.
13. Quoted in Lovell Clark, editor, *The Manitoba School Question: Majority Rule or Minority Rights?* (Toronto: The Copp Clark Publishing Company, 1968), p. 42.
14. Council of Ministers of Education, Canada, "The State of Minority Language Education in the Ten Provinces of Canada" (Toronto: Council of Ministers of Education, Canada, 1978).

Chapter 6: Canada's Absorptive Capacity
1. See Warren E. Kalbach and Wayne W. McVey, *The Demographic Bases of Canadian Society*, Second Edition (Toronto: McGraw-Hill Ryerson Limited, 1979), p. 204.
2. *Ibid.*, p. 190.
3. *Canada Year Book 1978-79* (Ottawa: Supply and Services Canada, 1978), p. 152.
4. Kalbach and McVey, p. 35.
5. *Canada Year Book 1978-79*, p. 152.
6. Kalbach and McVey, p. 47.
7. Raymond N. Morris and C. Michael Lanphier, *Three Scales of Inequality: Perspectives on French-English Relations* (Don Mills, Ontario: Longman Canada Limited, 1977), pp. 224-225.
8. Pierre Elliott Trudeau, *Federalism and the French Canadians* (Toronto: Macmillan of Canada, 1968), p. 199.
9. Carl Berger, *The Sense of Power: Studies in the Ideas of Canadian Imperialism 1867-1914* (Toronto: University of Toronto Press, 1970), p. 152.
10. James S. Woodsworth, *Strangers Within Our Gates: Or Coming Canadians* (Toronto: University of Toronto Press, 1972), p. xvii. Originally published in 1909.
11. See Section III, Ethnicity and Education, in Martin L. Kovacs, editor, *Ethnic Canadians: Culture and Education* (Regina: Canadian Plains Research Center, 1978), particularly the papers by Marilyn J. Barber, Raymond J.A. Huel, Nanciellen C. Sealy, Cornelius J. Jaenen, and Savelia Curnisky.
12. Quoted in Howard Palmer, editor, *Immigration and the Rise of Multiculturalism* (Toronto: Copp Clark Publishing, 1975), p. 61.
13. Freda Hawkins, *Canada and Immigration: Public Policy and Public Concern* (Montreal and London: McGill-Queen's University Press, 1972).

14. Anthony H. Richmond, *Post-War Immigrants in Canada* (Toronto: University of Toronto Press, 1967).
15. *Ibid.*, p. 252.
16. CTV, September 30, 1978.
17. See Palmer, 1975, Part One, for a representative selection of opinion.
18. John F. Kennedy, *A Nation of Immigrants*, Revised and enlarged edition (New York: Harper & Row, Publishers, 1964).
19. Hawkins, 1972, p. 35.
20. See Anthony H. Richmond, "Black and Asian Immigrants in Britain and Canada: Some Comparisons," *New Commentary* 4:4 (1975-1976), pp. 501-516.
21. See particularly John Porter, *The Vertical Mosaic: An Analysis of Social Class and Power in Canada* (Toronto: University of Toronto Press, 1965) and *The Measure of Canadian Society: Education, Equality, and Opportunity* (Toronto: Gage Publishing Limited, 1979).

Chapter 7: The Issue of Ethnicity

1. See particularly Nathan Glazer and Daniel Patrick Moynihan, *Beyond the Melting Pot: The Negroes, Puerto Ricans, Jews, Italians, and Irish of New York City* (Cambridge, Massachusetts: The M.I.T. Press, 1963); Nathan Glazer and Daniel Patrick Moynihan, editors, *Ethnicity: Theory and Experience* (Cambridge, Massachusetts: Harvard University Press, 1975); and Michael Novak, *The Rise of the Unmeltable Ethnics* (New York: Macmillan, 1971).
2. Alex Haley, *Roots* (Garden City, New York: Doubleday & Company, Inc., 1976).
3. Wsevolod W. Isajiw, "Olga in Wonderland: Ethnicity in a Technological Society," in Leo Driedger, editor, *The Canadian Ethnic Mosaic: A Quest for Identity* (Toronto: McClelland and Stewart Limited, 1978).
4. William Darcovich and Paul Yuzyk, editors, *A Statistical Compendium on the Ukrainians in Canada 1891-1976* (Ottawa: University of Ottawa Press, 1980), p. 7.
5. Wsevolod Isajiw, "Definitions of Ethnicity," in Jay E. Goldstein and Rita M. Bienvenue, editors, *Ethnicity and Ethnic Relations in Canada: A Book of Readings* (Toronto: Butterworth & Co. (Canada) Ltd., 1980), p. 24.
6. Joshua A. Fishman, *Language Loyalty in the United States* (The Hague: Mouton, 1966), p. 27.
7. See John M. Kralt, "Ethnic Origin in the Canadian Census, 1871-1981," in W. Roman Petryshyn, editor, *Changing Realities: Social Trends Among Ukrainian Canadians* (Edmonton: The Canadian Institute of Ukrainian Studies, 1980).
8. *Book I, Report of the Royal Commission on Bilingualism and Biculturalism* (Ottawa: Queen's Printer, 1967), p. xxiv.
9. Fishman, 1966, p. 408.
10. See Howard Palmer, *Immigration and the Rise of Multiculturalism* (Toronto: Copp Clark Publishing, 1975), pp. 176-185.
11. Warren E. Kalbach and Wayne W. McVey, *The Demographic Bases of Canadian Society*, Second Edition (Toronto: McGraw-Hill Ryerson Limited, 1979), p. 216.
12. *Ibid.*, p. 240.
13. *Ibid.*, pp. 320-323.
14. John Porter, *The Vertical Mosaic: An Analysis of Social Class and Power*

*in Canada* (Toronto: University of Toronto Press, 1965), p. 558.

15. Frank G. Vallee and Norman Shulman, "The Viability of French Group-ings Outside Quebec," quoted in John Porter, *The Measure of Canadian Society: Education, Equality, and Opportunity* (Toronto: Gage Publishing Limited, 1979), p. 126.

16. Porter, 1979, p. 129.

17. *Ibid.*, p. 133.

18. See Jeffrey G. Reitz, "Immigrants, Their Descendants, and the Cohesion of Canada," in Raymond Breton, Jeffrey G. Reitz, and Victor F. Valentine, editors, *Cultural Boundaries and the Cohesion of Canada* (Montreal: The Institute for Research on Public Policy, 1980), particularly pages 331-333.

Chapter 8: Group Survival and Language Maintenance

1. Warren E. Kalbach and Wayne W. McVey, *The Demographic Bases of Canadian Society*, Second Edition (Toronto: McGraw-Hill Ryerson Limited, 1979), p. 153.

2. Jeffrey G. Reitz, *The Survival of Ethnic Groups* (Toronto: McGraw-Hill Ryerson Limited, 1980), pp. 138-139.

3. See Leo Driedger, "Ukrainian Identity in Winnipeg," in Martin L. Kovacs, editor, *Ethnic Canadians: Culture and Education* (Regina: Canadian Plains Research Center, 1978), pp. 147-165.

4. Warren E. Kalbach and Madeline A. Richard, "Differential Effects of Ethno-Religious Structure on Linguistic Trends and Economic Achieve-ments of Ukrainian Canadians," in W. Roman Petryshyn, editor, *Changing Realities: Social Trends Among Ukrainian Canadians* (Edmon-ton: The Canadian Institute of Ukrainian Studies, 1980), p. 90.

5. Nathan Glazer and Daniel Patrick Moynihan, *Beyond the Melting Pot: The Negroes, Puerto Ricans, Jews, Italians, and Irish of New York City* (Cambridge, Massachusetts: The M.I.T. Press, 1963).

6. William Darcovich, "The 'Statistical Compendium': An Overview of Trends," in Petryshyn, 1980, p. 12.

7. Olga M. Kuplowska, "Language Retention Patterns Among Ukrainian Canadians," in Petryshyn, 1980, p. 159.

8. Leo Driedger, "Urbanization of Ukrainians in Canada: Consequences for Ethnic Identity," in Petryshyn, 1980, p. 129.

9. Kalbach and Richard, in Petryshyn, 1980, p. 94.

10. Evelyn Latowski, "Three Toronto Synagogues: A Comparative Study of Religious Systems in Transition." Unpublished doctoral thesis, University of Toronto, 1969.

11. See Gordon Hirabayashi, "Japanese Heritage, Canadian Experience," in Harold Coward and Leslie Kawamura, editors, *Religion and Ethnicity* (Waterloo, Ontario: The Calgary Institute for the Humanities, 1978).

12. Vandra L. Masemann, "Multicultural Programs in Toronto Schools," *Interchange 9:1* (1978-1979), pp. 29-44.

13. K.G. O'Bryan, J.G. Reitz, and O.M. Kuplowska, *Non-Official Languages: A Study in Canadian Multiculturalism* (Ottawa: Supply and Services Canada, 1976).

14. *Ibid.*, p. 165.

15. Reitz, 1980, pp. 130-133.

Chapter 9: A Multicultural Society

1. See Leo Driedger, editor, *The Canadian Ethnic Mosaic* (Toronto:

McClelland and Stewart Limited, 1978), pp. 9-12.

2. See the statement by J.B. Rudnyckyj in *Book I, Report of the Royal Commission on Bilingualism and Biculturalism* (Ottawa: Queen's Printer, 1967), pp. 155-169.

3. *Multiculturalism and the Government of Canada* (Ottawa: Supply and Services Canada, 1968).

4. *Ibid.*, p. 16.

5. *Loc. cit.*

6. *Ibid.*, p. 35.

7. *Ontario and Multiculturalism: A Survey of Recent Developments* (Toronto: Ministry of Culture and Recreation, 1978).

8. K.G. O'Bryan, J.G. Reitz, and O.M. Kuplowska, *Non-Official Languages: A Study in Canadian Multiculturalism* (Ottawa: Supply and Services Canada, 1976).

9. *Ibid.*, p. 176.

10. Iaacov Glickman, "Ethnic Boundaries and the Jewish Parochial School in Toronto: The Inevitability of False Expectations," in Danielle Juteau Lee, editor, *Emerging Ethnic Boundaries* (Ottawa: University of Ottawa Press, 1979), p. 176.

11. O'Bryan, Reitz, and Kuplowska, 1976, pp. 175-176.

12. *Ibid.*, p. 168.

13. See Bohdan Bociurkiw, "The Federal Policy of Multiculturalism and the Ukrainian Canadian Community," in Manoly R. Lupul, editor, *Ukrainian Canadians, Multiculturalism, and Separatism: An Assessment* (Edmonton: The Canadian Institute of Ukrainian Studies, 1978), pp. 98-128.

14. Jeffrey G. Reitz, *The Survival of Ethnic Groups* (Toronto: McGraw-Hill Ryerson Limited, 1980), pp. 241-242.

15. *Ibid.*, p. 233.

16. John W. Berry, Rudolf Kalin, and Donald M. Taylor, *Multiculturalism and Ethnic Attitudes in Canada* (Ottawa: Supply and Services Canada, 1977).

17. *Ibid.*, p. 241.

18. Harold Barclay, "The Muslim Experience in Canada," in Harold Coward and Leslie Kawamura, editors, *Religion and Ethnicity* (Waterloo, Ontario: The Calgary Institute for the Humanities, 1978), p. 111.

19. Howard Palmer and Harold Troper, "Canadian Ethnic Studies: Historical Perspectives and Contemporary Implications," *Interchange 4:4* (1973), p. 21.

20. *Ibid.*, p. 22.

21. See Bociukiw, 1978, p. 99.

22. David R. Hughes and Evelyn Kallen, *The Anatomy of Racism: Canadian Dimensions* (Montreal: Harvest House, 1974), p. 190.

23. *Ibid.*, p. 191.

Chapter 10: Unheard Voices

1. Victor F. Valentine, "Native Peoples and Canadian Society: A Profile of Issues and Trends," in Raymond Breton, Jeffrey G. Reitz, and Victor F. Valentine, editors, *Cultural Boundaries and the Cohesion of Canada* (Montreal: The Institute for Research on Public Policy, 1980), p. 81.

2. Barbara J. Burnaby, "Roles of Languages in Education for Native Children in Ontario." Unpublished doctoral thesis, University of Toronto, 1979, p. 48.

3. *The Globe and Mail*, Toronto, December 12, 1980, p. 12.
4. James S. Frideres, *Canada's Indians: Contemporary Conflicts* (Scarborough, Ontario: Prentice-Hall of Canada Ltd., 1974), pp. 157-163.
5. Burnaby, 1979, pp. 20-29.
6. W.T. Stanbury, *Success and Failure: Indians in Urban Society* (Vancouver: University of British Columbia Press, 1975).
7. Thomas R. Berger, *Northern Frontier, Northern Homeland: The Report of the Mackenzie Valley Pipeline Inquiry: Volume One* (Ottawa: Supply and Services Canada, 1977).
8. *Ibid.*, p. 181.
9. *Ibid.*, p. 182.
10. *Ibid.*, p. 184.
11. Howard Adams, *Prison of Grass* (Toronto: New Press, 1975), p. 155.
12. Burnaby, 1979, Chapters III and IV.
13. See Mel Watkins, editor, *Dene Nation—The Colony Within* (Toronto: University of Toronto Press, 1977).
14. Berger, 1977, p. 168.
15. Rene Fumoleau, *As Long As This Land Shall Last: A History of Treaty 8 and Treaty 11 1870-1939* (Toronto: McClelland and Stewart Limited, 1975).
16. Berger, 1977, p. 196.

# BIBLIOGRAPHY

Adams, Howard, *Prison of Grass*, Toronto: New Press, 1975.

Andrew, J.V., *Bilingual Today: French Tomorrow*, Richmond Hill, Ontario: BMG Publishing, 1977.

Ares, Richard, *Les Positions—Ethniques, Linguistiques at Religieuses—des Canadiens Francais a la Suite du Recensement de 1971*, Montreal: Les Editions Bellarmin, 1975.

Arnopolous, Sheila McLeod, and Clift, Dominique, *The English Fact in Quebec*, Montreal: McGill-Queen's University Press, 1980.

Beattie, Christopher, *Minority Men in a Majority Setting: Middle-Level Francophones in the Canadian Public Service*, Toronto: McClelland and Stewart Limited, 1975.

Berger, Carl, *The Sense of Power: Studies in the Ideas of Canadian Imperialism 1867-1914*, Toronto: University of Toronto Press, 1970.

Berger, Thomas R., *Northern Frontier, Northern Homeland: The Report of the Mackenzie Valley Pipeline Inquiry: Volume One*, Ottawa: Supply and Services Canada, 1977.

Berry, John W., Kalin, Rudolf, and Taylor, Donald M., *Multiculturalism and Ethnic Attitudes in Canada*, Ottawa: Supply and Services Canada, 1977.

Boissevain, Jeremy, *The Italians of Montreal: Social Adjustment in a Plural Society*, Studies of the Royal Commission on Bilingualism and Biculturalism, Number 7. Ottawa: Information Canada, 1970.

Breton, Raymond, Reitz, Jeffrey G., and Valentine, Victor F., *Cultural Boundaries and the Cohesion of Canada*, Montreal: The Institute for Research on Public Policy, 1980.

Burnaby, Barbara J., "Roles of Languages in Education for Native Children in Ontario." Unpublished doctoral thesis, University of Toronto, 1979.

*Canada Year Book 1978-79*, Ottawa: Supply and Services Canada, 1978.

Carty, R. Kenneth, and Ward, W. Peter, Editors, *Entering the Eighties: Canada in Crisis*, Toronto: Oxford University Press, 1980.

Choquette, Robert, *Language and Religion: A History of English-French Conflict in Ontario*, Ottawa: University of Ottawa Press, 1975.

Clark, Lovell, *The Manitoba School Question: Majority Rule or Minority Rights?* Toronto: The Copp Clark Publishing Company, 1968.

Clement, Wallace, *The Canadian Corporate Elite: An Analysis of Economic*

*Power*, Toronto: McClelland and Stewart Limited, 1975.

Commissioner of Official Languages, *Annual Report*, Ottawa: Supply and Services Canada, 1971- .

Cook, Ramsay, *The Maple Leaf Forever: Essays on Nationalism and Politics in Canada*, Toronto: Macmillan of Canada, 1969.

Coons, W.H., Taylor, Donald M., and Tremblay, Marc-Adelard, *The Individual, Language and Society in Canada*, Ottawa: The Canada Council, 1977.

Council of Ministers of Education, Canada, "The State of Minority Language Education in the Ten Provinces of Canada." Toronto: Council of Ministers of Education, Canada, 1978.

Coward, Harold, and Kawamura, Leslie, Editors, *Religion and Ethnicity*, Waterloo, Ontario: The Calgary Institute for the Humanities, 1978.

Darcovich, William, and Yuzyk, Paul, Editors, *A Statistical Compendium on the Ukrainians in Canada 1891-1976*, Ottawa: University of Ottawa Press, 1980.

Driedger, Leo, Editor, *The Canadian Ethnic Mosaic: A Quest for Identity*, Toronto: McClelland and Stewart Limited, 1978.

Fishman, Joshua A., *Language Loyalty in the United States*, The Hague: Mouton, 1966.

Fournier, Pierre, *The Quebec Establishment: The Ruling Class and the State*, Montreal: Black Rose Books, 1976.

Frideres, J.S., *Canada's Indians: Contemporary Conflicts*, Scarborough, Ontario: Prentice-Hall of Canada Ltd., 1974.

Fumoleau, Rene, *As Long As This Land Shall Last: A History of Treaty 8 and Treaty 11 1870-1939*, Toronto: McClelland and Stewart Limited, 1975.

Glazer, Nathan, and Moynihan, Daniel Patrick, *Beyond the Melting Pot: The Negroes, Puerto Ricans, Jews, Italians, and Irish of New York City*, Cambridge, Massachusetts: The M.I.T. Press, 1963.

Glazer, Nathan, and Moynihan, Daniel Patrick, Editors, *Ethnicity: Theory and Practice*, Cambridge, Massachusetts: Harvard University Press, 1975.

Goldstein, Jay E., and Bienvenue, Rita M., Editors, *Ethnicity and Ethnic Relations in Canada: A Book of Readings*, Toronto: Butterworth & Co. (Canada) Ltd., 1980.

Gordon, David C., *The French Language and National Identity (1930-1975)*, The Hague: Mouton Publishers, 1978.

Guindon, Hubert, "The Modernization of Quebec and the Legitimacy of the Canadian State," in Glenday, Daniel, Guindon, Hubert, and Turowetz, Allan, Editors, *Modernization and the Canadian State*, Toronto: Macmillan of Canada, 1978, pp. 212-246.

Haley, Alex, *Roots*, Garden City, New York: Doubleday & Company, Inc., 1976.

Hawkins, Freda, *Canada and Immigration: Public Policy and Public Concern*, Montreal and London: McGill-Queen's University Press, 1972.

Henripin, Jacques, *Immigration and Language Imbalance: Canadian Immigration and Population Study*, Ottawa: Information Canada, 1974.

*Les Heritiers de Lord Durham*, Ottawa: Federation des Francophones hors Quebec, 1977.

*How to Live French in Ontario*, Toronto: The Ontario Educational Communications Authority, 1978.

Hughes, David R., and Kallen, Evelyn, *The Anatomy of Racism: Canadian*

*Dimensions*, Montreal: Harvest House, 1974.

Jackson, John D., *Community and Conflict*, Toronto: Holt, Rinehart & Winston of Canada, 1975.

Joy, Richard J., *Languages in Conflict: The Canadian Experience*, Toronto: McClelland and Stewart Limited, 1972. First published 1967.

Joy, Richard J., *Canada's Official-Language Minorities*, Montreal: C.D. Howe Research Institute, 1978.

Kalbach, Warren E., and McVey, Wayne W., *The Demographic Bases of Canadian Society*. Second Edition, Toronto: McGraw-Hill Ryerson Limited, 1979.

Kelner, Merrijoy, "Ethnic Penetration into Toronto's Elite Structure," *The Canadian Review of Anthropology and Sociology 7:2*, 1970, pp. 128-137.

Kennedy, John F., *A Nation of Immigrants*. Revised and Enlarged Edition, New York: Harper & Row, Publishers, 1964.

Kovacs, Martin L., Editor, *Ethnic Canadians: Culture and Education*, Regina: Canadian Plains Research Center, 1978.

Lamy, Paul, Editor, *Language Maintenance and Language Shift in Canada: New Dimensions in the Use of Census Language Data*, Ottawa: University of Ottawa Press, 1977.

Latowski, Evelyn, "Three Toronto Synagogues: A Comparative Study of Religious Systems in Transition." Unpublished doctoral thesis, University of Toronto, 1969.

Laurin, Camille, *Quebec's Policy on the French Language*, Quebec: L'Editeur Officiel du Quebec, 1977.

Lee, Danielle Juteau, Editor, *Emerging Ethnic Boundaries*, Ottawa: University of Ottawa Press, 1979.

Lieberson, Stanley, *Language and Ethnic Relations in Canada*, New York: John Wiley & Sons, 1970.

Lupul, Manoly R., Editor, *Ukrainian Canadians, Multiculturalism, and Separatism: An Assessment*, Edmonton: The Canadian Institute of Ukrainian Studies, 1978.

Mallea, John R., Editor, *Quebec's Language Policies: Background and Response*, Quebec: Les Presses de l'Universite Laval, 1977.

Masemann, Vandra L., "Multicultural Programs in Toronto Schools," *Interchange 9:1*, 1978, pp. 29-44.

Maxwell, Thomas R., *The Invisible French: The French in Metropolitan Toronto*, Waterloo, Ontario: Wilfrid Laurier University Press, 1977.

McWhinney, Edward, *Quebec and the Constitution 1960-1978*, Toronto: University of Toronto Press, 1979.

Morin, Claude, *Quebec Versus Ottawa: The Struggle for Self-Government 1960-70*, Toronto: University of Toronto Press, 1976.

Morris, Raymond N., and Lanphier, C. Michael, *Three Scales of Inequality: Perspectives on French-English Relations*, Don Mills, Ontario: Longman Canada Limited, 1977.

*Multiculturalism and the Government of Canada*, Ottawa: Supply and Services Canada, 1978.

*A National Understanding: The Official Languages of Canada*, Ottawa: Supply and Services Canada, 1977.

Newman, Peter C., *The Canadian Establishment*, Toronto: McClelland and Stewart Limited, 1975.

Novak, Michael, *The Rise of the Unmeltable Ethnics*, New York, Macmillan, 1971.

# 266 LANGUAGE AND NATIONHOOD

O'Bryan, K.G., Reitz, J.G., and Kuplowska, O.M., *Non-Official Languages: A Study in Canadian Multiculturalism*, Ottawa: Supply and Services Canada, 1976.

*Ontario and Multiculturalism: A Summary of Recent Developments*, Toronto: Ministry of Culture and Recreation, 1978.

Palmer, Howard, *Immigration and the Rise of Multiculturalism*, Toronto: Copp Clark Publishing, 1975.

Palmer, Howard, and Troper, Harold, "Canadian Ethnic Studies: Historical Perspectives and Contemporary Implications," *Interchange* 4:4, 1973, pp. 15-23.

Petryshyn, W. Roman, Editor, *Changing Realities: Social Trends Among Ukrainian Canadians*, Edmonton: The Canadian Institute of Ukrainian Studies, 1980.

Porter, John, *The Vertical Mosaic: An Analysis of Social Class and Power in Canada*, Toronto: University of Toronto Press, 1965.

Porter, John, *The Measure of Canadian Society: Education, Equality and Opportunity*, Toronto: Gage Publishing Limited, 1979.

*A Preliminary Report of the Royal Commission on Bilingualism and Biculturalism*, Ottawa: Queen's Printer, 1965.

Reitz, Jeffrey G., *The Survival of Ethnic Groups*, Toronto: McGraw-Hill Ryerson Limited, 1980.

*Report of the Royal Commission on Bilingualism and Biculturalism*, Ottawa: Queen's Printer, 1967.

Richmond, Anthony H., *Post-War Immigrants in Canada*, Toronto: University of Toronto Press, 1967.

Richmond, Anthony H., "Black and Asian Immigrants in Britain and Canada: Some Comparisons," *New Commentary* 4:4, 1975-76, pp. 501-516.

Sheppard, Claude-Armand, *The Law of Languages in Canada*, Studies of the Royal Commission on Bilingualism and Biculturalism, Number 10. Ottawa: Information Canada, 1971.

Simeon, Richard, Editor, *Must Canada Fail?* Montreal and London: McGill-Queen's University Press, 1977.

Smiley, Donald V., *Canada in Question: Federalism in the Eighties*. Third Edition, Toronto: McGraw-Hill Ryerson Limited, 1980.

Stanbury, W.T., *Success and Failure: Indians in Urban Society*, Vancouver: University of British Columbia Press, 1975.

Task Force on Canadian Unity, *A Future Together: Observations and Recommendations*, Ottawa: Supply and Services Canada, 1979.

Thorson, J.T., *Wanted: A Single Canada*, Toronto: McClelland and Stewart Limited, 1973.

Trudeau, Pierre Elliott, *Federalism and the French Canadians*, Toronto: Macmillan of Canada, 1968.

Watkins, Mel, Editor, *Dene Nation—The Colony Within*, Toronto: University of Toronto Press, 1977.

Woodsworth, James S., *Strangers Within Our Gates: Or Coming Canadians*, Toronto: University of Toronto Press, 1972. Originally published 1909.

Young, Crawford, *The Politics of Cultural Pluralism*, Madison: The University of Wisconsin Press, 1976.

# Index

Printed in Canada

## DATE DUE
### DATE DE RETOUR

| | | | |
|---|---|---|---|
| FEB 2 0 1989 | | | |
| DEC 0 8 1990 | | | |
| APR 05 1995 | | | |
| APR 1 3 1995 | | | |
| DEC 0 6 1995 | | | |
| NOV 2 6 1996 | | | |
| NOV 1 1 1996 | | | |
| NOV - 1 1996 | | | |
| FEB 0 7 2005 | | | |
| APR 2 1 2005 | | | |
| | | | |
| | | | |
| | | | |
| | | | |
| | | | |
| | | | |